Deep Rivers

José María Arguedas

Deep Rivers

translated by
Frances Horning Barraclough

WAVELAND
PRESS, INC.
Long Grove, Illinois

For information about this book, contact:
  Waveland Press, Inc.
  4180 IL Route 83, Suite 101
  Long Grove, IL 60047-9580
  (847) 634-0081
  info@waveland.com
  www.waveland.com

Contents

Translator's Note

José María Arguedas is one of the few Latin American authors who have loved and described their rural natural surroundings, and he ranks among the greatest writers of any place and any time. He saw the beauty of the Peruvian landscape, as well as the grimness of social conditions in the Andes, through the eyes of the Indians who are a part of it.

He succeeded in instilling into his Spanish the sentence structure, the rhythm, and even some of the vocabulary of the Andean people. Although it is impossible to convey all of the nuances of his writing in English, I have translated *Deep Rivers* in the belief that English speakers deserve a chance to become acquainted with him and to experience the reality of life in Peru as it still exists today, even though the novel describes a period of about fifty years ago. I have tried to salvage, at least in part, the characteristics of the Quechua-Spanish created by Arguedas in the simplest manner possible, by attempting to be scrupulously faithful to the original. The Quechua songs presented in the book have been translated by transposing the author's rather free Spanish version of them into English.

I am grateful to Carlin Baraona and José Sabogal Weisse for their assistance in translating the Spanish and Peruvian idioms. I also wish to thank Martin Wolf and Claire Eisenhart, who read the English version and made many useful editorial suggestions.

F.H.B.

Introduction

"You may be surprised if I confess to you that I am the handiwork of my stepmother. My mother died when I was two and a half. My father remarried; his new wife already had three children. I was the youngest and, as I was so small, my father left me in the house of my stepmother, who owned half the town; she had many indigenous servants and with it the traditional contempt for and lack of awareness of what an Indian was. Since I was the object of as much of her scorn and rancor as the Indians, she decided that I was to live with them in the kitchen, eating and sleeping there. My bed was a wooden trough of the kind used to knead bread. . . . Resting on some sheepskins and covered with a rather dirty but very sheltering blanket, I spent the nights talking and living so well that if my stepmother had known it she would have removed me to her side. . . .

"I lived thus many years. When my father would visit I was hauled back to the dining room, my clothes were dusted off; but Sunday passed, my father went back to the provincial capital and I to my trough, to the lice of the Indians. The Indians, particularly their women, saw me as one of them, with the difference that being white I needed even more comforting than they did, and this they gave me in full. But consolation must contain within it both sadness and power; as those tormented comforted those who suffered even more, two things were sadly driven into my nature from the time I learned to speak: (1) the tenderness and limitless love of the Indians, the love they feel for each other and also for nature, the highlands, rivers, and birds; and (2) the hatred they felt for those who, almost as if unaware and seeming to follow an order from on high, made them suffer. My childhood went by, singed between fire and love."

(Opening remarks made by the Peruvian author before reading some of his work at a public gathering of fiction writers in Arequipa on June 14, 1965.)

José María Arguedas wrote three types of literature. There was fiction such as *Deep Rivers*, written in Spanish. Second, he wrote poetry, almost all of it in Quechua.[1] Many of his poems were collected posthumously in *Katatay*. After 1953 he earned his living as a museum curator and ethnographer of peasant life in the Andes. When we compare his technical, ethnological accounts with his novels, we see that the themes are almost always the same, but the language of the analytical reports, standard Spanish, was for him a third language, the only one of the three that he did not create.

When Arguedas first came down from the highlands of Peru in the thirties, he meant to be a Quechua writer. Everyone he met while working at the post office and studying part-time at the university discouraged him; there were, in fact, no Quechua writers. His earliest stories in Spanish were well received; the few intellectuals in Lima interested in the Andes encouraged him to write and publish; it was opportune, they said, to do so in the language the influential city people read and understood.

But, as he regretfully told me in later years, he was finally talked out of his plan to write in Quechua not by Lima pessimists, but by Moises Sáenz, the Mexican revolutionary, then his country's ambassador to Peru. Here was the representative of the proindigenous President Cárdenas, of the one successful modern revolution in the Americas—a man who cared enough about the Andean populations of Ecuador and Peru to write books about them. Sáenz assured him that the native languages had no chance as literary vehicles in the Americas of our time. Before Arguedas died, by his own hand, in 1969, as he began to write fiction again, after a long, dry (if anthropologically active) writing spell, he regretted this early decision. The Quechua poems of his last period, few in number but dealing with themes that do not always surface in his fic-

---

1. Quechua is spoken by millions of people in the five countries located in the Andes. There are at least as many Quechua speakers in the world as there are people speaking Swedish.

tion, were very important to him. He frequently published them himself, sometimes, but not always, providing a Spanish translation.

There are few translations of José María Arguedas into English and fewer still of his longer work done in the sixties; the daring of Frances Barraclough in undertaking this translation deserves our praise and gratitude. There are excellent reasons for hesitating; Arguedas did not write with us in mind. He was not surprised when a Scottish poet told him he found *Los Ríos Profundos* [*Deep Rivers*] untranslatable. He had given up Quechua in fiction, but he still saw himself as talking not only about the Andean peoples, but for and *to* them.

This immediately differentiates Arguedas from other *indigenista* writers of Mexico, Ecuador, or his own country. He not only knew Quechua well and had an emotional commitment to it and its speakers, but, unlike the other proindigenous novelists, he was also aware of its literary potential. "We Quechua speakers know very well that Quechua and Aymara are languages with vast expressive possibilities," he once said in 1966.[2] "These possibilities imply an equally vast development of human thought and experience." He not only saw the suffering of the Andean peoples, but used his anthropological work to argue that when conditions were even halfway favorable, they were likely to domesticate and interiorize the dominant culture, incorporating European features into Andean institutional forms.

When highlanders speak Spanish, they do so on Quechua grammatical underpinnings. It is not a matter of a surviving vocabulary, but of sentence structure; even when every word is Spanish, these have been rearranged according to the rules of Quechua syntax, of which the speaker is usually unaware, since the Andean mother tongues are not taught in the primary schools. Speakers and students of creole and pidgin languages in the Caribbean and elsewhere and readers of George Lamming and Errol Hill will have less difficulty imagining the magnitude of Arguedas's undertaking—how to transmit to the reader of Spanish not only compassion for the oppressed, but a sense that the latter also had a perception, a world view of their own, in which people, mountains, animals, the rain, truth, all had dimensions of their own, powerful, revealing, and utterly unlike the Iberian ones.

In creating this language, Arguedas did not just translate what his characters said, nor was he content with a caricature like the

2. *Mesa redonda sobre el monolinguismo quechua* . . . (Lima, 1966) p. 50.

speech of Hemingway's Spaniards. He took the very turns of phrase for which Andean speakers of Spanish are mocked, and used them in his fiction, so that their outlandishness, their "incorrectness," conveys to the middle-class reader of Spanish that he is missing another cultural context. I particularly remember the conversation in which a friend, a literary critic of note and the promoter of the linguistic study of the Andean languages, complained to Arguedas that his characters, like highlanders one met every day, insisted in repeating the same verb (*decir*, "to say"), twice in almost every sentence. They would interrupt the narrative, repeating *diciendo, dijo*, "so saying, he said," or *diciendo, dicen*, "so saying, they say." Arguedas explained that the genius of Andean languages required that the speaker indicate in *each* sentence if his account dealt with hearsay, was the report of an eyewitness, or was a quotation. In the last case one had to verbalize our quotation marks by saying each time after quoting: *nispa*, "so saying." If you then also indicate whom you were quoting, it sounds strange to outsiders: *nispa ninchis*, "saying, we say"; *nispa ninku*, "saying, they say."

When Arguedas insisted on using these rules, which seemed to make his literary language clumsy or archaic, his aim was to convey to the Spanish-reading public the grammatical, but in the context also the ethical, requirements of Andean speech.[3] He went beyond revelation of character and plot in his artistic creation; this includes the very language in which he communicates Andean experience to us. Alberto Escobar, a careful student of Arguedas's art, concludes: "The author was forced to undertake an extremely risky confrontation with the Spanish language, as a result of which it has emerged revitalized and more expressive."

The urban middle classes have received this message with extraordinary ambivalence. On the one hand, they are proud of him. Arguedas was even in life one of the nation's glories, with prizes, translations, and constant invitations to visit and lecture abroad. When he tried, unsuccessfully, to commit suicide in April, 1966, the radio transmitted bulletins about his condition and hundreds gathered at the hospital; cabinet ministers called on him and promised the moon if only he would get well. On the other hand, Arguedas reminded them constantly of the highland population whose very existence they tried to forget, convinced that soon the truck, the monetary economy, the transistor radio, and migration to the cities would eliminate the need to contemplate those who

3. No one has yet undertaken to translate Arguedas into Quechua.

insisted on speaking Andean languages, raising Andean crops, and praying to the snow-covered Andes, their ancestors.

Arguedas was continually criticized from the right and the left as a romantic, a visionary, and an antiquarian. In later years he did most of his writing abroad. One of his major works is dedicated to Dr. Lola Hoffman, a Jungian psychoanalyst in Santiago, Chile. It was my sad privilege to witness one public attack, organized by his colleagues, many of them his friends and fond of him, particularly when he sang in Quechua, but merciless when he told them that their "development" plans, xeroxed from alien models, did not take into account what Andean man could do for himself, out of his own perception of his own needs and their satisfaction. The night after this attack, during which few had defended him, Arguedas wrote a poem, *Huk Docturkunaman Qayay*, which in English is approximately "A Call upon or to Some Doctors":

They say that we don't know anything, that we are backwardness, that they'll exchange our heads for others, better ones.

They say that our heart also does not match the times, that it is full of fear, tears, like the calendar lark; like the heart of a huge, butchered bull; and thus (saying) we are impertinent.

They say that some doctors tell this about us; doctors who multiply in our land, who grow fat here, get golden. . . .

What are my brains made of? Of what the flesh of my heart?

The rivers run roaring in their depth. Gold and night, silver and the fearsome night shape the rocks, the walls of the canyons the river sounding against them; of that silver and gold night-rock are my mind, my heart, my fingers.

What's there, at river's edge, unknown to you, doctor?

Take out your binoculars, your best lenses. Look, if you can.

Five hundred kinds of flowers of as many kinds of potatoes grow on the balconies unreached by your eyes; they grow in the earth; mixed with night and gold, silver and day. Those five hundred flowers are my brains, my flesh.

Why did the sun stop for an instant, why have the shadows disappeared? Why, doctor?

Start your helicopter and climb here, if you can. The condor's feathers, those of smaller birds, light up, are now a rainbow.

The hundred flowers of *quinua* which I planted at the summit
    bubble their colors in the Sun; the black wings of the condor
    and of the tiny birds are now in flower.

It is noon; I am close to the lord-mountains, the ancestor-peaks;
    their snow now yellow flecked, now with red patches, is shin-
    ing in the Sun.

.   .   .   .

Don't run away from me, doctor, come close!
    Take a good look at me, recognize me.
    How long must I wait for you?

Come close to me; lift me to the cabin of your helicopter. I will
    toast you with a drink of a thousand different flowers, the life
    of a thousand crops I grew in centuries, from the foot of the
    snows to the forests of the wild bears.

I will cure your weariness, which clouds you; I will divert you
    with the light of a hundred *quinua* flowers, with the sight of
    their dance as the winds blow; with the slight heart of the
    calendar lark which mirrors the whole world;

I will refresh you with the singing water which I will draw out of
    the black canyon's walls . . .

Did I work for centuries of months and years in order that some-
    one I do not know and does not know me,
    cut off my head with a small blade?

No, brother mine. Don't sharpen that blade; come close,
    let me know you; look at my face, my veins;
    the winds blowing from us to you, we all breathe them;
    the earth on which you count your books, your machines,
    your flowers,
    it comes down from mine, improved, no longer angry,
    a tamed earth.

.   .   .   .

We know that they want to misshape our face with clay;
    exhibit us, deformed, before our sons.

We don't know what will happen. Let death walk towards us,
    let these unknown people come.

We will await them; we are the sons of the father
of all the lord mountains; sons of the
father of all the rivers. . . . . .

John V. Murra

Deep Rivers

1. The Old Man

He inspired respect, in spite of his old-fashioned and dirty appearance. The important people of Cuzco greeted him courteously. He always carried a gold-headed cane; his wide-brimmed hat cast a slight shadow on his forehead. It was uncomfortable to go out with him, because he knelt down before all the churches and chapels and ostentatiously took off his hat to every priest he met.

My father hated him. He had worked as a clerk on the Old Man's haciendas. "From the mountaintops he shouts with the voice of the damned, letting his Indians know that he is everywhere. He stores up the fruit from his orchards and lets it spoil; he doesn't think it's worth taking to sell in Cuzco or in Abancay, and says it's too dear to leave for his *colonos*.[1] He'll go to hell," my father said of him.

They were relatives and hated each other. My father, however, had conceived some peculiar plan concerning the Old Man; and although he told me we were traveling to Abancay, we set out from a distant town for Cuzco. According to my father we were just passing through Cuzco. I was eager to arrive in the great city. And my first meeting with the Old Man was to be an unforgettable occasion.

---

1. Indians belonging to the haciendas.—Author. (See glossary for Spanish and Quechua words not explained in the notes.—Trans.)

We entered Cuzco by night. The train station and the wide avenue along which we proceeded slowly, on foot, surprised me. The electric street lights were dimmer than those of some small towns I had known. Iron or wooden railings protected gardens and modern houses. This couldn't be the Cuzco my father had described to me a thousand times.

My father walked along close to the walls, hiding within the shadow. Cuzco was his native city and he did not want to be recognized. We must have looked like fugitives, but we weren't coming home in defeat; instead we were carrying out an important plan.

"I'll make him do it. I can ruin him!" my father said, referring to the Old Man.

When we came to the narrower streets, my father walked behind me and the men who were carrying the luggage.

Carved balconies and imposing, harmonious façades began appearing, and we caught glimpses of streets winding along the slope of the mountain. But not one ancient wall!

I was already familiar with those overhanging balconies, stone façades and sculptured entryways, and the great, arched courtyards, having seen them beneath the sun of Huamanga. I examined the streets, looking for Inca walls.

"Look over there," my father told me. It was the palace of an Inca.

When my father indicated the wall, I paused. It was dark, rough; its inclined surface was alluring. The white wall of the second story continued upward in a straight line from the Inca wall.[2]

"You'll have time to see it later. Let's try to find the Old Man," he told me.

We had come to the Old Man's house. It was on the same street as the Inca wall.

We entered the first courtyard. It was surrounded by a porch with stone arches and columns that supported the second story, which in turn had arches, but narrower ones. Dim light bulbs enabled us to see the outline of the completely silent courtyard. My father called out. A mestizo came down from the second floor, followed by an Indian. The stairway was rather narrow compared to the vastness of the courtyard and its porches.

The mestizo carried a lamp and led us to the second courtyard. It had neither arches nor a second story, only a porch with wooden

2. In Cuzco, as in other Inca towns, the Spaniards used the remains of the ancient walls as a base on which to construct the second stories of modern houses or churches.—Trans.

columns. It was dark; there was no electric lighting. We saw lamps in some of the rooms. People were talking loudly in some of them. The rooms must have been rented. The Old Man lived on the largest of his Apurímac haciendas; he came to the city from time to time for business or religious festivals. Some of the tenants came out to watch us go by.

A *cedrón*[3] tree shed its fragrance over the courtyard, although it was low, with shabby branches. The little tree showed white scars on its trunk, where the children must have made a martyr of it.

The Indian carried our bundles. I observed him carefully because I assumed he was the *pongo*.[4] His very tight pants reached only to the knee. He was barefoot; the muscles of his legs were like hard, shiny knots. "The Old Man must make him wash himself here in Cuzco," I thought. He was frail and spindly, and not tall. The straw frame showed through the edge of his bowl-shaped felt hat. He did not look at us. Beneath his hat brim I could see his aquiline nose, his sunken eyes, and the tendons that stood out on his neck. The expression of the mestizo was, on the other hand, almost insolent. He wore riding pants and boots.

They took us to the third courtyard, which had no porches at all.

I smelled the reek of a dung heap there. But the image of the Inca wall and the perfume of the *cedrón* tree continued to comfort me.

"Here?" asked my father.

"That's what the gentleman said. He chose it," answered the mestizo.

He kicked open the door. My father paid the porters and sent them away.

"Tell the gentleman that I'm coming, that I'll go to his bedroom immediately. It's urgent," my father commanded the mestizo.

The latter put the lamp on the adobe seat that was built against the wall of the room. He started to say something, but my father looked at him sternly and the man obeyed. We were left alone.

"It's a kitchen! We're in the animals' courtyard," my father exclaimed.

He took me by the arm.

"It's the mule drivers' kitchen," he told me. "We'll leave the first thing tomorrow for Abancay. Don't cry. I'm not going to risk

3. Lemon verbena, whose leaves are used for tea.—Trans.
4. Hacienda Indians who are obliged to take turns working as unpaid servants in the landowner's house.—Author

being sent to hell for trying to squeeze something out of a wicked old man."

I noticed that his voice was breaking and I hugged him.

"We're in Cuzco!" I said.

"That's why!"

He went out. I followed him to the door.

"Wait for me, or go to see the wall," he told me. "I must speak with the Old Man right away."

He crossed the courtyard rapidly, as if it were lighted.

The room they had given us was a kitchen for Indians. Spots of soot reached up to the ceiling from the Indian *tullpa*, a stone hearth in the corner. Adobe seats were built against the walls all around the room. A carved wooden bedstead with a kind of canopy of red cloth contradicted the lowliness of the kitchen. The spotless green silk spread which covered the bedstead heightened the contrast. "The Old Man," I thought. "So this is the way he welcomes us."

I didn't feel out of place in that room. It was quite similar to the kitchen in which they had made me live when I was a small child—the dark chamber where I had been cared for and where I had heard the music, the songs, and the low, sweet speech of the Indian servants and the *concertados*.[5] But this carved bedstead, what did it mean? The outrageous soul of the Old Man, his mad desire to offend the recent arrival, the globetrotting relative, who dared to return. We did not need him. Why had my father come to him? Why did he want to ruin the Old Man? It would have been better to let him continue to rot away with sin.

Forewarned, the Old Man had chosen the best way to offend my father. We would leave at dawn to cross the Anta Plain! It was settled. I ran to see the wall.

It turned a corner, ran the length of a wide street and continued along a narrower, dark one that climbed the hill and reeked of urine. I walked along the wall, stone by stone. I stood back a few steps, contemplating it, and then came closer again. I touched the stone with my hands, following the line, which was as undulating and unpredictable as a river, where the blocks of stone were joined. In the dark street, in the silence, the wall appeared to be alive; the lines I had touched between the stones burned on the palms of my hands.

For a long time no one came down the street. But while I was stooping to look at one of the stones, a man appeared from an

---

5. Hacienda workers who are paid by the year.—Author

upper street corner. I stood up. Before me was a high, half-ruined adobe wall. I leaned against it. The man urinated in the middle of the street and then walked on. "He'll disappear," I thought. "He'll sink out of sight." Not because he had urinated, but because he stopped walking and seemed to wrestle with the shadow of the wall. He paused a moment, completely hidden in the darkness that flowed from the stones, then came to where I stood and stumbled past me. He reached the lighted corner and turned. He must have been a drunkard.

My examination of the wall and the rapport that was developing between it and me had not seemed to affect him. My father had spoken to me of his native city, of its palaces, temples, and plazas, during the trips we made across Andean Peru, from east to west and from north to south. I had grown up on those journeys.

When my father confronted his enemies, and even more when he stood contemplating the mountains from the town plazas and it seemed as if rivers of tears might flow from his blue eyes— tears which he always seemed to hide beneath a mask—I would think of Cuzco. I knew that in the end we would arrive in the great city. "We will find eternal happiness," my father exclaimed one afternoon in Pampas, where we had been closed in by a wall of hatred.

The stones of the Inca wall were larger and stranger than I had imagined; they seemed to be bubbling up beneath the whitewashed second story, which had no windows on the side facing the narrow street. Then I remembered the Quechua songs which continually repeat one pathetic phrase: *yawar mayu*, "bloody river"; *yawar unu*, "bloody water"; *puk'tik yawar k'ocha*, "boiling bloody lake"; *yawar wek'e*, "bloody tears." Couldn't one say *yawar rumi*, "bloody stone," or *puk'tik yawar rumi*, "boiling bloody stone"? The wall was stationary, but all its lines were seething and its surface was as changeable as that of the flooding summer rivers which have similar crests near the center, where the current flows the swiftest and is the most terrifying. The Indians call these muddy rivers *yawar mayu* because when the sun shines on them they seem to glisten like blood. They also call the most violent tempo of the war dances, the moment when the dancers are fighting, *yawar mayu*.

"*Puk'tik yawar rumi*," I exclaimed, facing the wall.

And as the street remained silent, I repeated the phrase several times.

Just then my father reached the corner. He heard my voice and came up the narrow street.

"The Old Man has pleaded with me and apologized," he said,

"but I know it's all crocodile tears. We'll leave tomorrow. He says all the rooms in the first courtyard are full of furniture, bags, and junk; that he's had them bring down my father's bedstead for me. It's all lies. But I'm a Christian and we'll have to attend mass at dawn with the Old Man in the cathedral. We'll leave immediately afterward. We weren't really coming to Cuzco, we were just passing through on the way to Abancay. We'll go on with our trip. This is the palace of the Inca Roca.[6] The Plaza de Armas[7] is nearby. We'll take our time and also go to see the temple of Acllahuasi. Cuzco is the same as ever. The drunkards and passers-by still urinate here. Later on there'll be other filth . . . Memories are better. It's time to leave."

"Let the Old Man damn himself to hell," I told him. "Is someone living in the palace of the Inca Roca?"

"Ever since the Conquest."

"Are they living there now?"

"Haven't you seen the balconies?"

The colonial structure overhanging the wall had the appearance of a second story. I had forgotten about it. On the narrow street the whitewashed Spanish wall seemed to have no other purpose than that of brightening the Inca wall.

"Papa, every stone is talking. Let's wait a moment."

"We won't hear anything. It's not that they're talking. You're just confused. They get into your mind and disturb you."

"Each stone is different. They're not chiseled. They're moving."

He took my arm.

"They seem to be moving about because they're all different, more different than field stones. The Incas made the stones out of mud. I've told you that many times."

"Papa, it seems as if they're walking, that they move about and then become still again."

I hugged my father. Leaning against him, I contemplated the wall once more.

"Is someone living in the palace?" I asked again.

"A well-born family."

"Like the Old Man?"

"No. They're well-born, and at the same time misers, but not so miserly as the Old Man. Not like the Old Man! All the gentry of Cuzco are misers."

6. "The Inca" is the term of rank used for the ruler of the Incas.—Trans.
7. The main square which the Spaniards always established in the center of the cities they founded in the New World.—Trans.

"Does the Inca allow them to live there?"

"The Incas are dead."

"But not this wall. If the owner's a miser, why doesn't the wall swallow him up? This wall can walk; it could rise up into the sky or travel to the end of the world and back. Aren't the people who live in there afraid?"

"Son, the cathedral is close by. The Old Man has upset us. Let's go and pray."

"Wherever I go the Inca Roca's stones will go with me. I should like to swear to it right here."

"Swear to it? You're all excited, son. Let's go to the cathedral. It's too dark here."

He kissed me on the forehead. Although his hands were trembling, they were warm.

We walked down the street, crossed another very wide one, and then went along an alley which came out into the Plaza de Armas. We saw the domes of the cathedral. My father took me by the arm. The portico with its white arches came into view. We were in the shadow of the church.

"There's no one in the plaza now," my father said.

It was the largest one I had ever seen. It was as if the arches were on the distant perimeter of some silent plain in the icy highlands. What if we suddenly heard the call of a *yanawiku*, one of the wild ducks that forage around the ponds of those plains!

We entered the plaza. The little trees that had been planted in the park and the arches seemed intentionally dwarfed in the presence of the cathedral and the Jesuit church.

"They must not have been able to grow," I said. "They couldn't, in front of the cathedral."

My father led me up the steps to the terrace at the entrance of the cathedral and removed his hat as we neared the large central door. It took us a long time to cross the terrace. Our footsteps resounded on the stone. My father prayed as we walked along, not repeating the usual prayers, but talking freely to God. We were in the shadow of the façade. He did not tell me to pray; I just stood with my head uncovered, completely subdued. It was an immense façade; it seemed to be as wide as the base of the mountains that rise up from the shores of some highland lakes. In the silence, the towers and the terrace echoed the smallest sound, like the rocky mountains that border the icy lakes. The rocks send back deep echoes of the cry of the ducks or of the human voice. The echo is diffused, and seems to spring from the very breast of the traveler, who is alert to the silence and oppressed by it.

We recrossed the terrace, descended the steps, and entered the park.

"This was the plaza where the Incas held their ceremonies," said my father. "Take a good look at it, son. It's not square; it's longer from north to south."

The Jesuit church and the wide cathedral surrounded us with their rows of small arches that extended the lines of the walls. The cathedral was in front of us and the Jesuit church to one side. Where could I go? I wanted to fall down on my knees. Some people were walking about under the archways and I saw lights in a few stores, but no one crossed the plaza.

"Papa, the cathedral seems bigger when it's seen from farther off. Who made it?"

"The Spaniards, with the Inca stones and the hands of the Indians."

"The Jesuit church is higher."

"No, it's just narrower."

"And it has no terrace in front of it. It rises up out of the ground."

"It is not a cathedral, son."

The domes were partially visible in the darkness of the night.

"Does it ever rain on the cathedral? Does the rain fall on the cathedral?"

"Why do you ask?"

"The sky lights it, to be sure. But neither the lightning nor the rain must be able to touch it."

"The rain falls on it, but the lightning never does. The cathedral seems larger in the rain, in a shower or a downpour."

A patch of trees stood out on the mountainside.

"Eucalyptus?" I asked.

"They must be. They weren't there before. Behind them is the Fortress of Sacsayhuaman.[8] You won't get a chance to see it. We're leaving early and can't go there at night. The walls are dangerous. They say they devour children. But the stones are like those of the Inca Roca's palace, except that each one is higher than the top of the palace."

"Do the stones sing at night?"

"They might."

"Like the largest river boulders or cliff rocks. The Incas must have known the history of all the 'enchanted' stones and have had

8. A stone fortress more than a third of a mile long, built by the Incas in the fifteenth century.—Trans.

them brought to construct the fortress. And what about the ones they used for the cathedral?"

"The Spaniards reworked them. Look at the chiseled edge of the corner of the tower."

Even in the twilight one could see the edge; the lime that joined the cut stones made it stand out.

"Chiseling them must have broken their 'enchantment.' But perhaps the domes on the tower retain the radiance they say there is in heaven. Look, papa; they're glowing."

"Yes, son. As a child you see some things we older people cannot see. God's harmony exists on earth. We'll forgive the Old Man, since it was through him you came to know Cuzco. We'll come to the cathedral tomorrow."

"Is this plaza Spanish?"

"No, not the plaza. The arches and temples are, but not the square. The Inca Pachakutek', Renewer of the Earth, made it. Isn't it different from the hundreds of squares you've seen?"

"It must be because this one glows with the radiance of heaven. Look how the light is reflected on us from the sides of the towers. Let's stay here until dawn, papa!"

"It may be that God is more at home in this plaza because the Inca chose it to be the center of the world. It's not true that the world is round. It's oblong. Remember, son, that we have always walked the length and breadth of the world."

We approached the Jesuit church. Instead of being overpowering, it made me rejoice. I felt like singing in the doorway. I had no desire to pray. The cathedral was too big, as the gates of glory must seem to those who have suffered up until the hour of their death. Before the portal of the church, which I could easily take in at a glance, I suddenly wanted to sing a hymn, one different from those I had heard the Indians chorusing in Quechua as they wept in the small churches of the towns. No, not a song with tears.

We walked briskly to Amaru Cancha—the palace of Huayna Capac[9]—and the temple of the Acllas.

"Was the Jesuit church made of Inca stones, too?" I asked.

"What other stones would the Spaniards have used in Cuzco, son? You'll soon see."

The walls of the palace and the Inca temple formed a narrow street that led into the plaza.

"There's not a single door on this street," said my father. "It's

9. Amaru Cancha means "Snake Enclosure." Huayna Capac was one of the Inca emperors.—Trans.

the same as when the Incas were here. It's only a passageway. Come. Let's go on."

It seemed to be cut from the living rock. We always call unhewn rock that is covered with parasites or red lichen "living rock." This street was like the walls carved out by rivers, between which passes no one[10] but the waters, tranquil or turbulent.

"It's called Loreto Quijllu," said my father.

"*Quijllu*, papa?"

This is the Quechua name given to clefts in the rocks. Not for those found in ordinary stones, but for those enormous, endless crevasses that zigzag across the cordilleras of the Andes, beneath the snowfields that blind travelers with their glare.

"Here are the ruins of the Temple of Acllahuasi[11] and of Amaru Cancha," exclaimed my father.

The walls were serene, of perfect stones. The Temple of Acllahuasi was very high, and the other low, with serpents carved on the doorpost.

"Doesn't anyone live there?" I asked.

"Only in Acllahuasi—the Santa Catalina nuns live there, far from us. They're cloistered nuns. They never go out."

The Amaru Cancha, palace of Huayna Capac, was a ruin, gradually crumbling away at the top. The difference in height between its walls and those of the temple permitted light to enter the street, tempering the shadows.

The street was luminous, not rigid. Had it not been so narrow, the straight stones might perhaps have moved out of line. As it was, they fit tightly; they weren't bubbling or talking, nor did they have the spontaneity of those that frolicked in the wall of the palace of the Inca Roca; it was the wall who commanded silence, and if someone were to sing out clearly, the stones would echo, with perfect pitch, the very same music.

We stood together, and I was thinking of the way my father had described Cuzco on our journeys, when I heard a musical sound.

"The María Angola," I cried.

"Yes, be still. It's nine o'clock. It can be heard five leagues away on the Anta Plain. Travelers stop and cross themselves."

The world must have been changed into gold at that moment—

10. One of the first examples of Arguedas's personification of natural things.—Trans.

11. *Aclla*, "chosen woman"; *huasi*, "house." The *acllas* were women chosen from the upper ranks of the Inca empire and dedicated to religious service or to the service of the Inca emperor.—Trans.

I, too, as well as the walls and the city, the towers, and the façades I had seen.

The voice of the bell welled out again. And I seemed to see before me the image of my protectors, the Indian *alcaldes*[12]—Don Maywa and Don Victor Pusa, praying on their knees before the façade of the whitewashed, adobe church of my village, while the evening light sang instead of glowing. In the pepper trees the hawks—the *wamanchas* so greatly feared because they were carnivorous—lifted their heads, drinking in the light, drowning in it.

I knew the voice of the bell carried a distance of five leagues. I thought the plaza would explode with sound. But the vibrations expanded slowly, at spaced intervals—growing stronger, piercing the elements, transmuting everything into that Cuzco music that opened the doors of memory.

On the large lakes, especially those that have islands and clumps of giant cattail reeds, there are bells that ring at midnight. At their mournful tolling, bulls of fire, or of gold, emerge from the water dragging chains; they climb to the mountain peaks and bellow in the frost, because in Peru the lakes are in the highlands. I thought that those bells must be *illas*,[13] reflections of the María Angola, which would change the *amarus*[14] into bulls. From the center of the world the voice of the bell, sinking down into the lakes, must have transformed the ancient creatures.

"Papa," I said when the bell had stopped tolling, "didn't you tell me we were coming to Cuzco to find eternal happiness?"

"The Old Man is here," he said. "The Antichrist!"

"We're leaving tomorrow. He'll go off to his haciendas, too. The bells that are in the lakes we've seen in the highlands—mightn't they be *illas* of the María Angola?"

"Perhaps, son. You still think as a child."

"I've seen Don Maywa when he was ringing the bell."

"That's how it is. Its voice revives old memories."

The carved serpents over the door of Huayna Capac's palace were writhing in the darkness. They were the only things moving in that paved *quijllu*. They followed us, slithering, to the house.

The *pongo* was waiting in the doorway. He took off his hat and, bareheaded, followed us through to the third courtyard. He came soundlessly, his tousled hair on end. I spoke to him in Quechua.

12. Indian community leaders.—Trans.

13. For the explanation of this word see the beginning of chapter 6.—Trans.

14. Snakes.—Trans.

He looked at me, startled. "Doesn't he know how to talk?" I asked
my father.

"He doesn't dare," he told me. "Even though he is coming with
us to the kitchen."

In none of the hundreds of towns where I had lived with my
father were there any *pongos*.

"*Tayta*,"[15] I said to the Indian in Quechua, "are you from
Cuzco?"

"*Mánan*,"[16] he answered. "From the hacienda."

He wore a very short, ragged poncho. He asked permission to
leave, bowing like a worm asking to be crushed.

I clung to my father after he lit the lamp. The perfume of the
cedrón tree came in to us. I couldn't hold back my sobs. I wept as
if I were on the shore of a great unknown lake.

"It's Cuzco," my father told me. "That's what it does to the
sons of those who have left. It must also be the song of the María
Angola."

He didn't want to lie on the Old Man's bed.

"Let's make our own pallets," he said.

We spread our bedding on the floor, as we used to on the
porches of the houses where we lodged in the towns. My eyes filled
with tears. I saw the hacienda Indian, his bewildered face, the little snakes of Amaru Cancha, the lakes rippling to the sound of
the bell. The bulls must be plodding off now, seeking the mountain peaks.

We prayed aloud. My father asked God not to listen to the prayers that the Old Man intoned with his filthy mouth in all the
churches and even in the streets.

The following day he awakened me, calling, "It's growing light;
time for them to ring the bell."

He held in his hands the triple-lidded gold watch that he had
inherited from his father. He had never sold it. Sometimes he
looked like a madman winding that elaborate watch, while he was
dressed in threadbare clothing and too depressed even to shave.
In the town where the children massacred the birds and where we
were besieged by hunger, my father used to go out onto the porch.
Standing before the thicket of poisonous weeds that grew in the
courtyard, he would polish his watch, making it shine in the sun,
and the reflected light strengthened him.

15. Father, also used as an affectionate and respectful form of address.—
Trans.
16. No.—Trans.

"We'll get up after the bell rings, at five," he said.

"The gold that Doña María Angola gave to be melted to make the bell, was it jewelry?" I asked.

"We know that she gave a hundred pounds of gold. That metal was from Inca times. Perhaps they were fragments of the Sun of Inti Cancha[17] or of the walls of the temple, or of the idols. It could have been just pieces, or whole ornaments made from that gold. But the gold used to cast the bell wasn't just a hundred-weight; it was much more. María Angola alone brought a hundred pounds. The gold, my son, resounds so that the voice of the bells can rise up to heaven and return to earth with the song of the angels."

"And the ugly bells in the towns that had no gold?"

"They're forgotten towns. God will hear them, but what angel could they persuade to come down with such a noise? Man is also powerful. You'll never forget what you saw last night."

"Papa, I saw Don Pablo Maywa kneeling before the chapel in his town."

"But remember, son, the small bells in that town had gold in them. That was a mining town."

At that moment the first stroke of the María Angola rang out. Our room, covered with soot to the ceiling, began to vibrate with the slow reverberations of sound. The vibration was a sad one; webs of soot swayed back and forth like black rags. We knelt to pray. The final waves could still be felt, dying out in the air, when the second, even more sorrowful stroke sounded.

I was fourteen years old; I had spent my childhood in an alien house, always tended by cruel people. The master of the house, the father, had reddish eyelids and thick eyelashes and took pleasure in making the servants and animals who depended on him suffer. Afterwards, when my father rescued me and I wandered with him through the towns, I found that people everywhere suffered. Perhaps the María Angola mourned for all of them, here in Cuzco. I had never seen anyone more humiliated than the Old Man's *pongo*. At every stroke the bell became more mournful and its sound penetrated everything.

"Who made it, papa?" I asked, after the last stroke.

"The bellmakers of Cuzco. That's all we know."

"It couldn't have been a Spaniard."

"Why not? They were the best workmen, the master craftsmen."

17. A great, round, golden disk that hung on the wall in the Temple of the Sun in Cuzco. *Inti*, "sun"; *cancha*, "enclosure."—Trans.

"The Spaniard suffered too?"

"He believed in God, son. The more important he was, the more he humbled himself to him. And they killed each other, too. But now we must hurry to get our things ready."

It must have been almost daylight. The Old Man's carved bedstead exhibited itself clearly in the middle of the room. Its absurd canopy and silken coverlet irritated me. Against the humiliating background of soot it would have looked better in pieces.

We repacked my father's mattress, the three sheepskins on which I slept, and our blankets.

As we left, many of the tenants from the second courtyard, who were gathered around a water fountain, holding buckets and pots, looked at us in surprise. The *cedrón* tree, planted in the middle of the courtyard in the driest, hardest earth, had a few red flowers on its top branches. The bark was almost completely peeled off the trunk up to where it began to branch.

The walls of the courtyard, which hadn't been painted for perhaps a hundred years, were crisscrossed with simple lines and pictures drawn in charcoal by the children. The courtyard stank of urine and stagnant water; but the most unhappy being of all who lived there must have been the *cedrón*. "If it should die, if it should wither, the courtyard would look like an inferno," I said in a low voice. "Nevertheless they'll undoubtedly kill it by peeling off all the bark."

We found the first courtyard clean and silent; it was the owner's. Above us, the bareheaded *pongo* stood next to a second-story pillar. He disappeared, but when we climbed to the second floor we found him leaning against the rear wall.

He greeted us and, bowing, went over to my father and kissed his hands.

"Child, little child!" he said to me, and followed us, whimpering.

The mestizo stood guard by the carved door.

"The gentleman is waiting for you," he said, opening the door.

I entered quickly behind my father.

The Old Man was seated on a sofa. It was a very large room, unlike any I had ever seen, with the entire floor covered with a rug. Mirrors with wide, dark, gilded frames decorated the walls; a crystal chandelier hung from the center of the paneled ceiling. Tall high-backed chairs were upholstered in red. The Old Man did not get up; we went to him. My father did not shake hands, but presented me.

"Your uncle, the owner of the four haciendas," he said.

The Old Man looked at me as if he were trying to make me sink into the rug. I saw that his coat was rather frayed at the lapel and that it had an unpleasant sheen to it. In Huamanga a tailor friend of mine and I had guffawed at the ancient coats some miserly grand *señores* sent to be mended.[18] "This mirror is useless," exclaimed the tailor in Quechua. "The only one who sees his face here is the devil who stands watch over the *señor* to carry him off to hell."

I bowed and shook hands with the Old Man. The large room had confused me. I had been so frightened as I crossed it that I hardly knew how to walk. But the grimy sheen I observed on the Old Man's coat set me at ease. The Old Man kept staring at me with the smallest, brightest eyes I had ever seen. He was trying to make me give in! Why? His thin lips were pressed tightly together. Then he looked at my father. Being impetuous and good-hearted, my father would have preferred to be by himself, out walking through the towns, among Indians and mestizos.

"What is your name?" the Old Man asked, again training his eyes on me.

I was ready for him this time. I had seen Cuzco. I knew that misers lived within the walls of the Inca palaces. "He called me *tú*,"[19] I thought, staring back. The far-carrying sound of the great bell and the snakes from the palace door were still with me. We were in the center of the world.

"I have the same name as my grandfather, *señor*," I told him.

"*Señor*? Am I not your uncle?"

I knew that the convent friars prepared grand evening receptions for him, that the clergy greeted him in the streets; but he had had us sent to the kitchen of his house; he'd ordered that carved bedstead set up before the soot-covered wall. This man could not be more wicked or powerful than my guardian with the eyebrows that met over his nose, who had also made me sleep in the kitchen.

"You're my uncle. It's time for us to go now, *señor*."

I saw that my father was delighted despite his almost solemn expression.

The Old Man arose, smiling, without looking at me. Then I

18. Throughout this book *señor* is used in the sense of a *seigneur*—a feudal lord or lord of a manor. An hacienda owner is called *señor* by Indians belonging to him.—Trans.

19. The familiar form of "you," used by superiors to address inferiors, among friends, and in addressing children and animals.—Trans.

noticed his ashen complexion and his leathery skin that looked as
if it were falling from his bones. He went to a cabinet where there
hung many canes, all of them with golden heads.

The door of the parlor had been left open, and I could see the
pongo, clothed in rags, his back to the balcony railing. Even from
this distance one could sense the invisible weight that oppressed
his breathing and the effort that he was making just to appear to
be alive.

The Old Man handed my father a black cane; its golden handle
was shaped like the head and neck of an eagle. He insisted on my
father's taking it and carrying it. They didn't look at me. My father took the cane and leaned on it; the Old Man chose one with a
plainer head, like the staff of an Indian *alcalde*.

When he passed me I noticed that the Old Man was very short,
almost a dwarf; nevertheless he walked with a pretentious air and
looked imposing even from behind.

We went out onto the balcony. The bells began to ring. The
sound of all the others could be heard early over the background
of the very deliberate strokes of the María Angola.

The *pongo* tried to approach us; the Old Man shooed him away
with his cane.

It was cold in the street, but the bells brought cheer to the city.
I waited for the voice of the María Angola. Above its reverberations that embraced the whole world, the pealing of all the other
church bells could be heard. The ponderous tolling revived in my
mind the humiliated image of the *pongo*, his deep-set eyes, the
bones of his nose—the only energetic-looking thing about him—
and his bare head with hair that seemed to be purposely tousled
and covered with filth. "He has no father nor mother, only his
shadow," I kept repeating to myself, remembering the words of a
huayno,[20] as with each step I awaited a new stroke of the immense
bell.

The ringing call to mass ended, and I was free to take a better
look at the city by daylight. We were to leave within the hour. The
Old Man was talking.

"Built by the Inca Roca. Shows the chaos of the heathens, of
primitive minds." His voice was penetrating and didn't seem to be
that of an old man who was gray-haired with age, but still vig-
orous.

The lines of the wall frolicked in the sun; the stones had neither

20. A folk song and dance of Inca origin.—Author

angles nor straight lines; each one was like a beast that moved in the sunlight, making me want to rejoice, to run shouting with joy, through some field. I would have done so, but the Old Man kept on with his preaching, choosing his words, as if trying to over-whelm my father.

When we came to the corner of the main square, the Old Man knelt and removed his hat. He bowed his head and slowly crossed himself. Although many people recognized him, no one laughed. A few boys approached us. My father stood leaning on his cane a short distance from the Old Man. I waited for a *huayronk'o* to appear and spit blood on his forehead, because these flying insects are harbingers of the devil or of the damnation of the saints. The Old Man got up and hurried off. He didn't put his hat back on, but walked with his gray head bare. My father followed him po-litely. In a moment we arrived at the door of the cathedral. The Old Man was arrogant; I should have liked to take hold of his shoulders and shake him, but he probably wouldn't have fallen, for he seemed to be very heavy, as if he were made of iron, and he walked quite energetically.

We went into the church and the Old Man knelt on the tiles. Among columns surrounded by an aura of gold, I felt subdued by the towering arches. From somewhere above came a sound more like the buzzing of bumblebees than the praying of a men's chorus. There were very few people in the church. Indian women, their heads covered by multicolored shawls, were weeping. The cathedral did not glow as it had before. The light that filtered through the alabaster windows was different from sunlight. As in the legends, it seemed as if we had fallen into some city hidden in the center of a mountain, under layers of inextinguishable ice that sent us light through the rocks. A high choir loft of polished wood rose up in the center of the church. The Old Man stood up and led us to the nave on our right.

"Our Lord of the Earthquakes," he said, showing us an altar-piece that extended upward to the top of the arch. He looked at me as though I weren't a child.

I knelt near him, with my father on the other side.

A forest of candles burned before the crucifix. The Christ could be seen through the smoke, with a gilt altar screen in the back-ground between columns and arches on which figures of angels, fruit, and animals had been carved.

I knew that when this crucifixion image appeared at the door of the cathedral all the Indians of Cuzco made an outcry that caused the whole city to tremble, and that afterwards they took delicate red flowers called *ñujchu*, and with them covered the streets, the roads, and the litter which carried the image of the Lord.

The face of the crucified Christ was dark and gaunt, like that of the *pongo*. In the processions, with his arms outstretched, his wounds deep, his hair fallen to one side, he would advance like a black spot against the brilliance of the plaza, with the cathedral, mountains, and winding streets behind him, intensifying the afflictions of the suffering, showing himself to be the one who, unceasingly, suffers the most. Now, through the smoke of the flickering light of the candles and the morning, he appeared over an altar, seething with gold as if seen through a sunset over the ocean in some torrid zone, where the golden light is soft and gleaming, and not heavy and flaming as it is in the clouds over the high, cold Andes, where the setting sun rends its awesome mantles.

Blackened, suffering, the Christ maintained a silence that did not set one at ease. He made one suffer; in such a vast cathedral, in the midst of the candle flames and the daylight that filtered down dimly, the countenance of the Christ caused suffering, extending it to the walls, to the arches and columns, from which I expected to see tears flow. But the Old Man was there, praying rapidly in his metallic voice. The wrinkles on his forehead jutted out in the candlelight; it was these furrows that gave the impression that his skin had come away from his bones.

"There isn't time for more," he said.

We did not hear mass. We left the church and hurriedly returned to the house, with the Old Man in the lead.

We did not go into the church of the Society of Jesus; I did not even get another look at its façade; I saw only the shadow of its towers on the square.

At the door of the house we found a truck. The mestizo with boots was talking with the driver. They had put our gear up onto the truck. We had no need to go into the courtyard again.

"Everything is ready, sir," said the mestizo.

My father handed the Old Man his cane.

I ran back to the second courtyard. I said good-bye to the little tree. As I stood before it, looking up at its shabby branches and the few dark flowers that trembled there, I feared Cuzco. The visage of the Christ, the voice of the big bell, the perpetually frightened expression of the *pongo*, and the Old Man on his knees in the cathedral, even the silence of the Loreto Quijllu depressed me. Nowhere else must human beings suffer so much as here. The shadow of the cathedral and the voice of the María Angola at dawn were reborn; they came back to me. I went out. It was time to leave.

The Old Man shook hands with me.

"We shall see each other again," he said.

I thought he looked happy. A short distance away the *pongo* stood leaning against the wall. Through the torn places in his shirt one could see parts of his chest and arms. My father was already in the truck. I went up to the *pongo* and said good-bye. This time he wasn't so startled. I hugged him without shaking his hand. He started to smile, but whined instead, exclaiming in Quechua, "Little child, now you are going; now you are leaving! Now you are leaving!"

I ran to the truck. The Old Man raised the two canes in a gesture of farewell.

"We should go to the church of the Society of Jesus," my father told me when the truck began to move. "There are some balconies near the main altar; yes, son, some carved balconies with golden lattices that conceal those who hear mass there. They were for the cloistered nuns. But I know that at dawn the littlest angels come down there and hover about, singing beneath the dome, at the very moment the María Angola is rung. Their happiness reigns throughout the church for the rest of the day."

He had forgotten the Old Man, who had been in such a hurry to send us off without even hearing mass, and remembered only the city, his beloved Cuzco, and the churches.

"Papa, the cathedral makes people suffer."

"That's why the Jesuits built their church. They represent the world and salvation."

Once we were on the train, I watched the city spread out before me in the blazing sunlight that shone upon the tiled roofs and the domes of stone and lime, and I spied the Fortress of Sacsayhuaman beyond the hill where the eucalyptus trees had been planted.

In broken ranks the walls settled into the gray, grassy slope. Some black birds, smaller than condors, soared over the rows of walls or plummeted down from the depths of the sky. My father saw me contemplating the ruins and did not speak to me. Farther up, when Sacsayhuaman appeared, encircling the mountains, and I could distinguish the rounded, blunt profile of the angles of the walls, he said to me, "They are like the Inca Roca's stones. They say they will last until Judgment Day, and that the archangel will blow his trumpet here."

Then I asked about the birds that soared over the fortress.

"They're always there," he told me. "Don't you remember that *huaman* means 'eagle'? *Sacsay huaman* means 'satiated eagle.' "

"Satiated? They must fill themselves with air."

"No, son. They don't eat. They're the fortress eagles. They don't need to eat, just soar over the fortress. They never die. They'll be at the Final Judgment."

"On that day the Old Man will appear looking even worse, and more ashen, than he does now."

"He won't appear. The Final Judgment is not for devils."

We crossed over the summit to Iscuchaca. There we rented horses in order to continue our trip to Abancay. We would go by the Anta Plain.

As we trotted across that immense plain, I saw Cuzco in my mind—the church domes in the sunlight, the long plaza where the trees were unable to grow. How then had those eucalyptus trees developed on the slopes of Sacsayhuaman? Perhaps all the miserly *señores* who had dwelt on those ancient sites since the Conquest had poisoned the earth of the city with their breath. I recalled the image of the little *cedrón* at the Old Man's house.

My father went along tranquilly. The joy he felt at the start of every long trip showed in his blue eyes. His plans had been frustrated, but we were riding along at a trot. The smell of the horses made us happy.

In the afternoon we arrived at the summit of the high mountain ranges that bordered the Apurímac. "God-who-speaks" is the meaning of the name of this river.

A stranger comes upon it almost suddenly, seeing before him an endless chain of alternating black and snow-clad mountains. The sound of the Apurímac rises faintly from the gorge to the peaks, like a murmur from outer space.

The river runs through blackish woods and patches of canebrakes that grow only in the hot lowlands. The canebrakes snake along the steep slopes or seem to hang suspended over the cliffs. The clear air of the highlands becomes denser near the bottom of the valley.

Suddenly the traveler enters the gorge. The voice of the river, the profundity of the dusty gorge, the sparkle of the distant snows, and the rocks that shine like mirrors all awaken in his mind primeval memories, the most ancient of dreams.

As he descends to the bottom of the valley, the newcomer feels transparent, like a crystal in which the world is vibrating. Buzzing gnats appear in the subtropical zone; clouds of poisonous mosquitoes prick his face. The traveler from the cold highlands nears the river in a state of confusion, feverish, with swollen veins. The voice of the river grows louder, but doesn't become deafening; instead it makes one feel excited. It charms children, giving them intimations of unknown worlds. The plumes of the reed thickets sway by the riverside. The current rushes down as though keeping time with the hoofbeats of horses, of great wild horses.

"*Apurímac mayu! Apurímac mayu!*" the Quechua-speaking children repeat with tenderness and a touch of fear.

2. The Journeys

My father could never find a place to settle down; he was a restless, wandering country lawyer. With him I came to know more than two hundred towns. He feared the hot valleys, only passing through them on his travels; he would stop off to live for a time in towns of milder climates: Pampas, Huaytará, Coracora, Puquio, Andahuaylas, Yauyos, Cangallo . . . all of them near streams with large, shiny boulders and small fish. The myrtle, the *lambras*, the weeping willow, the eucalyptus, the *capulí*, and the *tara* are all clean-wooded trees whose branches and leaves may be trimmed frequently. Contemplating them from afar, whoever seeks shade approaches them and rests under a tree that sings alone in a deep voice in which water, earth, and sky mingle.

Enormous boulders hold back the water of these streams to form eddies, pools, falls, and fords. Wooden bridges, suspension bridges, and hanging baskets for carrying people or things over the rivers are supported by them. They glisten in the sun. Because they are almost always smooth and polished, it is difficult to climb them. But from these stones one can see how the river flows, how it winds, and how the woods are reflected in its water. Men swim out to the largest stones; cutting through the water, they reach them and fall asleep there, for from no other place can the sound of the water be heard so clearly. Not everyone can reach the boulders in the big, wide rivers. Only the bravest swimmers, the heroes, can; the others, the faint-hearted and the children, are left behind. From the banks they watch the strongest men swim through the current in the deepest part of the river, reach the solitary rocks, climb them with difficulty, and then stand on them to contemplate the valley, to breathe in the light of the river and the power with which it rushes down to disappear into unknown regions.

But my father would decide to leave one town for another just when the mountains, the roads, the playing fields, the places where the birds sleep, and the details of the town were beginning to become a part of me.

My father liked to listen to *huaynos*. He didn't know how to sing, and he danced badly, and yet he remembered each town, community, or valley for its songs. A few days after arriving in a town, he would seek out the best harp, *charango*,[1] violin, or guitar player. He would call them in and they would spend the whole night in our house. In those towns only the Indians played harps and violins. The places my father rented were always the cheapest ones, in the middle of town. They had dirt floors and walls made of bare adobe or plastered with mud. A kerosene lamp gave us light. The musicians would play in one corner of the huge rooms. The Indian harpists played with their eyes closed. The voice of the harp seemed to flow from the darkness inside of its box; and the *charango* became a whirlwind that recorded the words and music of the songs in my memory.

In the small towns, at certain hours, the birds can be seen flying toward accustomed places. To the stony fields, to the orchards, to the shrubs that grow on the shores of the ponds. Their flights vary with the time of day. The people who live there do not observe these details, but travelers, people who must leave, never forget them. The *tuyas* prefer the tall trees; the goldfinches sleep or rest in the yellow bushes; the *chihuaco* sings in the dark-leaved trees, such as the alder, the eucalyptus, or the *lambras*; it doesn't go to the weeping willows. The doves seek out the old, hollowed-out walls. The wild pigeons fly to their groves in the valleys that seem to be far away; they prefer to be heard from a distance. The sparrow is the only one that may be found in all the towns and is everywhere. The widow bird swings on the large thorn bushes; it opens its black wings, flutters them, and then calls. The large parrots are migratory. The small parrots prefer the cactus and the thorn trees. As darkness begins to fall, the birds scatter through-

1. An instrument like a mandolin.—Trans.

out the sky; from each town they take off in different directions and those who have seen them never forget their flight patterns or confuse them in their minds.

Once we came to a town whose prominent citizens were hostile to strangers. It was a large town, with few Indians. The hillsides were covered with broad fields of flax so that the whole valley seemed to be sown with ponds of the blue flower, which was the color of highland waters. The fields look like shimmering lakes, forming ripples or waves depending on the strength of the wind.

All the roads near the town are lined with *capulíes*, tall, leafy trees with luminous trunks, the only fruit tree in the valley. The heavy-beaked birds—the *tuya*, the widow bird, and the *chihuaco* —could be found in the orchards, to which all of the children in town would rush at midday and in the afternoon. No one who had seen it could ever forget the war that the children of that town waged against the birds. In the wheat-growing towns, the children arm themselves with slings and empty cans; they walk along the paths that cross the wheatfields making their slings whir, singing, and beating on the cans. They entreat the birds and warn them, singing, "They're poisoning the wheat! Go away, go away! Fly, fly! This wheat belongs to the priest! Get out of here! Look for other fields!" In the town of which I am speaking, all of the children were armed with rubber slings; they hunted down the birds like enemies of war, collecting the bodies at the entrance to the orchards, in the road, and counting them: twenty *tuyas*, forty *chihuacos*, ten widow birds.

A high, steep hill was the lookout point for the town. On its summit stood a cross, the largest and strongest one I had ever seen. In May it was brought down to the town to be blessed. A host of Indians came from the valley communities and met with the few *comuneros* who lived in town at the foot of the hill. They were already drunk, and carried wineskins full of brandy. Then they climbed the hill, shouting and weeping. They removed the cross and carried it down bodily. They came along the thorny, barren slopes of the mountain, arriving after nightfall.

I left that town while the Indians were holding a vigil by their cross in the middle of the plaza. They had met with their women by the light of lamps and small bonfires. It was past midnight. On the street corners I nailed up some notices on which I bade farewell to the prominent people of the town, cursing them; then I set out on foot for Huancayo.

In that town they had tried to starve us out; they had posted a watchman at each corner to threaten any clients who came to my father's law office; they hated strangers like plagues of locusts. My father was to leave in a truck, at dawn; I departed on foot in the night. The cross lay in the plaza. There was little music; the sound of a few muted harps was lost on the plain.

The Indians usually move about during vespers, but in that plaza men and women still lay about on the ground; they were talking near the cross, in the shadow, like giant bullfrogs croaking in the swamps.

Far from there, when I had already reached the high mountain ranges, I came upon other towns that kept vigil by their crosses. They sang without much enthusiasm. But they were well lighted; hundreds of candles shone on the walls, against which they had propped the crosses.

In the pass, before crossing over the top of the ridge, I remembered the rows of *capulíes* that lined the town walls; how the birds wounded by the slingshots fell, entangling themselves in the branches; the tranquil stream without large stones, silently crossing the flax fields; the little fish whose flanks glistened in the sun; and the unforgettable, aggressive look on people's faces.

It had been a hostile town that lived in anger, infecting others with it. There was a store on a street corner where sorrel weeds grew, concealing many crickets and toads. A tall, young, blue-eyed girl lived there. Night after night I went to this corner to sing *huaynos* that had never before been heard in the town. From the mountain pass I could see the corner; it was almost at the end of town. I paid her disinterested homage. I would steal corn in the evenings; then my father and I would cook the ears in an earthenware pot, the only one in our house. Once we had eaten, we could spend some time hating the town and planning our escape. Finally we would lie down; but I would get up as soon as my father began to snore. Beyond the dry courtyard of our house was a long patio covered with tall weeds that were poisonous to animals. The *capulíes* in the neighboring garden stretched their long branches out over the yard. Fearing this dense undergrowth, in the midst of which thousands of wart-covered toads were hopping about, I never went near the branches of those *capulíes*. When I went out at night the toads would croak at intervals, their chill chorus accompanying me for many blocks. I would reach the corner and, in front of the store of the young girl, who seemed to be the only one in the town who did not look upon strangers with a disapproving eye, I would sing the *huaynos* of Querobamba, of Lambrama, of Sañayca, of Toraya, of Andahuaylas . . . of the most distant towns—songs of the deep valleys. I unburdened myself; I would pour out the bitter scorn and hatred with which that town looked upon us, fiery stories of my journeys through the high Andes, images of many rivers, of bridges that overhang desperately rushing waters, of the radiant light and shadow of the highest, most awesome clouds. Then I would slowly return home, thinking clearly of the time when I would be old enough and determined enough to approach a pretty woman, who would be all the more beautiful if she lived in some hostile town.

Across from Yauyos is the village of Cusi. Yauyos is in a small valley on a tributary of the Cañete River. The little stream originates on one of the few snow-clad mountains that lie on that side of the high ranges; the water comes tumbling down to reach the big river that flows through the far-off depths of the valley, through a gorge hidden between mountains that rise up abruptly without leaving space for clearings or bottom lands. Man plants the craggy slopes, leaning uphill to keep his balance. The bulls that pull the plow lean over, like the men, and at the end of the furrow take a half turn like circus animals, with careful, measured steps. In Yauyos the stream has three bridges: two made of concrete that are steady and safe, and an old one of eucalyptus logs covered with dried mud. Near the old bridge there is a eucalyptus plantation. From time to time flocks of parrots would come to perch in those huge trees. The parrots clung to the branches; they squawked and crept out to the very end of the limbs; they seemed to converse in screams, celebrating their arrival. But scarcely would they have begun to enjoy their rest when their cries would re-echo from the rocky cliffs. The hunters would come out of their houses, running, gun in hand, toward the wood. The call of the big parrots I have heard only in places where the sky is deep and unclouded.

I would reach the wood in Yauyos before the hunters, and watch the parrots and listen to their screams. Then the sharpshooters would come. The marksmen of Yauyos were said to be famous for their standing shots because they trained by shooting parrots. They would take aim, and at each shot a parrot fell; sometimes, with luck, two would be knocked down. Why didn't the flock scatter? Why didn't they take off at the sound of the explosions, when they saw the wounded falling all about them? Instead they stayed in the branches, screeching, clambering, hopping from one tree to another. I would make a noise, throw stones at the tree, shake cans full of stones; the hunters only made fun of me and kept on killing parrots with great formality. Groups of school children came to pick up the dead birds and string them up. Once the practice was over, the boys went off carrying lines that stretched the width of the street; from each line dangled thirty or forty blood-spattered parrots.

We spent only a few days in the town of Huancapi. Of all the provincial capitals I have known it is the poorest. It is in a wide, cold valley, high in the Andes. All the houses are thatched with straw, and only the outsiders—the judge, the telegraph operator, the sub-prefect, the schoolteachers, and the priest—are not Indians. On the mountain slopes, the dry grasses quiver in the wind; on the valley floor and in some ravines grows the *k'eñwa*, a low tree with red bark. The mountain, behind which the sun rises, ends in a precipice of dark, lustrous rocks. At the foot of this cliff, among the stones, also grow small-leaved, red puna trees, their trunks rising from the stony river terraces and their branches twisting among the rocks. In the evening the precipice glows with a yellow light and from the distant town one can discern the red tree trunks, for when the light of the clouds is reflected from the stone, the trees that grow among the rocks stand out. On that high precipice the kestrels of the valley have their nests. When the condors and eagles fly too close to the precipice, the kestrels attack them; these smaller birds plummet onto the enormous wings of the larger birds and sink their claws into their backs. The condor is helpless before the kestrel; he cannot defend himself and beats his wings as he flies, and the kestrel clings to him, if it manages to catch him. Sometimes the eagles complain and shriek as they cross the valley with flocks of little kestrels in pursuit. The little bird attacks the condor and the eagle for the fun of it; it strikes at them and soars back up into the sky, plunging down again to wound its victim.

In May the Indians sing a warlike *huayno*:

Killinchu yau,	Kestrel, hear me,
Wamancha yau,	little eagle, hear me,
urpiykitam k'echosk'ayki	your dove I must steal from you,
yanaykitam k'echosk'ayki.	I must steal your love from you.
K'echosk'aykim,	I shall take her from you,
k'echosk'aykim	I shall take her from you,
apasak'mi apasak'mi	I will carry her off, I will carry her off,
killincha	little kestrel!
wamancha	little eagle!

The challenge is the same to kestrel, eagle, or condor. By the high mountains, near the cliffs where the birds of prey build their nests, the Indians sing this in the dry, frosty month of May. It's a song of the cold regions, of the high valleys, of the steppe towns of the south.

We left Huancapi before dawn. There was snow on the thatched roofs and frost on the crosses atop the houses. The earthenware bulls fastened to the sides of the crosses seemed larger at that hour. With their heads raised, they had an air of living animals sensitive only to profundities. Frost-covered grass and weeds lined the ditches. Imprisoned by the snow, the branches overhanging the water stirred sluggishly as the wind or water moved them. The kestrels' cliff was quite visible; by its peak flowed the Milky Way. We went down toward the bottom of the gorge taking the Cangallo road, following the course of the valley. The night was cold and we didn't talk; my father went on ahead, I after him, and the peon followed close behind on foot. We went along looking for the great river, the Pampas. It is the widest river of all those that flow through the temperate regions. The riverbed is broad and covered with sand. In May or June the sandy or stony shores stretch out to a great distance from the edges of the river, and beyond them lies a long belt of low, flowering broomwood, a virgin forest where doves, small birds, and clouds of yellow butterflies dwell. A dove takes a long time to cross from one side of the river to the other. The pack animals' ford is wide, a hundred yards of water so clear one can see the shadow cast by the fish when they dart in under the stones to hide. But in summer the river is a muddy torrent; then there are no fords and one has to walk a long way to reach a bridge. We descended by the road that comes down into the Cangallo ford.

It must have been almost daylight. We had reached the area of the *lambras*, the *taras*, and the pepper trees when, suddenly, through the gorge where the rapids began, a light appeared and shone on our backs. It was a star—colder and more luminous than the moon. When its light fell upon the valley, the leaves of the *lambras* sparkled like snow; the trees and the grasses seemed as taut as drumheads; the very air took on a sort of solid transparency. My heart pounded as if it were inside a luminous cavity. The star grew brighter with an uncanny light; the white dirt road was now visible only in the distance. I ran to overtake my father; he had averted his face; his black hair had also begun to shine, and his shadow moved along like a gray spot. It was as if we had gone into a sheet of water that reflected the sparkle of a snowy world. The peon came up to us, calling out, "A great morning star, *werak'ocha*, a great morning star." He felt the same exaltation we did at this sudden light.

The star rose slowly. We reached the shadow of a high cliff that jutted out sharply from the rock, and went into the darkness as if seeking refuge in it. It was the last bend of the rapids. Around the turn lay the river, the wide blue valley—the great placid Pampas River, as it looks in wintertime. Of the star only a white pool remained in the sky, a circle that took a long time to dissolve. We crossed the ford; the animals splashed through the clear stream, trembling with joy. We reached the *lúcumo* woods that grow around the houses of the small haciendas near Cangallo. They were tall trees with straight trunks and high, leafy crowns. Doves and *tuyas* flew out of the trees toward the countryside.

From Cangallo we continued our journey to Huamanga, across the plain of the Morochuco Indians.

The Morochucos are horsemen with European features, legendary cattle thieves, descended from the excommunicated troops of Diego de Almagro, who took refuge on this cold, and, to all appearances, inhospitable and barren, plain. They play the *charango* and the *wak'rapuku*, abduct women, and fly across the steppe on little horses that run like vicuñas. The mule driver who guided us never ceased praying the whole time we were trotting across the plain. But we didn't see a single troop of Morochucos on the road. Near Huamanga, as we went slowly down the hill, about ten of them passed us; they descended by a short cut at a gallop. I could scarcely see their faces. They rode along enveloped in ponchos, with scarves around their necks; their long ponchos fell down over the flanks of their horses. Over their shoulders several carried *wak'rapukus*, the trumpets made of bull's horn trimmed with silver rings. Much lower down, near a woods glittering with pepper trees, they blew these *wak'rapukus*, announcing their arrival in the city. The song from the horns rose up to the mountain peaks like a chorus of angry, rutting bulls.

We continued our journey with an inexorable slowness.

3. The Leave-Taking

One day my father declared to me, rather more emphatically than usual, that our pilgrimage would end in Abancay.

We had to cross three departments to reach that quiet little town.[1] It was the longest and strangest journey we ever made together, some thirteen hundred miles in a series of rigorous daily marches. He went through Cuzco, where he was born, had studied, and had begun his career; but he didn't stop there; on the contrary, he passed through as if going through fire.

We crossed the Apurímac, and I saw in my father's innocent blue eyes the look they always held when discouragement compelled him to set out on new journeys. As I struggled along through the furnace of a valley, he walked beside me, silent and abstracted.

"He's still the same old scoundrel," he once exclaimed.

And when I asked him of whom he was speaking, he answered. "The Old Man!"

Amank'ay is the name of a wildflower, a yellow lily, and *awankay* the term used for the soaring flight of the large birds. *Awankay* means to glide, gazing down into profundity. Abancay! It must have once been a town lost amid groves of *pisonayes* and unfamiliar trees, in a valley of immense corn fields that stretched down to

1. Peru is divided politically into departments, which in turn are divided into provinces.—Trans.

the river. Today its tin roofs shine with a horrible glare, blackberry patches separate one neighborhood from another, and the sugar cane extends from the town to the Pachachaca. The town is a prisoner of the hacienda, on whose alien land it was built.

The day we arrived the bells were ringing. It was four o'clock in the afternoon. All of the women and most of the men were kneeling in the streets. My father got down from his horse and asked a woman why the people were praying and why the bells were ringing in the streets. The woman told him that at that very moment Father Linares, the saintly preacher of Abancay and Rector of the school, was undergoing an operation at the school. He ordered me to dismount and kneel by his side. For almost half an hour we prayed on the sidewalk. No one came along the street, while the bells kept ringing as if calling people to mass. The wind blew and the street litter swirled around us, but no one got up or went on their way until the pealing had stopped.

"He must be the Rector of your school," my father said. "I've heard he's a saint, Cuzco's best preacher, and a fine mathematics and Spanish teacher."

The first night we stayed at the home of a notary public who had been a classmate of my father's. On the long journey he had spoken to me of this friend and of his belief that the notary would send him clients in Abancay, so that he could start to work from the very beginning. But the man was almost completely ineffectual. Stooped and pale, he was so feeble that he could hardly walk. His clerk did the notarial work and cheated him mercilessly.

My father felt sorry for his friend, and all the time we were in Abancay he lamented having gone to stay at the home of this sick gentleman instead of at an inn. They made up two pallets for us on the floor in the children's bedroom. The children slept on sheepskins, and we on the pallets.

"Gabriel! Forgive me, brother, forgive me!" said the notary.

The woman went about with downcast eyes, not daring to speak or to look at us. We would have liked to leave that place under any pretext. "We should go to a *tambo*, to any inn!" exclaimed my father, softly.

"After such a long time, and you coming from so far away, and me being unable to take care of you," lamented the invalid.

My father thanked him and apologized, but couldn't bring himself to ask him to let us leave. It was impossible. It seemed as if his friend's voice might be extinguished at any moment; he spoke with great difficulty. The children helped their mother; they didn't

really distrust me, but they feared my father and didn't dare look
at him.

My father wore an old suit, made by a village tailor. His appearance was complex. Although he seemed to be from a small village,
his blue eyes, blond beard, and refined Spanish and manners were
confusing. No, we shouldn't make trouble, nor could we hurt people's feelings, even though they were very poor. Nevertheless, it
was a painful situation. And we were glad the next day when we
could sleep on benches of adobe bricks in a store with rough
shelves that we had rented near the center of the town.

Our life in Abancay began abruptly, in this way. And my father
knew how to take advantage of these first inconveniences to justify
the failure of the main purpose of that journey. He could not stay
here; he did not set up his law office. For ten days he bemoaned
the ugliness of the town, its quietness, poverty, torrid climate, and
lack of legal activity. There were no small landholders in the province; what lawsuits there were were of a criminal nature—petty
trials that never came to an end; all of the land belonged to the
haciendas; the very city of Abancay was unable to grow because it
was surrounded by the Patibamba hacienda, whose owner would
sell land to neither the poor nor the rich; and the gentry had only
a few ancient lawsuits amongst themselves, and these had already
been before the courts for decades.

I was registered at the school and would sleep in the dormitory.
I understood that my father would leave. After all the years of
traveling together, I would have to remain behind, and he would
go off alone. As always, some chance circumstance would determine his direction. Where to go, and by what road? These calcu-
lations were being made by each of us alone this time. He wouldn't
take the road to Cuzco again; he would leave by the other side of
the valley, crossing the Pachachaca and seeking the highland
towns. In any case he would begin by going down into the bottom of the valley. And then he'd climb the mountain range that
lay before us; he would see Abancay for the last time from a remote mountain pass, from some blue summit where he'd be invisible to me. And he would go into the next valley or plain alone
this time; his eyes would see neither sky nor distance in the same
way; trotting along between stones and bushes he would be unable
to speak; and in the valleys or on the mountain peaks he would
feel much more deeply, with great cruelty and silence inside him,
how the horizon fell away before him. Because when we traveled

together, the world was our dominion; its joy and its shadows passed from him to me.

No, he could not stay in Abancay. Neither a city nor a town, Abancay drove my father to despair.

He wished to show me, however, that he really did not want to break his promise. He polished his lawyer's plaque and fastened it to the wall in the doorway of the store. He divided the room with a cloth screen, and laid out his blankets on an adobe bench behind it. Seated in the doorway of the store, or pacing back and forth, he awaited clients. Beyond the top of the wooden partition one could see the shelves of the store. Sometimes, tired of walking or of sitting, he would fling himself down on the bed. I would find him like this, in despair. When he saw me he would try to hide his feelings.

"Perhaps some big landowner will give me a case. And just one would be enough," he would say. "Even though I had to stay in this town for ten years, your future would be assured. I would look for a house to live in with a large garden and you wouldn't have to stay at school."

I would agree with him. But he was accustomed to living in houses with large courtyards, chatting in Quechua with dozens of Indian and mestizo clients, and drawing up his cases as the sun lit up the earth of the courtyard and then spread cheerfully across the wooden floor of his "office." Now he cowered in depression within the walls of a store that had been built for hucksters.

That was why, when he came to visit me one afternoon at the school, accompanied by a stranger who had the look of an hacienda owner, I had a premonition that his departure had been resolved. His face shone with an expression of uncontainable joy. They had both been drinking.

"I've come by for a moment with this gentleman," he told me. "He's just arrived from Chalhuanca to consult a lawyer, and we're in luck. His lawsuit is a simple matter. You already have permission to leave the school. Come by the office after class."

The stranger shook my hand.

They said good-bye immediately. The stranger's riding pants with leather patches, his dark leggings, his short jacket, his necktie with its small knot at the wide collar of his shirt, the color of his eyes, his diffidence, and his wide-brimmed hat closely resembled those of all the hacienda owners from the Indian districts.

In the afternoon I went to see my father. I found the Chalhuanquino in the office, sitting on one of the benches. The door of the store was almost closed. On the table were several bottles. My father poured the stranger a glass of dark beer.

"Here is my boy, sir, the sun that lights my way," he said.

The man stood and approached me respectfully.

"I'm from Chalhuanca, young man. Your father, the attorney, honors me."

He laid his hand on my shoulder. A vicuña scarf hung around his neck; he wore purple shirt buttons. He had light-colored eyes, but in his sunburnt face they looked like the eyes of an Indian. He was exactly like all the friends my father had in the towns.

"You are the doctor's joy; you are his heart. Me, I'm just passing through. To him, Doctor!"

"To him!"

And they drained their glasses.

"He's a man now, Don Joaquín," said my father, pointing to me. "With him I've crossed the cordillera five times; I've walked the sands of the coast. We've slept on the punas, just below the snowfields. A hundred, two hundred, five hundred leagues on horseback. And now he's a student at a religious boarding school. After having ridden at a trot through so many places, how will he like being shut in day and night?" Then he spoke to me. "But you're in your school! You're in your rightful place. And no one shall move you until you finish, until you go to the university. Only you must never, ever become a lawyer! It's bad enough that I should have to contend with such great evils."

He was restless. He paced the length of the room. There was no need to say any more. There was the traveler, with his vicuña scarf, hat of Indian manufacture, yellow-buckled leather leggings, and purple shirt buttons, his long hair damp with perspiration and those eyes that were as green as if they had been diluted by the cold. He spoke to me in Spanish. When he spoke Quechua, he would take off his scarf or wrap it around his neck, as was proper.

"Young man, I'm from Chalhuanca. I'm bringing suit against a large hacienda owner. I'll skin him alive. This time I'll really do it. Like a kestrel that tears an eagle apart in midair. Even if your father only advises me from a distance. Why should he have to come along to my town with me? Isn't that right, Doctor?"

He had been speaking to my father; but the latter kept still with his back turned.

"Don't you be imagining anything, young man. I'm from Chalhuanca; I've come seeking advice on my lawsuit. The attorney, here, sees as keenly as an eagle. My hands were tied before. But a lawyer is a lawyer, and knows more than a shyster. Worthless little shysters! Now they'll see! *Payhunak'a nerk'acha . . . !*''

And he went on unburdening himself in Quechua.

My father was unable to control himself any longer. It was no use hiding the fact that he would leave. His friend's innocent attempts to avoid telling the news only proclaimed his departure, and finally succeeded in upsetting him. He laid his head down on the table and cried. The Chalhuanquino tried to console him. He spoke to him in Quechua, offering him all the rewards and the worlds the Indian language can offer until he succeeded for a moment in making him forget his great sorrow. Then he addressed me:

"It's not far to Chalhuanca, young man,'' he told me. "It's just beyond these mountains, in a little valley. We'll come for you and take you there. We'll shoot off rockets when you come into the plaza. We'll make the Indian dancers perform. You can fish with dynamite in the river and ride across all the hills on horseback. You'll go hunting deer, viscachas, wild boars . . .''

I left him talking and went over to my father. We sat for a long while together. The Chalhuanquino kept on talking Quechua, circling around us noisily, repeating the words in a voice that grew ever louder and kinder:

"It's better in Chalhuanca. There's a river right by the town. We like strangers there. No lawyer has ever gone there, ever! You'll be treated like a king, Doctor. Everybody will bow down when you go by, they'll take off their hats to you, as they should. You'll buy lands; we'll give you a horse with good metal trappings for the boy. You'll dash through the ford at a gallop! On my hacienda you can crack a bullwhip and herd cattle! We'll hunt ducks in the hills along the river; you'll fight the brave bulls of the hacienda with a cape. Damnit! You mustn't cry. It's a sort of a miracle of the patron saint of Chalhuanca! He has chosen that town for you. Your health, Doctor! Lift up your head. Stand up, my brave boy! Your health, Doctor! Because you're taking leave of this dismal town!''

And my father stood up. The Chalhuanquino poured me half a glass of beer.

"You're a big boy now, and equal to the occasion. *Salud!*''

It was the first time I had ever drunk with my father. And suddenly he became happy once more, repeating the same glowing plans he always made on the eve of our departure.

"I shall remain in Chalhuanca, son. I'll be a townsman at last.

And I'll be waiting for you at vacation time, as the gentleman says, with a lively horse on which you can climb the hills and gallop across the rivers. I'll buy a lot by the river, and we'll build a stone mill. Who knows, perhaps we might bring Don Pablo Maywa here to set it up! One has to settle down, not just keep going like this, like the Wandering Jew . . . Poor Alcilla will be your guardian until December."

And we parted almost joyfully, with the same hopefulness that always brightened the beginning of another journey after the tedium of a town.

He would climb to the top of the high ridge that rose up on the other side of the river, crossing the Pachachaca on the triple-arched bridge of stone and lime. From the pass he would bid farewell to the valley and look down upon new country. And while he would miss me, as he talked with friends in Chalhuanca, playing the role of the newly arrived stranger, I would explore the great valley and the town inch by inch; and I would feel the force of the sad and powerful current that buffets children who must face, all alone, a world fraught with monsters and fire and great rivers that sing the most beautiful of all music as they break upon the stones and the islands.

4. The Hacienda

The small-town landowners contribute huge earthenware jars of *chicha*[1] and big pans of peppery food for the community work projects. When there are fiestas they dance and sing *huaynos* together in the streets and squares. Ordinarily they go around wearing leggings and suits of corduroy or rough wool cloth, and have vicuña or alpaca scarves around their necks. They ride gaited horses, use bronze spurs and always cover their saddles with sheepskins. They oversee their Indians themselves, and when their workers ask for more pay than is usually considered reasonable, they lash them across the face, kick them, and drag them off to jail personally. On holidays, or whenever they go to the provincial capitals, they wear serge suits, ride on *sampedrano* sheepskins, and use ornate tack covered with silver rings, stirrups trimmed with wide metal bands, and spurs with long steel rowels. They seem transformed; they dash across the plaza at a gallop, or force their horses to trot rapidly and lift their hoofs elegantly. When they become drunk, dressed in this fashion, they spur their horses so savagely that they score their flesh, and spurs and stirrups are bathed in blood. Then they race headlong through the streets and make their horses rear at the street corners. Trembling, the animals slide across the paving stones, and the riders force them to back step. Sometimes, the animals stop and buck; but then the spurs are sunk even deeper into their flesh and they are reined in even more cruelly.

1. A mild alcoholic drink made from corn.—Trans.

The riders are quite demanding; their pride forces them to be so. People gather round in groups to watch them. Scarcely ever does a horse manage to seize the reins and run off down the road, dragging the rider along over the ground behind him.

The Indians are quite familiar with the houses of the landowners, who sleep in antique brass beds with canopies supported by gilded rods. The hacienda mansion has a courtyard and a corral, both large; an arcaded porch; a pantry; a stable; a parlor furnished with antique benches and large wooden chairs; and a kitchen which is always far off on the other side of the courtyard because that is where the workmen eat. The landowner also organizes and finances religious fiestas. His position does not permit him to entertain the populace less lavishly than an Indian, unless he has already lost all his self-respect as a landowner.

Abancay is closed in by the lands of the Patibamba hacienda. The whole valley, from north to south, from one mountaintop to the other, belongs to the haciendas.

The grounds of the Patibamba mansion were better kept and larger than the main plaza of Abancay. Luxuriant trees shaded its stone benches. Beds of roses and lilies lined its stone-paved paths. The house had a silent, white, arcaded porch with a gleaming tiled floor and high wooden-barred windows. The garden stretched on out of sight; its paths were edged with flowers and coffee trees. A tall aviary stood in one corner of the garden; its dome touched the treetops. The cage had several levels, holding dozens of linnets, larks, and other birds. The house appeared to be surrounded by whitened walls. An iron gate guarded the arched entrance.

The owner and his family lived like lost souls inside the immense mansion. I often went to look in through the gate; the grounds and porches were always silent and empty. Common butterflies, their red wings spotted with black, skimmed the flowers, rising as high as the top branches of the *pisonay* trees. Only once did I hear the voice of a piano from that place; someone was playing it inside the mansion, and the music seemed to come from the orchard around the house.

A wide lane led from the owner's house to the sugar mill and the quarters where the Indian farm workers lived. This lane was covered with sugar cane trash almost the whole way to the mansion. The mill stood in a stone-paved courtyard. Over the years a soft, spreading pile of cane trash had accumulated there and had been strewn along the lane to the quarters and even beyond it, almost completely covering a reed fence.

The sun blazed down on the dried molasses, on the white remains of the ground cane. When it rained, the trash steamed; it smelled like brandy and permeated the whole settlement with its fumes. The houses had low walls of narrow adobe bricks, and were roofed with a ragged, dusty thatch of sugar cane leaves.

The Indians and their women didn't speak with strangers.

"*Jampuyki mamaya.* (I am coming to see you, little mother.),"
I would call from the doorways of the houses.

"*Mánan! Ama rimaychu!* (No, I don't want you to! Don't speak to me!),'' they would answer.

They looked like the Old Man's *pongo*; black sweat ran down their heads onto their necks. But they were even dirtier than he and were barely able to remain standing on the dusty ground of the quarters and the factory amid the clouds of mosquitoes and wasps that swarmed over the cane trash. All of them wore hats made of wool, stiffened with grease from long usage.

"*Señoray, rimakusk'ayki!* (Let me talk to you, *señora!*),'' I often insisted, in my attempts to enter a house. But the women would look at me fearfully and suspiciously. They would no longer even listen to the language of the *ayllus*;[2] they must have been compelled to forget it, because when I spoke to them using those words and tones of voice they paid no attention to me.

And I would have to go back to town. Bewildered and lost in the valley, I would walk through the steaming lanes that led to the sugar cane fields. At dusk, when only the mountain peaks remained in sunlight, I would reach the town, afraid that I would find no one I knew, that no one would accept me. When the Rector saw me come into school covered with dust, he would call me "madman" and "wandering fool." For many days afterwards I would be unable to play or to remember what I studied. At night I would get up and decide to run away, to make a bundle of my clothing, cross the Pachachaca in the darkness, climb to the top of the next mountain, and stride across the puna until I came to Chalhuanca. But I knew how to respect my father's wishes, and waited, observing everything, storing it all up in my memory.

In those days of confusion and depression I recalled the farewell song that the women had sung to me in the last Indian *ayllu* in which I had taken refuge while my father wandered from town to town to avoid persecution.

To escape cruel relatives, I had thrown myself on the mercy of an Indian community that grew corn in the smallest, happiest val-

2. Indian communities.—Author

ley I have ever known. The flame-blossomed thorn trees and the song of the wild doves illumined the corn fields. The family chiefs and the older women, the *mamakunas* of the community protected me and instilled in me that kindness in which I live and which I can never repay.

When the political persecution against my father had ceased, he came looking for me at the home of the relatives with whom he had left me. Having struck my guardian on the head with his revolver butt, he came down into the valley, where he got drunk with the Indians and danced with them for several days. Then, he asked the vicar to come and say high mass in the *ayllu's* chapel. As my father left mass, to the bursting of rockets and the ringing of bells, he stopped in front of the church to hug the community leaders, Don Pablo Maywa and Don Victor Pusa. In the plaza, we immediately mounted our horses and set out on our long journey. As we left the village and started up the hill, the women sang this farewell *jarahui*:

Ay warmallay warma	Do not forget, my little one,
yuyaykunkim, yuyaykunkim!	do not forget!
Jhatun yuark' ork'o	White hill,
Kutiykachimunki;	make him return;
abrapi puquio, pampapi puquio	mountain freshet, pampa spring,
yank'atak' yakuyananman.	never let him die of thirst.
Alkunchallay, kutiykamunchu	Falcon, bear him on your wings
raprachaykipi apaykamunki.	and make him return.
Riti' ork'o, jhatun riti ork'o	Deep snow, father of snows,
yank'tak ñannimpi ritiwak';	do not harm him on the road.
yank'atak wayra	Evil wind,
ñannimpi k'ochpaykunkiman.	do not touch him.
Amas pára amas pára	Rainstorm,
aypankichu;	do not overtake him.
amas k'ak'a, amas k'ak'a,	No, chasm, terrible abyss,
ñannimpi tuñinkichu.	do not surprise him!
Ay warmallay warma	My son,
kutiykamunki	you must return,
kutiykamunkipuni!	you must return!

"It doesn't matter if you cry. Cry, son, because if you don't your heart may break," exclaimed my father when he saw that I was riding along in silence with my eyes tightly shut.

From then on, we never stopped traveling. From town to town, from province to province, until we came to the deepest of all valleys, to these feudal sugar estates. My father left Abancay too soon,

when I was just beginning to discover the true hell it was, when
hatred and desolation had once more begun to overwhelm me.

The hacienda owners came to the school only to visit the Rector.
They would cross the courtyard without looking at anyone.
"The owner of Auquibamba!" cried the boarding students.
"The owner of Pati!"
"The owner of Yaca!"
And they seemed to be announcing the largest stars. The Rector
would go out to the hacienda chapels to say mass for them. But on
certain Sundays the hacienda owners would come to town. Then
there would be sermons and singing in the church.

The Rector began his sermons softly. He praised the Virgin
Mary in moving tones; his voice was high and pleasant, but he
easily became excited. He hated Chile and always found ways to
pass from religious themes to the praise of his country and its
heroes. He preached a future war against the Chileans. He called
on the young men and boys to be prepared and to never forget
that to obtain revenge was their greatest duty; and thus, exalted
and speaking in violent terms, he would remind the men of their
other duties. He would praise the landowners—they were the
foundation of the republic, the pillars of its wealth. He referred
to the piety of the gentry, to the care they took of the hacienda
chapels and the way they made the Indians go to confession, take
communion, get married, and be content with their humble lot.
Then he would once more lower his voice to recite some passage
on Calvary.

After mass, the town officials and the landowners would wait in
the church doorway for the Rector to come out, and then accompany him to the school.

Those Sundays the Rector would have lunch with the boarding
students; he'd preside over the dining hall, watching us with a
kindly expression on his face. He beamed with joy, joking with
the boys and making them laugh. He was ruddy, with an aquiline
nose; his gray hair, which was combed back high on his head,
made him look elegant and imposing in spite of his age. The
women adored him; the men and boys thought he was a saint; and
he came before the hacienda Indians as an apparition. I confused
him in my dreams, sometimes seeing him as a fish with a luxuriant, waving tail, swimming among the algae of the river pools or
pursuing the minnows that lived in the shelter of the water plants
by the river's edge. At other times he became Don Pablo Maywa,
clasping me to his breast on the edge of the immense corn fields.

5. Bridge over the World

*"Pachachaca! Bridge over the world
is the meaning of this name."*

There was only one lively quarter in town—Huanupata. In the olden times it must have been the dump for the Indian communities, because its name means dung heap. In that quarter lived the marketwomen, the laborers and the porters, who did the daily work of the city, the policemen, and the clerks from the few stores. Here also were found the inns where litigants from the country, mule drivers, and mestizo travelers stayed. It was the only quarter with *chicha* bars. On Saturdays and Sundays they played harp and and violin in the most popular ones and danced *huaynos* and *marineras*. It was said that at those revels one could find women of easy virtue and even mestizas who earned their living as prostitutes.

Huge waves of flies surged around the doorways of the *chicherías*. On the ground, a thick layer of them swarmed over the trash that was tossed out. Whenever anyone entered a *chicha* bar a whirlwind of flies rose from the ground. People had trampled the floors down hard; the tables were low and the benches small. Everything was black with grime and soot. Several mestizas served the public. They wore shawls of Castilian cloth[1] trimmed with silk, whitened

1. Coarse, fuzzy factory-made cloth.—Trans.

straw hats, and wide, bright-colored sashes. Indians and *cholos*[2] stared at them with equal insolence. The *chicha* bars often owed their popularity to the beauty of the mestiza waitresses, and their gaiety and availability. But I knew that the struggle for them was long and arduous; it was not easy to get to dance with them. The women who ran the bars watched them and taught them with the help of their long experience in trickery. And many men from other towns broke down and wept on their way home through the mountain passes because they had wasted their time night after night, drinking *chicha* and singing until dawn.

The *chicherías* opened to the public at noon, but the musicians went there only on weekends. Anyone could request them to play his favorite *huayno*. It was hard to find one the musicians did not know. More outsiders went to the *chicha* bars than to the inns. But sometimes a customer would come from a distant, quite different part of the country, from Huaraz, from Cajamarca, from Huancavelica, or from the provinces of Collao, and would ask them to play a completely unfamiliar *huayno*. Then the harpist's eyes would shine with joy; he would call the stranger over and ask him to sing it softly. Just once was enough. The violinist would learn it and play it with the harp accompanying him. The stranger almost always corrected him several times: "No, it's not like that; that's not the right way." And he would sing it in a loud voice, trying to force them to play it correctly. It was impossible. Even when playing the identical melody, the musicians would change the song into an Apurímac *huayno*, with a lively, tender rhythm. "*Mánan*," the men from the cold country would shout; those from Collao would grow angry, and, if they were drunk, would silence the musicians by threatening them with big glasses of *chicha*. "It is the same, sir," the harpist would protest. "No, *alk'o* (dog)!" a man from Collao would shout. Both were right. But the Collavino would sing it again. The people from the valley could not dance well to his singing; it had a slow, hard rhythm, as if someone were grinding metal, and if it were a sad *huayno*, it seemed as if the wind from the highlands, the air that ruffles the dry grass and makes the little steppe plants tremble, was blowing through the *chichería*. Then we travelers would remember the highland clouds, always menacing, cold, and pitiless, or the gloomy rain and the endless snowfields. But the Collavinos were feted. The mestiza

2. Indians who have adopted the speech, clothing, and manners of the whites; can be derogatory.—Trans.

waitresses, who had never left those fly-filled caverns, those dives reeking of *chicha* and cane liquor, would pause to listen to them.

They knew only the *huaynos* of the Apurímac and Pachachaca valleys, of the warm country where sugar cane and fruit trees grow. When they sang with their high voices, they evoked another landscape—the rustling of large leaves; the sparkle of cascades tumbling down between bushes and white-flowered cactus; the heavy, tranquil rain falling on the cane fields; the canyons flaming with *pisonay* flowers, full of red ants and voracious insects:

Ay siwar k'enti!	O, hummingbird!
amaña wayta tok'okachaychu,	pierce the flowers no longer,
siwar k'enti.	emerald wings.
Ama jhina kaychu	Do not be cruel.
mayupataman urayamuspa,	Come down to the river bank,
k'ori raphra,	emerald wings,
kay puka mayupi wak'ask'ayta	and see me weeping
k'awaykamuway.	by the red water,
K'awaykamuyway	see me weeping.
siwar k'enti, k'ori raphra,	Come down, golden hummingbird,
llakisk'ayta,	and see,
purun wayta kirisk'aykita,	all my sorrow,
mayupata wayta	wounded flower of the fields,
sak'esk'aykita.	flower of the rivers,
	that you abandoned.

I went to the *chicherías* to hear the singing and to look for hacienda Indians. I never lost the hope that I would be able to talk to them. Once some ragged Indians, whose hair was dirtier and longer than a usual, came into a *chicha* bar. I went up to them and asked if they belonged to an hacienda. One of them answered scornfully, "*Mánan haciendachu kani!* (I'm not from an hacienda!)." Later, when I had become convinced that the *colonos* never got to town, I went to the *chicherías* just to listen to the music and reminisce. As I accompanied the singing in a low voice I would think about the fields and stones, the squares and churches, and the streams where I had once been happy. And I could spend hours at the harpists' side or in the entrance of the bars, listening; for the hot valley, scorching air, and weed-choked ruins of the other sections of the city were hostile to me.

Departmental officials, storekeepers, some landowners, and a few impoverished families of ancient gentry stock lived in the other sections of Abancay. Most of the houses had large gardens with fruit trees whose shadows extended to the streets. Many orchards were neglected or abandoned, with walls that had in many places crumbled away almost to the foundations. One could see the roots of the spiky plants that had been stuck into the top of the walls, and the old sidewalks were all broken and covered with branches and layers of damp leaves. Toads crawled about in the grass. Irrigation ditches, with an abundance of clean, wasted water, crossed the orchards.

In those districts there were whole blocks without buildings, fields overgrown with bushes and thorny shrubs. Between the main square and the river there were only two or three houses, and beyond them a vacant lot with thickets of castor-oil bushes, populated with toads and tarantulas. The boys from school played in that field. Here the patriotic sermons of the Rector were put into practice; gangs of "Peruvian" and "Chilean" students did battle; we shot the castor beans from our rubber slings and then rushed to the attack, pummeling one another with our fists and wrestling. The "Peruvians" always had to win. The best friends of the school champions were enlisted in this group because we obeyed their orders and always let them choose sides.

Many boys went back to school with bloody noses, black eyes and swollen lips. "Most of them are 'Chileans,' Padrecito," the leaders would report. The Rector would smile and take us off to the medicine chest to doctor us.

Añuco[3] was a shrewd, frightening "Chilean." He was the only boarding student who came from a landowning family.

It was well known in Abancay that Añuco's grandfather had been a large landholder, a rake, a gambler, and a ladies' man. He had mortgaged his largest hacienda and initiated his son to vice.

Añuco's father had come into his inheritance as a young man, and, like his grandfather, had devoted his life to gambling. He would establish himself in the country house of a large estate owner, invite the neighboring *hacendados*, and organize a gambling casino in the mansion parlor. He would play the piano, sing, and be attentive to the landholders' daughters and wives. His visits to the hacienda palaces became unforgettable occasions. But in the end he was left without a foot of land. His two haciendas fell into the hands of an immigrant who had managed to start a factory in Cuzco and had decided to buy land to experiment with cotton growing.

In Abancay people spoke of the way Añuco's father had spent the last three years of his life in that city. He had lived in his own

3. This nickname means "one who is about to die" in Quechua.—Trans.

house, a broken-down mansion with an orchard full of unproductive trees and grass that dried up in the winter and came to life again with the summer rains. Almost every day this gentleman resolved to kill himself. He would go to the church and pray, bid farewell to the world as he contemplated the sky and mountains, and then, with a determined stride, walk homeward. At first his neighbors and the few friends he had in town would watch him fearfully and with a certain feeling of relief. They knew what he had decided. But the next morning the door would open and the gentleman would reappear, always clad in a voluminous Spanish cape. People spoke of how they had once seen him, just before evening prayers, tying a hangman's noose to an orange tree in his garden, and told how he had left the rope dangling and had brought out two boxes from inside his house, setting them up one atop the other. So it seemed as if everything had been settled. But the ex-landowner hesitated, leaning against the tree. And when the bells rang for the rosary, he went out into the street, walked slowly to the church, and then came back again. But this time he stayed inside the house and did not go out into the garden. Nor did he dismantle the gallows in the days to come, and the boxes were left under the tree.

Añuco was that gentleman's illegitimate son. The school priests had taken him in when he was nine years old, shortly before his father died. The house had been sold to pay the gentleman's last debts.

Although he was penniless, Añuco was an aristocrat at school. The large landholders who came to visit the priests sometimes spoke to him, and it was said that some left him money for books and other expenses. But he strongly denied this and would attack anyone who suggested it. "The priests support me!" he would shout.

Añuco had a defender—Lleras, champion pole-vaulter and sprinter, and indispensable back of the soccer team. Lleras was the dullest student in the school; his origin was obscure and he was a ward of the priests. He had repeated the ninth grade three times, but was the strongest boy in the school, and the townspeople never lost their fear of him. He had beaten up all the students and town boys who had fought with him. He was arrogant, sullen, abusive, and moody. Nevertheless, many times after the Sunday soccer matches, when the school team had beaten clubs from town or from other provinces, we students would carry him on our shoulders from the stadium to the school, shouting his name as we went. He would go along in the middle of the crowd with a cold, peevish expression on his face, our applause scarcely ever seeming to affect him. On such occasions Añuco played the vain hero. We always made room for him in front of the champ, and he'd dash about all by himself, screaming Lleras's name, cursing and shouting imprecations. He made up another separate crowd, holding his own celebration. Sometimes after an important match which Lleras had won for us, at the end of the game he would begin to get dressed slowly, wearing a defiant expression. Añuco would hand him his clothes and pack up his soccer shoes and sweater. Both would stand up. "Get out of here!" Lleras would shout, with Añuco adding, "Beat it, you mangy dogs!" And they'd make us scatter across the field. At such times no one could congratulate them; not even the Rector dared to approach Lleras. Only in the evening would he take him to the school chapel. He would put his arm around Lleras, and they would walk together to the chapel like that. Almost always Lleras came out with sunken eyes, but with a peaceful expression on his face. And for several days afterward he did not tease the younger boys; he would eat lunch and dinner without speaking to anyone. The same cloud dominated Añuco.

Añuco would suddenly appear in the midst of the "Chileans." He attacked like a hellcat. He was thin, and must have been about fourteen years old at the time. His skin was soft and so disgustingly white that it made him look sickly; but when the battle began, his tough skinny arms turned into deadly weapons—he struck out with both fists as if he were attacking people with the ends of two clubs. No one respected him. New boys, from distant provinces, spoke to him for the first few days. Añuco tried to make them hate and distrust all the boarding students. He was always the first to approach the new boys, but in the end they invariably grew tired of him and he would become their first enemy. If they were older, he teased them by insulting them with the filthiest of words until they attacked him, so that Lleras would intervene; but if he were quarreling with a smaller boy he would beat him unmercifully. When he played war, he was quite violent. With his sling he shot stones rather than castor beans. Or he would fight on his own in the free-for-all, kicking from behind and knocking down boys who had their backs turned. And he changed from the "Chilean" to the "Peruvian" side, depending on which had the easier adversaries, either because they were smaller or because they were surrounded by the largest number of enemies. He didn't follow the rules. He was glad when someone was knocked down during a group struggle, because that made it possible to trample the face of the boy who had fallen, or kick him, as if it were all an accident because he was blinded by the game. Despite the fact that he sometimes behaved very differently, it reached the point where Añuco was forbidden to play "war." Even against Lleras's wishes, we disqualified him in a large meeting, as a "traitor" who had sold out his country. But he almost always participated, whenever he wasn't going off with Lleras to climb mountains, drink *chicha*, or molest the mestiza women and the Indians. Suddenly he would appear, emerging from the castor-bean thickets, leaping down from a mud wall, or climbing up out of the bottom of some ditch; and sometimes he fought for any small boy who was being chased or who had been taken prisoner and put under heavy guard in the "stockade." He would rush out like a little wild beast, growling, biting, scratching, and dealing hard, decisive blows.

"Out of here, you mangy dogs! I've got rabies!" he would shout, with a terrifying gleam in his eyes. Then he'd really begin to fight, and his opponents would run away. But often when Añuco fell among a group of boys who really hated him, he would be beaten mercilessly. Squealing like a stuck pig, he would call for help and his screams could be heard as far away as the center of town. He exaggerated his injuries and whimpered about them for days afterwards. And the hatreds never died out; instead they spread and grew more complex.

At night some of the boarding students would play the harmonica on the porch of the main courtyard, while others preferred to sneak out to the playground to smoke and tell stories about women. The main courtyard was paved with stone. To the right of the large wooden gate at the entrance of the school was the main building; on the left there was only a high, bare, damp wall. By that wall was a large water pipe with a small, rectangular water tank made of stone and lime. The courtyard was lined with old wooden pillars which supported the balcony. Three electric bulbs shed a feeble light over the porch, leaving the courtyard in semi-darkness. At dusk some toads would come to the fountain to swim in the little tank or to float near the edge and croak. In the daytime they'd hide in the weeds where the water flowed out of the tank.

Often three or four boys would compete with each other in playing *huaynos*. A fair audience of boarding students would gather to listen and to act as judges. One night each contestant played more than fifty *huaynos*. These harmonica players liked to have me sing. While some repeated the melody, others played the "accompaniment" on the bass, swaying back and forth or bobbing up and down enthusiastically in time to the music. But none surpassed Romero, the tall, Indian-like harmonica player from Andahuaylas.

The inner courtyard, which served as a playground, was not paved. A long dirt passageway led to it from the first courtyard. On the right of this passage, near the first courtyard, was the dining hall; in the rear, behind an old board fence at the far end of the playground, several empty boxes were set up over a ditch to serve as toilets. The ditch water flowed out of a little pond.

In the daytime more than a hundred boys played in this dusty little courtyard. Some of the games were cruel; the bigger and stronger boys chose them so they could hit one another, or hurt the younger and the weaker ones and make them cry. But even so, many of the smaller and weaker students preferred those rough games, strangely enough, even though they would go around limping and complaining, pale and humiliated, for several days afterwards.

At night the playground was left in darkness. The last light was the one that shone down on the dining hall doorway, ten yards from the playground.

On certain nights a feeble-minded woman who worked in the kitchen would come walking slowly into that playground. She had been picked up in a nearby town by one of the priests.

She was not an Indian; her hair was light and her face white, even though it was covered with dirt. She was short and fat. She was sometimes seen in the morning leaving the bedroom of the priest who had brought her to the school. At night, when she went to the playground, she walked silently, brushing against the walls. They would discover her when she was already quite close to the board fence around the toilets, or was pushing open one of the doors. This caused confusion and terror. The biggest boys would come to blows trying to be the first to reach her or would stand guard near the toilets in a short line. We younger, smaller boys stayed next to the nearest walls, trembling with anxiety, not speaking to one another, watching the uproar or the tense waiting of those who were in line. Presently, while some were still waiting or pummeling one another on the ground, the woman would come out and run away. But almost always someone would still catch up with her on the way and try to knock her down. The uproar, insults, and fist fights among the older boys would continue after she had disappeared down the passageway.

They never fought more savagely; they even kicked those who

fell down, trampling their heads or the most sensitive parts of their bodies with the heels of their shoes. The younger boys would not go near them. We'd listen to the filthy curses of the older boys and watch how they chased one another in the darkness, and how some of them fled, with the winner threatening them and ordering them loudly to stay in the corner with the little boys the next night. The struggle never ended until the bell rang summoning us to the dormitory, or until one of the priests would heard the insults and the uproar and call to us from the dining room doorway.

On moonlit nights the feeble-minded woman did not go to the playground.

Añuco and Lleras were tremendously scornful of those who were injured in the nightly battles. Some evenings they would watch the fighting from the corner of the passage. They would get there after the struggle had begun, or when the violence was waning, and the youths were forming a line out of sheer desperation.

"Come on now, babies! Get in line, get in line!" Añuco would shout as Lleras laughed loudly. He would be speaking to us younger boys who had withdrawn to the corners of the courtyard. The older ones would either remain quietly in line, or else all rush out together to attack Lleras; he'd run off toward the dining hall, and those who were chasing him would stop.

An abyss of hatred separated Lleras and Añuco from the older boarding students, but they did not dare to fight the school champ.

Until one night something happened which brought the hatred against Lleras to a head. One of the smallest and shyest of the students who lived at the school was a boy called Palacios. He came from a village in the high Andes. He could hardly read and did not understand Spanish very well. He was the only student in the school who came from an Indian *ayllu*. His origin and slowness in learning made him timid. Several of us students tried to help him with his lessons, but it was no use; he couldn't understand and remained hopelessly withdrawn from the school atmosphere, from the teachers' explanations, and from the content of his textbooks. He was condemned to the torment of the boarding school and of the classroom. And yet his father stubbornly insisted on keeping him in the school. He was a tall man who dressed like a mestizo, wearing a necktie and leather leggings. He visited his son every month. He would sit with him in the parlor, and we could hear him shouting angrily. He spoke Spanish, but when he became annoyed he lost control of himself and insulted his son in Quechua.

Palacitos[4] would wail and implore his father to take him out of the boarding school. "Take me to the government school, *papacito!*" he would beg in Quechua.

"No! In this school!" the *cholo* would insist vehemently.

And then he would go off after leaving expensive gifts for the Rector and the other priests. He usually brought four or five slaughtered sheep and several bushels of corn and potatoes.

The Rector would call Palacitos in after each of his father's visits. After a long talk, Palacitos would come out even more tearful than he had been after seeing his father, meeker and more intimidated, looking for a quiet place to cry. Sometimes the cook could get him to go into her room, taking care not to let the priests see him. We would make excuses for him to his teacher, and Palacitos would spend the afternoon until dinner time at the rear of the kitchen, covered with some dirty blankets. Only then would he calm down. He would leave the kitchen with his eyes rather swollen, but with a clear, almost shining look in them. He would talk to us for a while and play. The feeble-minded woman would give him a look of recognition when he passed the door to the dining hall.

Lleras and Añuco wearied of teasing Palacitos. He would not fight back, and they lost interest in him. After a while, Añuco gave him a kick and never paid any more attention to him.

But one evening the feeble-minded woman went to the playground unexpectedly. She must have walked quite stealthily, because no one noticed her. Suddenly we heard Palacitos's voice, pleading, "No! No, I can't! I can't do it, little brother!"[5]

Lleras had undressed the feeble-minded woman, raising her skirt above her head, and was urging poor Palacitos to throw himself upon her. The feeble-minded woman wanted him and moaned, beckoning to the boy with both hands.

There was a stampede. We all ran. It wasn't very dark; the night was cloudless and starry. We saw Palacitos near the doorway, inside the board fence; and we also could see the body of the feeble-minded woman on the ground. Lleras was in front of the door.

"What do you want, you dogs!" he shouted. "Get out! Get out! Here's Doctor Palacios, Doctor Palacios!"

4. Diminutive form of Palacios.—Trans.
5. Here Palacios, the most Indian boy in the school, addresses the school bully, Lleras, with *hermanito*, the diminutive form of "brother." This is an example of Arguedas's use of the nuances of Quechua speech in Spanish;

He was going to laugh, but we all jumped on him. And then he cried out desperately for the priests, "Help, Padres, help!"

The madwoman was able to escape. She did not go to the passageway; instead, she was cunning enough to run toward the other end of the playground. Two priests came into the courtyard.

"They tried to *huayquear*[6] me, Father," complained Lleras.

The other boys were speechless.

"Why?" asked one of the priests.

"You know, Father. He's a bully and he abuses us," answered Romero, the oldest boy among us.

"What did I do? Tell them what I did!" asked Lleras cynically.

"He's a devil; he was trying to make Palacios do something dirty."

"Dirty! How's that?" asked one of the priests, obviously angered.

"Excuses, Padrecito," answered Añuco. "They're just jealous of him because he won us the championships."

"Spoiled brats' foolishness. To bed! Get going, all of you!" ordered the priest.

Lleras was the first to run off, with the rest of us following.

In the dormitory, Romero challenged Lleras.

"Tomorrow night," said Lleras.

"Right now!" insisted Romero.

"Right now!" we all shouted.

But the Rector had begun to pace back and forth outside the dormitory.

Palacios was afraid to look at anyone. He lay down, fully clothed, and covered his head with the blankets.

Before he got into bed, Añuco looked at Romero and said, "Poor thing, poor thing!"

But Romero had made up his mind, and did not answer, nor would he look at Añuco.

Then the Rector turned out the lights, and no one spoke again.

In spite of our great expectations the fight did not take place. The Rector forbade us to enter the playground for a week.

Lleras and his friend would smoke in some concealed spot on the porch, or walk about with their arms around each other's shoulders. No one went near them. Añuco would run to the foun-

---

-ito is used the same way as Quechua *-cha*—as a mark of respect, for something small, as an endearment, or to make a person or thing more one's own.—Trans.

6. For many people to beat one person.—Author

tain when he heard the toads croaking and throw pebbles into the water or beat the edges of the tank with a long stick. "Bastards, bastards!" he would exclaim, flailing furiously. "That makes one, Lleras! I broke his back!" he'd exclaim jubilantly. And he'd take the stick over to the light to see if it were bloody.

As the days went by Romero lost his courage. He stopped talking of his plans to defeat Lleras, and of how he would annoy and humiliate him. "The time has finally come," he assured us. "I'll break his nose for him. You'll see that damned bastard's blood flow." And he might have done it; Romero was thin, but agile and strong. He had powerful muscles in his legs and player center-half on the school team. He could bump into taller and stouter opponents and knock them down, or leap about like a monkey, skillfully eluding other players. We had great faith in him. Nevertheless, he grew quieter as the days went by. And nobody wanted to force him to fight. Lleras was tricky and wild and had had a lot of experience. "If he thinks he's losing, he might stab Romero with a knife," said one of the boys.

But Lleras did not remember his engagement either. The next Sunday he and his friend were the first to leave the school. We didn't see them in town, nor at the soccer field. Nor did they come back to school for lunch. Later they said they had gone mountain climbing and had reached the first snowfields on Ampay.

Palacios evaded Lleras and Añuco. He protected himself by always walking with us and sitting next to us. His fear made him trust his classmates a little more.

"If I catch him in my home town, my father and I will have him killed," he told me, trembling slightly as he spoke, on one of those days when we were still expecting the fight. His cheeks reddened, and for the first time I noticed his face glowing with a look of great determination.

His father came to visit him after the fight had been called off. Shortly after this visit Palacios called me into our classroom. Standing beside the teacher's desk, he whispered, "Here, little brother, take this to Romero. My father gave it to me because I promised to try to pass this year."

And in my hands he placed a shiny gold coin that looked as if it had recently been minted.

"What if he doesn't want it?"

"Beg him to take it. No one will know. Tell him if he doesn't I shall run away from school."

I found Romero and took him up to the dormitory. It was nearly six o'clock in the afternoon and all of the boys were in the courtyards; I handed him the gold piece. First he blushed as if he had been greatly insulted, then he told me, "No, I can't accept it. I'm no good. I'm a dog."

"You've already humbled Lleras," I answered him, loudly. "Don't you see? He doesn't bully us around or hit the little boys the way he used to. He shouts, growls, and threatens them but he doesn't have the courage to touch them. It's better you didn't fight. You've muzzled him without having to beat him." As he was still doubtful and kept staring at the ground, I went on talking to him. I was amazed to see him looking so downcast, he who was so much older than I and so many grades ahead of me. "Can't you see how much little Palacios has changed?" I asked. "It'll be your fault if he runs away from school." He took the coin and decided to look at me. "But I'm not going to spend it," he said. "I'll keep it to remember him by." And then he managed a smile.

And Palacios and Romero became good friends. Not all at once, but gradually. This fact in itself served as a sort of warning to Lleras. I believe this was when Lleras decided to run away from school, even though he knew he would have to abandon Añuco, leaving him so defenseless, so suddenly ruined.

The feeble-minded woman did not go into the dark courtyard again for several weeks.

Many of the boarding students grew impatient. One of them, who was quite cowardly in spite of his stout appearance, even began cursing. They called him "Wig" because his father was a barber. Wig would hide in the latrines and even under the cots when one of the priests brought the boxing gloves to the playground. He always wore a doleful expression, like a little boy who was about to burst into tears.

"Don't cry, Wig, don't be like that," his classmates and the boarding students would say to him. He would blush with anger, tearing up his notes and textbooks. And when he became exasperated because they all taunted him at once, he even began to cry.

"Don't be sad, Wiggy."

"I'll bring my grandmother to console you, Wiggy."

"Goo, goo, Wiggy," they would say.

He must have been about nineteen or twenty years old. He had a thick neck, with a nape as strong as a bull's, and huge hands. His legs were muscular; at vacation time he worked in the fields. At first we thought he would make a good boxer. The students told how he had trembled when they tied on his gloves, how in spite of everything his rival looked at him fearfully. But the first time he was hit in the face, Wig turned his back, cringed, and didn't want to keep on fighting. They insulted him; even the priests egged him on and made fun of him as sarcastically as possible. It was all in vain; he refused to face his opponent. Father Cárpena, who was a boxing fan, could not control himself and gave him a kick that knocked him headlong.

However, whenever he saw the feeble-minded woman come into the playground, Wig was completely transformed. He would take advantage of the confusion of the first few moments so as not to be left behind. It was said that at such times he behaved with a shrewdness that drove the other boys crazy. And afterwards he would run to the main courtyard to be near the priests. Often the others, blind with rage, would try to separate him from the feeble-minded woman by giving him a terrible beating, but they said she would cling to him with unconquerable strength. And Wig would receive a rain of blows when he emerged from the latrine. Seldom was he left out, and on one of those occasions he broke the board fence with one blow of his fist.

Having waited four weeks after the incident of Palacitos and the idiot, Wig was seized with a tremendous impatience. He said nothing, but paced about nervously, running up and down the stairs that led to the dormitories and cursing obscenely. He didn't even hear the insults and jeers that ordinarily hurt his feelings.

"Hey, Wig! Hey, you beast!" they shouted to him.

"What a little darling the idiot has!"

"He's dying, just dying for her!"

"Look how he's crying!"

And they'd all laugh.

But he no longer cared; he was much too immersed in his own impatience.

The self-isolation that Wig had managed to achieve as a result of his exhausting wait exasperated the boys who lived at the school. And they attacked him one night on the playground.

"Wig doesn't even hear us anymore," several of them complained.

"We should give him a good beating," recommended another.

There was a moon that night. The whitish earth of the inner courtyard and the limed walls illumined the playground. Wig came into the courtyard, alone. The boys formed a sort of ring around him, closing in on him. Wig didn't notice them at first and kept on walking. When he turned around, because he had come up to the students who were in front of him, he saw that he was surrounded. Then they began to call out to him:

"You're dying, Wig!"

"For the filthy *chola!*"

"For the idiot!"

"You jackass!"

"She's such a maiden!"

"The maiden! Bring the maiden to the poor little boy! To Wiggy!"

He stood paralyzed in the center of the ring. The boarding students kept on taunting him. Then he recovered his composure. Walking over to the oldest boys, he cursed them loudly and passionately.

"Silence! You *k'anras.*[7] Silence!"

He stopped in front of Ismodes and spoke to him. Ismodes was bristly-haired and pitted with smallpox.

"I've seen you, *k'anra!*" he told him. "I've seen you here on the ground by the boxes, rubbing yourself all alone like one of the damned. Your eyes were almost popping out, you pig!"

"And you, you Antichrist!" he said to Montesinos. "You too, in the same place! You were rubbing yourself against the wall, you dog!"

And he went on pointing them out one by one, accusing each of the same crime.

He addressed Romero in a special way.

"You, at midnight, in your bed panting like a rabid animal. Howling softly. Only Llebras and I are brave Christians! You will be damned to perdition, *k'anra!* All of you! All of you will welter in hell!"

No one stopped him. He left with his head held high, breaking through the circle, looking proud as none of the others could have.

The group dispersed, the boys trying to walk lightly and not make much noise, as if a *nakak*[8] were asleep in the courtyard.

Some of the smaller boys wept as they said the rosary after dinner. The Rector was very much surprised. But he felt quite satisfied with the intense sobbing of the students. For the first time the rosary was recited with great piety and fervor.

From that time on, the dark courtyard was even more frightening and unfathomable to many of the little boys. In the paved courtyard, where we sang funny, gay *huaynos,* where we talked peacefully and listened to and told interminable tales of bears, mice, pumas, and condors—even by the little river of Abancay, the

7. Disgustingly filthy person.—Author
8. A being who slits people's throats.—Author

clear Mariño, on those occasions when we dammed up the current to make ponds—never could we be free from sudden attacks of fear of that courtyard.

The Wig's words had expressed a long-felt foreboding. I knew that the corners of that courtyard, with its sound of water falling into the cemented ditch, the little weeds that grew hidden behind the boxes, and the damp ground on which the feeble-minded woman lay down and on which some of the boarding students would wallow after she had left, or the next day, or any afternoon—I knew that the whole place concealed by the board fence was under a curse. Its stench oppressed us, seeping into our dreams, and we smaller boys struggled with that evil burden, trembling before it. We tried vainly to save ourselves, as river fish do when they are swept into waters muddied by an avalanche. The morning illumined us and liberated us; the great sun shed its radiance even on the yellow weeds that grew in the dense atmosphere of the latrines. But the evening, with its wind, would awaken that horrible bird that flapped its wings in the inner courtyard. We never went there alone, in spite of being wracked by a dark desire to do so. Some of us, a few, would go, following the biggest boys. And they'd return in shame, as if they had bathed in a polluted stream; they looked at us fearfully, overcome by remorse. And when they thought we were all asleep, they would pray, almost aloud, in their beds.

One night I saw Chauca get up. Half dressed and barefooted, he went out onto the balcony. A dim red electric bulb shone feebly down on the dormitory. Chauca was thin and blond. He carefully opened the door and went out. In his hand he held a rubber belt. A short while later he returned, his eyes brimming over with tears and his hands trembling. He kissed the rubber belt and lay down very quietly. His bed was in front of mine, at one end of the dormitory. For a few moments he lay back against the iron bars of his cot, and kept on crying until he had covered himself with his blankets. The next morning he woke up quite cheerful. Singing a lovely carnival song from his home village, he went down to the fountain in the courtyard to bathe. He ran down the stairs, skipped into the courtyard, and danced around the little tank, joking with the little toads and sprinkling them with water. His gaiety and the sparkle in his eyes were infectious. Not a shadow darkened his soul; he was jubilant. The pupils of his eyes shone. I learned later that he had been whipping himself the night before in the doorway of the chapel.

I looked forward to Sundays, when I set out on long walks in the country. On other days I banished the evil from my mind by thinking of my father, by inventing great deeds to try to accomplish when I became a man, or by letting my thoughts dwell on that young girl with the beautiful countenance who lived in the cruel village of the *capulí* orchards. And as I recalled her image, other younger girls would come into my mind, one of whom might perhaps pay more attention to me and be able to divine and take for her own my dreams, my memories of journeys, of the rivers and mountains I had seen, of the sheer cliffs and wide plains populated with lakes that I had crossed. But she should be small and slender, with blue eyes and braids.

But on many afternoons I, too, would follow the bigger boys to the inner courtyard and contaminate myself watching them. They were like goblins, like the monsters who appear in nightmares, moving their hairy arms and legs. When I returned from the dark courtyard the expressions of some of them, the anguished, smothered, burning sounds they made as they moaned or howled triumphantly, followed me. There was still light at that hour; the setting sun illumined the rooftops. The sky, yellow as honey, seemed to be aflame. And we had nowhere to go. The walls, the ground, the doors, our clothes, the sky at that hour—so strange and shallow, like a hard roof of golden light—all seemed contaminated, lost, or full of anger. No thought, no memory could penetrate the mortal isolation that separated me from the world at such times. I, who felt as if even the things owned by others were mine. The first time I saw a line of beautiful weeping willows shimmering on the bank of a stream I could not believe that those trees might belong to someone else. The rivers were always mine, the bushes that grew on the mountain slopes, the village houses with their red roofs streaked with lime, the blue fields of alfalfa, the beloved valleys filled with maize. But at the time I'd return from the courtyard, at dusk, this maternal image of the world would fall from my eyes. And at nightfall my feelings of loneliness and isolation grew more intense. Even though I was surrounded by boys my own age and by other people, the dormitory was more frightening and desolate than the deep gorge of Los Molinos, where I had once been abandoned by my father when he was being pursued.[9]

The valley of Los Molinos was a rather steep-walled canyon,

9. For years, during Arguedas's childhood, his father suffered from political persecution.—Trans.

through the depths of which a little river flowed between giant boulders and spiky shrubs. The water swirled under the rocks. In the still pools, almost hidden in the shadow of the rocks, swam some swift, silvery, needlelike fish. Five stone mills, ranked one below another in the least precipitous part of the gorge, were turned by the same water. The water came through a narrow aqueduct of stone and lime which the Spaniards had made, cutting long tunnels through the living rock. The road uniting the valley with the nearest towns was almost as narrow as the aqueduct and, like it, clung to the face of the cliff, with long sections under a roof of rock; horsemen had to bend over there and could see the river rushing through the bottom of the ravine. The soil was yellow and sticky. In the rainy season the road stayed closed; even mountain goats slipped in the yellow clay. The sun rose late and disappeared soon after midday. Its rays crept slowly up the rocky walls of the canyon, rising like a warm liquid. And so, while the mountain peaks were alight, the valley of Los Molinos was left in shadow.

In that gorge I lived, abandoned, for several months; I wept aloud at night; I wanted to leave but feared the road, with its dark stretches tunneled through the living rock, and the narrow trail, a mere trace in the yellow clay which, in the blackness of the night, seemed aglow with a soft, hazy, blinding light. I'd get up at moonrise. The mill gear thundered; the immense river boulders crowned with dry bushes awaited me and I could not get by them. The little bridge of eucalyptus trunks covered with yellow dirt shook at the first tread of the traveler.

But even there, in that chill gorge that buried its inhabitants, alone, in the care of a feeble, old, almost blind Indian, I never lost hope. The fish in the pools, the great sun that sped across the sky, the goldfinches that hovered over the threshing floors, and the mills that laboriously ground out the flour, the dust-covered shrouds on the crosses hanging on the mill wall, the riverbed, tangled and wild as it was—all of these gave me courage. I lived trembling with fear, not because I had been left behind but because the gorge was so dark and until then I had always lived in level valleys bright with maternal fields of maize, and I needed companionship to conquer my fear and explore calmly and fearlessly the boulders, tunnels, and enormous upended rocks of that gloomy, uninhabited riverbed.

I recalled this, recalled it and relived it in moments of great loneliness. But what I really experienced those nights in the dormitory was a feeling of horror, not as if I had once again fallen into the gloomy, isolated gorge of Los Molinos, but rather into an ever wider and deeper crevasse in the ice, where no voice or encouragement from the busy world could reach me.

That was why I dashed out of school on Sundays to go walking through the fields until I'd become dazed by the fiery heat of the valley.

I'd go down the road to the sugar cane fields, seeking the big river. As I descended, the road became dustier and the heat more intense. The *pisonayes* formed patches of woodlands; the pepper trees became taller and thicker trunked. The Peruvian pepper tree, which in the warm mountains is translucent, with musical red seeds that chime like tiny cymbals when the wind blows, was here in the depths of the blazing valley transformed into a tall, large-crowned tree, covered with dirt, seemingly overcome with sleep, its fruit blurred by the dust, submerged, as I was, in the dense, scorched air.

Sometimes I managed, after hours of walking, to reach the river. I would come to it just as I was feeling sore and exhausted, and would contemplate it, as I stood on the side of the great bridge, leaning against one of the stone crosses that are set up on top of the central pillars.

A smooth bend of the river, the awesome Pachachaca, appeared before me, winding round the base of a cliff on which only blue-flowered vines were growing. The large migratory parrots use that cliff as a resting place; they cling to the vines and their shrieking calls come down from on high.

The calm, rippling current of the river flows slowly eastward; the long boughs of the *chachacomo* bushes graze the surface of its waters, are swept under, and spring back violently on freeing themselves from the current. It looks like a river of molten steel, blue and smiling, despite its solemnity and depth. A chill wind flows over the top of the bridge.

The Pachachaca bridge was built by the Spaniards. Its two high arches are supported by pillars of stone and lime, as powerful as the river. The abutments that canalize the waters are built upon the rocks and oblige the river to go rushing and tumbling along through the imposed channels. On the pillars of the arches, the river breaks and divides; the water rises to lap at the wall, tries to climb it, and then rushes headlong through the spans of the bridge. At dusk, the spray that splashes from the columns forms fleeting rainbows that swirl in the wind.

I didn't know if I loved the river or the bridge more. But both of them cleansed my soul, flooding it with courage and heroic dreams. All of the mournful images, doubts, and evil memories were erased from my mind.

And thus renewed and brought back to myself, I would return to town, resolutely climbing the dreadful slope, holding mental conversations with my old distant friends, Don Maywa, Don Demetrio Pumaylly, and Don Pedro Kokchi . . . those who had brought me up and made my heart like their own.

For many days afterward I felt alone, completely isolated. I felt I should be like the great river, crossing the land, cutting through the rocks, undetainably and serenely flowing through mountains and forests, and entering the sea accompanied by a huge nation of birds that sang from the heavens.

On those days I didn't need my little friends. I was exalted by my decision to march along invincibly.

"Like you, Pachachaca River!" I would say to myself.

And I could go into the dark courtyard, walk back and forth across its dusty ground, go up to the board fence, and return to the light of the main courtyard, feeling prouder and calmer. I even pitied the feeble-minded woman; I grieved to remember how she was beaten and fought over with implacable brutality, how they banged her head against the board fence and the base of the toilets, and how she fled down the passageway, running like a hunted bear. And the poor young men who pursued her, and then defiled themselves to the point of feeling the need to flagellate themselves and cry out under the weight of repentance.

Yes! I must be like that clear, imperturbable river, like its conquering waters. Like you, Pachachaca! Handsome, glossy-maned steed, who runs undetainably and unceasingly along the deepest of earthly roads!

6. Zumbayllu

The Quechua ending *yllu* is onomatopoeic. *Yllu*, in one form, means the music of tiny wings in flight, music created by the movement of light objects. This term is similar to another broader one —*illa*. *Illa* is the name used for a certain kind of light, also for monsters with birth defects caused by moonbeams. *Illa* is a two-headed child or a headless calf, or a giant pinnacle, all black and shining, with a surface crossed by a wide streak of white rock, of opaque light. An ear of corn with rows of kernels that cross or form whorls is also *illa*; *illas* are the mythical bulls that live at the bottom of solitary lakes, of highland ponds ringed with cattail reeds, where black ducks dwell. All *illas* bring good or bad luck, always to the nth degree. To touch an *illa*, and to either die or be resurrected, is possible. The term *illa* has a phonetic relationship and, to a certain extent, shares a common meaning with the suffix *yllu*.

Tankayllu is the name of the inoffensive humming insect that flies through the fields sipping nectar from the flowers. The *tankay-llu* appears in April, but may be seen in irrigated fields during other months of the year. Its wings whir at a mad pace to lift its heavy body with its ponderous abdomen. Children chase and try to catch it. The dark, elongated body ends in a sort of stinger, which is not only harmless, but sweet. Children hunt it to sip the honey with which the false stinger is anointed. The *tankayllu* is not easy to catch because it flies high over the bushes, looking for flowers. It is a strange, dark, tobacco color, and has a bright striped abdomen; and because its wings make such a loud noise, much too strong for such a tiny figure, the Indians believe that the *tankayllu* has something more inside its body than just its own life. Why does it have honey on the end of its abdomen? Why do its weak little wings fan the air until they stir it up and make it change direction? How is it that whoever sees the *tankayllu* go by feels a gust of air on his face? It cannot possibly get so much vitality from such a tiny body. It fans the air, buzzing like a big creature; its velvety body disappears, rising straight upward in the light. No, it is not an evil being; children who taste its honey feel for the rest of their lives the brush of its comforting warmth on their hearts, protecting them from hatred and melancholy. But the Indians do not consider the *tankayllu* to be a godly creature, like all the ordinary insects; they fear it may be a reprobate. The missionaries must have once preached against it and other privileged beings. In the Ayacucho towns there was once a scissors-dancer who has since become legendary. He danced in the town squares for important fiestas and performed diabolical feats on the eves of saints' days—swallowing bits of steel, running needles and hooks through his body, and walking about the churchyards with three iron bars in his teeth. That dancer was called Tankayllu. His suit was made of condor skins decorated with mirrors.

Pinkuyllu is the name of the giant flute that the southern Indians play at the community celebrations. The *pinkuyllu* is never played for home fiestas. It is a heroic instrument, not made of ordinary reed or cane, nor even of *mámak*, an extraordinarily thick jungle reed which is twice as long as bamboo. The hollow of the *mámak* is dark and deep. In areas where there is no *huaranhuay* wood, the Indians do make smaller flutes of *mámak*, but they do not dare to use the name *pinkuyllu* for these instruments. They simply call them *mámak* to distinguish them from ordinary flutes. *Mámak* means the mother, the source, the creator—it is a magic name. But there is no natural reed that can be used as material for the *pinkuyllu*. Man must make his own, fashioning a deeper, heavier *mámak*, unlike anything that grows, even in the jungle. A great bent tube. He removes the hearts from *huaranhuay* poles and then bends them in the sun, binding them together with bull sinews. The light that enters the hole at the smaller end of the hollow tube can be seen only indirectly, as a half-light flowing through the curve, a soft glow, like that on the horizon just after sunset.

The *pinkuyllu* maker cuts the instrument's finger holes, seeming to leave too much space between them. The first two holes should be covered with the thumb and either the index or the ring finger, the player opening the left hand as widely as possible; the other three holes are for the index, ring, and little fingers of the right hand, with the players' fingers spread quite widely apart. Indians with short arms cannot play the *pinkuyllu*. The instrument is so long that the average man who tries to use one has to stretch his neck and put his head back as if he were looking directly upward at the zenith. Troupes of musicians play them, with drum accompaniment, in town squares, in the fields, or in the corrals and courtyards, but never inside the houses.

Only the *wak'rapuku* has a deeper, more powerful voice than the *pinkuyllu*. But in areas where there are *wak'rapukus*, the *pinkuyllu* is unknown. Man uses both of them to express similar emotions. The *wak'rapuku* is a trumpet made of bull's horn, of the thickest, most crooked of horns, and is fitted with a silver or brass mouthpiece. Its damp, twisting tunnel is darker and more impenetrable than the *pinkuyllu*'s and, similarly, it can be played only by a chosen few.

Only heroic songs and dances are played on the *pinkuyllu* and the *wak'rapuku*. Drunken Indians work themselves into a frenzy singing the ancient war dances; and while some sing and play, others whip themselves blindly, to bleed and weep afterwards in the shadow of the lofty mountains, near the abysses, or before the cold lakes and the steppe.

During religious festivals the *pinkuyllu* and the *wak'rapuku* are never heard. Could the missionaries have forbidden the Indians to play these strange, deep-voiced instruments inside or in front of the churches, or alongside the images carried in Catholic processions? The *pinkuyllu* and the *wak'rapuku* are played at communal ceremonies such as the installation of new officials, during the savage fights between young men at carnival time, at the cattle branding, and at bullfights. The voice of the *pinkuyllu* or of the *wak'rapuku* dazzles and exalts the Indians, unleashing their strength; while listening to it, they defy death. They confront the wild bulls, singing and cursing; they build long roads or tunnel through the rock; they dance unceasingly, heedless of the change of light or the passage of time. The *pinkuyllu* and the *wak'rapuku* set the pace, stimulating and sustaining them; no probe, music, or element can penetrate deeper into the human heart.

The suffix *yllu* signifies the diffusion of this kind of music and *illa* is the diffusion of nonsolar light. *Killa* is the moon, and *illapa* the ray. *Illariy* names the dawn light which streams out over the edge of the world just before the sun appears. *Illa* is not the term for fixed light, like the resplendent, supernatural light of the sun. It represents a lesser light—a radiance, the lightning flash, the rays of the sun, all light that vibrates. Those kinds of light, only semi-divine, which the old men of Peru still believe to be intimately related to the blood and to all kinds of shining matter.

"*Zumbayllu!*" In the month of May, Antero brought the first *zumbayllu* to school. The smaller boys gathered round him.

"Let's go to the playground, Antero!"

"To the playground, brothers. Little brothers!"

Palacios ran off with the first of them, leaping over the bank onto the dusty playground, shouting, "*Zumbayllu, zumbayllu!*"

I followed them expectantly.

What could a *zumbayllu* be? What did this word, whose last syllables reminded me of beautiful and mysterious objects, mean? Timid Palacios was almost at the head of the group of boys who ran to see the *zumbayllu*. He made a tremendous leap in order to be the first to reach the playground. And there he was, looking down at the thing in Antero's hand. His face shone, as never before, with a look of great happiness and eagerness. His expression was quite similar to that of the Indian schoolboys who play in the shade of the pepper trees, on the roads that join remote huts to the villages. Even Añuco, pale, wizened, conceited Añuco, watched Antero from the edge of the group; there was an expression of tender anxiety on his sallow, bitter face, which was erect on his thin neck with its sharp, taut tendons. He looked like a new, recently converted angel.

I remembered the great Tankayllu, the mirror-bespangled dancer, making tremendous leaps in front of the church. I also recalled the real *tankayllu*, the flying insect we chased through flowering shrubs in April and May. I thought of the white *pinkuyllus* I had heard men playing in the southern towns. The *pinkuyllus* reminded me of the voice of the *wak'rapukus* and of how the sound of both of them resembled the prolonged bellowing with which ruttish bulls challenge one another across hill and river.

I couldn't see the little top, nor how Antero wound it. I had been left behind, near Añuco, and could only see Antero, in the center of the group, lash out with his right arm. Then I heard a delicate humming sound.

It was still early. The courtyard walls cast a long shadow. The sun kindled their limed surfaces from the east. The air of the deep valleys and their hot sunshine are not propitious to the diffusion of sound; they mute and absorb the songs of birds; in compensation these valleys have woods that allow one to get quite near the singing birds. In temperate or cold country the voices of people or birds carry a long way in the wind. In this oppressive sunlight, however, the song of the *zumbayllu* was diffused with a strange clarity; it seemed to have a sharp edge. All the air must have been filled with its delicate voice, and all the earth, that sandy ground from which it seemed to have sprung.

"*Zumbayllu, zumbayllu!*"

I said the word over and over, as I listened to the whirring of the top. It was like a chorus of big *tankayllus*, all fixed in one place, prisoners in the dust. And it made one happy to repeat this word, so much like the name of the sweet insects that disappear humming upwards into the light.

With a great effort, I pushed aside other bigger boys and reached the circle around Antero. In his hands he held a little top. The small sphere was made from a store coconut, one of those tiny, gray ones that come in tins. The tip was long and thin. The sphere had four round holes by way of eyes. Antero wound the top slowly, with a fine cord; making many turns he wound it right down to its sharpened tip and then cast it. The top hesitated for a moment in midair, then fell at the edge of the circle of boys, in the sunlight. Its long tip traced curves in the loose dirt; spinning, it gave off little gusts of air through the four eyeholes. It whirred like a large, singing insect, and then shifted, tilting on its axis. A gray shadow haloed its spinning head; a black circle divided the sphere in the middle. And its high-pitched song flowed out from the dark band made by the eyes—the four eyeholes that sank into the hard sphere as if into a liquid. A circle of very fine dust rose up around it, enveloping the little top.

The song of the top penetrated deep into my ear, reviving memories of rivers, and of the black trees that overhang the walls of the abysses.

I looked into Antero's face. No child ever watched a toy the way he did. What similarity was there, what current flowed between the world of the deep valleys and the body of that little mobile toy, almost protean, that hummed as it scrabbled about in the sand in which the sun seemed to have melted?

Antero was blond. On very sunny days his head seemed aflame. His complexion was also golden; but he had many birthmarks on his forehead. His classmates called him "Candle"; others used the Quechua nickname "Markask'a," "The Marked One," because of his birthmarks. Antero stared at the top with an infectious eagerness. As long as the top was spinning, everyone remained silent. Crouched there so intently, Antero, with his sharp face and high, aquiline nose, seemed to have appeared from outer space.

Suddenly, when the top still had not toppled over, Lleras shouted, "Get out of here, *akatank'as*![1] Watching Candle's sorcery. Out, you skunks!"

No one paid any attention to him. Not even Añuco. We kept on listening to the *zumbayllu*.

"Skunks, skunks! You poor *k'echas*,"[2] scolded Lleras, tonelessly.

The *zumbayllu* tilted over until it grazed the dust; as soon as it touched the ground, the sphere made a circle and stopped.

"Sell it to me!" I shouted to Antero. "Sell it to me!"

Before anyone could stop me, I flung myself to the ground and grasped the top. Its long tip was made of yellow wood. That tip and the top's black-rimmed eyes, made with a red-hot nail, with black edges that smelled charred, gave the top an air of unreality. To me it was a new kind of being, an apparition in a hostile world, a tie that bound me to the courtyard I hated, to that vale of sorrow, to the school. I stared at the toy as the other boys gathered around me in amazement.

"Don't sell it to the stranger!"[3] ordered Añuco in a loud voice.

"Don't sell it to that boy!" said another.

"Don't sell it to him," commanded Lleras. "I told you not to sell it."

Lleras pushed forward and stopped in front of Antero. I looked him in the eye. I knew how to hate, with a passing but uncontainable hatred. Lleras's eyes were like a kind of shallow mine, dirty and foul.

Had anyone ever held back the murky lightning of those eyes? Had any small boy ever stood motionless before him, staring at him with a growing hatred that swept all other emotions before it?

"I'll sell it to you, stranger. I'll give it to you, I'll give it to you!" exclaimed Antero, while Lleras's look still clashed with mine.

I hugged Markask'a, while the others shouted noisily, as though cheering for us.

"Don't pay any attention to those *k'echas*, champ," said Añuco, rather kindly.

---

1. Dung beetles.—Author
2. Bedwetters.—Author
3. Arguedas is probably using *foráneo*, "stranger," for *qala*, a Quechua word that is used to mean "outsider" in Indian communities.—Trans.

"I'm giving these away too!" declared Antero. And he tossed several *zumbayllus* into the air.

The boys fought happily over the tops. Lleras and Añuco went off to the main courtyard.

The owners of the other *zumbayllus* found some string; gathering in little groups, they set their tops spinning. We could hear the voices of some of the *zumbayllus*. From all corners of the courtyard came their light, penetrating humming. It was as if a small troop of singing insects that had come from some clump of flowering bushes and had strayed into the arid courtyard were rising and falling in the dust.

I begged Antero to cast his top. Most of the boys gathered around us once more. No one could make his top spin longer or faster than Antero. His hands wrapped around the top as if it were a great, impatient insect. When he pulled the string the gray sphere rose to the level of our eyes and fell slowly.

"Now it's your turn," he told me. "You saw how I did it."

I was sure I could wind the *zumbayllu* well and throw it correctly. I was impatient and timid. I grasped the top and began to wind the string around it, making it tight at the top, winding it slowly and pulling hard on it. I took the top in the fingers of my left hand and pulled the string with my index and ring fingers crooked, as I had seen Candle do.

"The stranger's showing off!"

"The little stranger."

"The fool!"

The Abancay boys began shouting, "This game's not for just any old stranger!"

But Antero, who had been watching me intently, exclaimed, "Now you've got it! Now you've got it, brother."

I pulled the string with my eyes closed. I could feel the *zumbayllu* spinning in the palm of my hand. I opened my fingers when all the string had unwound. The *zumbayllu* sprang whistling through the air; the boys standing beside me jumped back, leaving room for it to fall to the ground. As I watched it amid the silence of the other boys, the bell rang to announce the end of the recess period. Almost everyone ran off. Antero congratulated me solemnly in the presence of the two or three who still remained behind.

"It was luck!" said the others.

"A born top spinner," asserted Candle. "A top spinner like me."

The roots of his hair were almost black, and resembled the downiness of certain spiders who creep across the roads after torrential downpours. Between the color of the roots of his hair and the color of his birthmarks there was an indefinable but clear identity. And the blackness of his eyes seemed to be a result of the same inexplicable mystery of his race.

Until the morning he brought the *zumbayllus*, Antero had been conspicuous only because of the unusual color of his hair, and his large black birthmarks. His nickname made him unique but also made the strangeness of his face seem unimportant. "That's Candle, Markask'a," they told me when I asked about him. He was older than I, and was in the eighth grade, two years ahead of me. He was neither exceptionally bright nor dull in class, and had no close friends, being rather reserved. Nevertheless he had some power, some innate authority that prevented his companions from making him the laughingstock of the class, a scapegoat, a freak, or a favorite butt of their jokes. He was the only one to whom they gave a nickname which was used neither excessively nor in a joking manner.

When he left the school, or his classroom, his head attracted the attention of the new students. During recess he would lean against the porch pillars, watching the other boys play, and sometimes participating, but never taking part in the cruel games.

"Hey, Ernesto, they tell me you write like a poet. I'd like you to write a letter for me," said Markask'a, a few days after the debut of the *zumbayllus*.

He came to my classroom looking for me. Everyone else had gone out for recess and we were alone.

"I wouldn't ask the other boys to do this kind of favor for me. You're different."

"Sure. I'll be glad to do it, brother!" I told him. "I'll write you the most beautiful of letters. It's for a girl, isn't it?"

"Yes, for the princess of Abancay. You know who she is, don't you?"

"No, brother, tell me which girl is your princess."

"How stupid of me! I forgot that you're the stranger and don't know Abancay. You go walking in the Patibamba cane fields. You're a fool, brother. But I'll open your eyes. I'm going to show you around this town a bit. I've looked all the girls over, from a distance and close up too, and she's the princess of them all. Her name is Salvinia and she goes to the Colegio de las Mercedes. She lives on Condebamba Avenue, near the hospital. She has small, black eyes, and her forehead is covered with bangs. She's quite dark, almost black."

"Like a *zumbayllu*, Brother Markask'a!"

"That's it, Ernesto! Like a *zumbayllu* that's been spinning ever since dawn. But you must see her before you write the letter. You must take a good look at her. And since she's mine, you won't fall in love with her, will you?"

"Don't even say such a thing. It's as if she were already my sister."

"Tomorrow, Saturday, we'll go to my room. Tonight I'll make you a special *zumbayllu*. I have a *winku*[4] one, *cholo*. *Winkus* have a different hum. They have souls."

"I'll be thinking about the letter. Have you ever spoken to her?"

"No, not yet. But I've sent her messages with her servant. Her servant is from my home town."

The bell rang, and we went out to line up in the courtyard. In the doorway of our classroom we sealed our alliance with a handshake.

Markask'a crossed the courtyard and joined his classmates in the line.

Next morning after school, when the town boys had gone off, I stayed behind in my classroom, alone. I felt I should think about Markask'a's request.

How should I begin the letter? I could not remember seeing that little princess of Abancay. Condebamba Avenue was wide, with no sidewalks. It was called an avenue because of the mulberry trees that grew along it. It was said to have once been the entrance road to a large manor house. When I came to Abancay, it led from town to the soccer field. I could not recall ever having seen a girl with bangs in the doorway of any of the few houses behind the mulberry trees, nor looking out of any of the windows. The mulberries grew along the stone walls; their large, veined leaves cast deep shadows on the road. In the Andean towns there are no mulberry bushes. They had been brought to Abancay by a silk grower whose business had failed because the hacienda owners had managed to have a special tax levied against him. But the mulberries multiplied in the city's gardens. They grew with unrivaled luxuriance and became tall, large-crowned trees, tame and stately. Birds and children enjoyed their fruit. The stone walls were stained pink

4. Deformity in objects that should be round.—Author

by the berries. At picking time, the fruit-eating birds congregated in the town gardens to gorge themselves on the berries; their red droppings fell on the whitewashed walls, on the tin roofs, and sometimes on the straw hats of the passers-by.

In which house did Markask'a's princess live, and how far was it from the end of the avenue? It was a beautiful road on which to await one's beloved.

I did not know the young ladies of the town. On Sundays I would lose myself in the poorer sections of the city, in the *chicha* bars and in the neighboring settlements. I always thought of the young ladies as remote beings, in Abancay and in all the other towns. I feared and avoided them, although I adored their image as it was portrayed in the few stories and novels I was able to read. They were not of my world. They sparkled in another sky.

From the gateway of the huge hacienda that surrounded and strangled Abancay I often listened to an unfamiliar waltz being played on the piano. Hundreds of larks and goldfinches would be singing in the trees near the great porch. I was never able to see the person who played the piano, but I thought it must be a white woman with blond hair who played such slow music.

In the Apurímac valley, on the journey I had made with my father, we had had to put up for the night on an hacienda. The mule driver had taken us to the *tambo*, far from the owner's mansion. My face was swollen from the heat and the bites of the mosquitoes. We passed beneath the observatory of the residence. There was still sun on the snowy peaks; the yellow glow of that distant light seemed to be reflected on the plumes of the sugar cane. My heart was affected and beat faster; it was excited and feverish from the bites of the gnats, the insignificant noise of their wings, and the all-enveloping voice of the great river. But as I looked up at the high observatory atop the manor house, I saw a slender girl, dressed in yellow, contemplating the black rocks of the precipice opposite me. From those damp black rocks hung long cacti covered with Spanish moss. That night we slept among loads of fragrant alfalfa, near the horse stables. My face throbbed all night. And yet I was still able to recall the indifferent expression of that young white girl, her long chestnut locks, and her slender arms resting on the banister; her lovely image kept vigil all night long in my mind.

The music I heard coming from the Patibamba mansion bore a strange resemblance to the hair, hands, and posture of that girl. What distance lay between her world and mine? Perhaps the same that there was between the glassed-in observatory in which I had seen her and the dusty dung and alfalfa in which I had spent the night being flayed alive by the dance of the carnivorous insects.

I knew that, in spite of everything, I could cross that distance like an arrow, like a spark that flies upward. The letter I was to write for Markask'a's beloved would reach the gates of that world. "Now you can choose your best words," I said to myself. "By writing them!" It did not matter that the letter was for someone else; perhaps it was better to begin that way. "Take flight, blind hawk, roving hawk!" I exclaimed.

I burned with a new pride. And, like one who is about to go into combat, I began to write Markask'a's letter:

"You are the mistress of my soul, dear girl. You are in the sun, in the breeze, in the rainbow that glistens beneath the bridges, in my dreams, in the pages of my books, in the song of the lark, in the music of the weeping willows that grow by the clean water. My princess, princess of Abancay, princess of the flowering *piso-nayes*, I have gone to your door at daybreak. The sweet morning stars perched on your windowsill; dawn light surrounded your house, crowned it with light. And when the goldfinches came to sing from the branches of the mulberry trees, when the robins and the *calandrias* arrived, your avenue resembled heaven. I seemed to see you then, walking alone between two lines of illumined trees. Dear nymph, you played among the mulberry trees like a butter-fly . . ."

But a sudden discontent, an intense feeling of shame, made me interrupt the writing of the letter. I laid my arms and head down on the desk; with my face hidden, I paused to listen to those new feelings. "Where are you going, where are you going? Why don't you continue? What has frightened you; who has cut short your flight?" After asking these questions I went back to listening to myself eagerly.

"And what if they knew how to read? What if I could write to them?"

And they were Justina, or Jacinta, Malicacha, or Felisa, who had neither long hair nor bangs, nor wore tulle over their eyes. Only black braids, and wildflowers in the bands of their hats . . . "If I could write to them my love would flow like a clear river; my letter could be like a song that goes through the sky to reach its destination." Writing! Writing for them was useless, futile. "Go; wait for them on the roads and sing! But what if it were possible, if it could be started?" And I wrote:

"*Uyariy chay k'atik'niki siwar k'entita . . .*

"Listen to the emerald hummingbird who follows you; he shall speak to you of me; do not be cruel, hear him. His little wings are tired, he can fly no farther; pause a moment. The white stone where the travelers rest is nearby; wait there and listen to him; hear his sobs; he is only the messenger of my young heart; he shall speak to you of me. Listen, my lovely one, your eyes are like large stars; beautiful flower, do not flee any more, halt! An order from the heavens I bring you; they command you to be my tender lover . . . !"

This time my own sobbing made me pause. Fortunately, at that hour the boarding students were playing in the inner courtyard and I was alone in my classroom.

I wept from neither sorrow nor despair. I left the classroom erect, with a certain pride; as proudly as I had swum across the rivers in January, when they are laden with the heaviest, most turbulent waters. I paced the stone-paved courtyard for a few moments.

The little bell that was rung for a long while to tell us it was time to go to the dining hall aroused me from my rapture. When I entered the dining hall, the boarding students were standing by their seats. Brother Miguel prayed aloud and the boys repeated the prayer in chorus. I was still bewildered; my companions seemed to move about in a murky, undulating space; they looked elongated and strange.

"What's the matter?" Palacios asked me. "You look kind of scared. The *zumbayllus* are driving you crazy."

"Ernesto may read from the Carreño Manual,"[5] decreed Brother Miguel.

A servant handed me the book. I began to read the marked passage. The precision required for the reading of the Manual immediately clarified my thoughts. It was those public readings that had given me prestige. I was one of the largest boys in my class, and when I first entered the school I had not known how to read aloud. I failed the first time and was relieved after a few moments. This seemed to show that the reason for my backwardness was not the wandering life I had led, but something more serious. But two weeks later I asked to read again—I had practiced for many hours —and I surprised everyone. I read in a loud, clear, deliberate tone. The boys stopped eating their soup for a few moments and looked at me. From then on, all the priests who presided over the meals,

5. An etiquette book.—Trans.

and Brother Miguel, considered me one of their favorite readers. Now I had become quite calm by the time Romero replaced me, and I was able to say to Palacios, "It was because I was hungry, Palacitos! I'm not such a good friend of the cook's as you are."

Palacios stretched his neck and whispered in my ear, "I was in the kitchen. Tonight the idiot is going to the playground. Lleras asked her to go. Something is going to happen tonight, little brother. Lleras and Añuco have been talking together like a couple of sorcerers."

"That's all right. We won't go."

"We can play the harmonica with Chauca in the outer court-yard."

Lleras began to stare at us. Little Palacios became frightened and did not speak to me again.

"He noticed us. But don't be like that; don't be afraid!" I told him.

He was terrified and did not lift his head again. He ate his lunch meekly. I had to talk to Rondinel, who was sitting on my right; I had to speak with him, in spite of the fact that he always looked at me arrogantly. Lleras and Añuco continued watching us.

"You think you're such a good reader, now," Rondinel told me. "You think you're a master of the *zumbayllu*, too. You're a little Indian, even though you look white! A little Indian, that's all!"

"And you, you're white but useless. A useless nobody."

Some boys who heard me laughed heartily. Palacitos continued to be cautious.

"I challenge you for Saturday!" exclaimed Rondinel, giving me a furious look.

He was terribly thin, nothing but bone. His eyes, more sunken than any I had ever seen, and very small, made one feel sorry for him. They were surrounded by thick, jet black eyelashes, so long and curly as to seem artificial. "His eyes could be extremely beauti-ful," said Valle, who was a senior, a great reader, and quite ele-gant. "They could be extremely beautiful if they didn't look like those of a dead child."

That was why he evoked pity. One had the impression that only his eyelashes grew; and that they grew up into his ears; but that his eyes themselves would always be those of a month-old infant.

"Poor baby! Poor baby!" I said to him.

He turned pale with anger.

"I'm going to kick you to death Saturday," he told me.

I did not answer him, nor did we speak to each other again dur-ing the lunch hour.

On the way out of the dining hall, Lleras came over to me.

"You're a good actor, *cholito*," he said to me quite loudly so that Palacios might hear him. "But I know that Indian Palacios was telling you secrets about me."

"Not me, Lleras," answered Palacios, almost whining. "I was talking about my harmonica."

"Well, watch out! Rondinel will break the stranger's ribs. His arms and legs are hard as iron. They hurt. Oh *zumbayllito, zumbayllu!*"

He broke off with a laugh, giving me an ironical look. Taking Rondinel by the arm, he led him away.

"I'll be your trainer," he told him. "Don't worry. I guarantee you'll beat the chocolate out of the stranger."

It frightened me to hear him talk.

"You were scared," said Palacios, looking at me. "If he ever hits you he'll make a sheep out of you for the rest of the year."

Until then no one had ever formally challenged me to a fight. That must have been the first time, and I was afraid. I was unable to overcome that filthy, shameful feeling of terror.

"It's Lleras I'm afraid of, not Skinny," I said.

But this was not the truth. It was the other way around.

And Markask'a did not come to school that afternoon.

"Watch out," Romero told me. "The real skinny ones are dangerous. If you hit him first, you'll take him apart; but if he gets there ahead of you, he'll cut up your face."

The boarding students did not have much to say about the contest. The only one who cared about it was Valle.

"It will be an unusual fight," he said. "Something to see. A wiry mosquito against a gloomy stranger. We must make sure that it's not called off. It will be a strange spectacle."

Until that day I had been quite respectful of Valle. He was the only boy in the school who liked to read. He hid novels and other books under the mattress of his bed. The priests watched him carefully because he declared himself to be an atheist and lent books to the other boys. "God does not exist," he'd say as he entered the chapel. "I am my own God." He was very proud, but seemingly with justification. He lent me an *Anthology* of Rubén Darío. And as I memorized the longest poems he would make me recite them. Then, looking thoughtful, he'd say, "Emotive, sensitive, too much, too much." And off he'd go.

Valle courted the most aristocratic young girls in town. He was eligible, because he was in the last year of high school, and was quite elegant. He ironed his pants carefully, with enviable dexterity. His neckties were tied with a knot he had invented himself, for which, incredibly, he used a Quechua word, *k'ompo*. The *k'ompo* became stylish in Abancay. It was a wide, voluminous knot. Valle would use almost his whole necktie to make it. This attracted the young girls' attention. He was contemptuous of the high school girls, and his disdain for them was quite sincere. He said the doctor's wife was his great love, and proved it. On Sundays he would stand on the corner in front of the doctor's house. Highly perfumed, with his hat pulled down over his forehead, he would wait there, his enormous *k'ompo* so visible, so perfect, his shoes gleaming. Erect, and striking quite a distinguished pose, Valle would whistle on the corner.

Even though he looked like a gallant young man, and was fully eligible, he was not accepted into society. The doctor's wife gave him a kind look now and then; the other young girls tolerated his compliments, but he could not manage to get invited to social functions. Knowing that the schoolgirls noticed him, watched him, and whispered about him, he consoled himself with the thought that in any case he held a privileged position among the students. His atheism and "materialism" were notorious; he himself said that his culture was "encyclopedic." Enamored of form alone, he scorned the romantics and the "passionists." "Poor, unhappy Espronceda; and that other one, who was even more unfortunate, the weeper, Bécquer," he would say. Chocano[6] and Schopenhauer were his idols. He never participated in the struggles over the feeble-minded woman, nor did he have any friends. He lent novels and poetry books courteously, but rather disdainfully. There was one book by Schopenhauer, however, that he kept locked up in a little suitcase and never lent to anyone. "This is reading matter for the strong, for giants; only gold can hold this liquid without dissolving. You would be accursed if you were to read it, and wouldn't understand it anyway," he told us.

Valle spoke to Rondinel. Waiting until he saw us nearby, and knowing I was listening, he demonstrated to my rival that, in view of our relative advantages, Rondinel had every chance of beating me, of giving me a good drubbing. Then he came over to me and said, "You are in an honorable position. If you win, it will be because of your bravery and nothing but your bravery. I offer you my felicitations; I should really like to have such an opportunity."

6. José Espronceda y Delgado (1808–1842), Spanish politician and romantic poet; Gustavo Adolfo Bécquer (1836–1870), Spanish poet and author of romantic narratives; José Santos Chocano (1875–1934), famous Peruvian poet.—Trans.

His language was always flowery, like that. And as we all thought he had a right to speak that way, because of his reading, we were neither hurt nor surprised by his style. On the contrary, many of the boys were influenced by him and tried to imitate him.

Valle was the only student who did not speak Quechua; he understood it well, but did not speak it. His ignorance of the language was not just a pose. The few times I heard him try to pronounce some words he failed completely; no one had taught him as a child.

"I am not in the habit of speaking Indian," he would say. "The words resound in my ear, but my tongue refuses to manufacture those sounds. Fortunately I shall not need the Indians; I am thinking of living in Lima or abroad."

Rondinel's challenge gave Valle an opportunity to amuse himself.

"Only your courage can save you," he repeated. "Fortunately sentimentalists are either quite brave or else quite cowardly."

And he looked at me sharply.

I began to feel a sort of impotent rage against him. He guessed or really knew about the fear that oppressed me, that was about to overwhelm me. Perhaps he had once felt that same despicable terror.

"The vinelike Rondinel should win," he proclaimed. "A Quixote from Abancay will topple a Quechua, a singer of *jarahuis*. What a fight, boys, what a noble, Homeric combat. A new duel between the races. By Beelzebub! It will be a spectacle to merit the attention of the whole boarding school. It even deserves an epic poem of praise!"

Rondinel was aroused by Valle's predictions. He paced back and forth nervously. He no longer accepted Lleras's advice. He stretched out his scrawny arm—he was completely under the influence of Valle's language and gestures—and told Lleras, "Don't you give me any advice. I can knock that little *cholo* down all by myself. I'll tear him apart."

Añuco sought me out and, walking by my side, shouted to me, "How sad you look *zumbayllero*! What about the long-awaited duel?"

"He's right," agreed little Palacios. "You've turned yellow. Rub your face and ears, brother. It's better to make the blood come."

The boarding students who were my own age did not speak to me. They preferred to await further developments. Romero encouraged me, but in pitying tones.

Although I wished to commend myself to God that evening, as

we recited the rosary, I was unable to do so. Shame bound my tongue and thoughts.

Then, as I trembled with shame, there flashed into my mind the image of my regional god, Apu K'arwarasu.[7] And I spoke to him, just as the scholars of my native village used to commend themselves to him when they had to compete in races, wrestling, or tests of courage.

"You alone, Apu, and Markask'a!" I told him. "I shall dedicate my fight to you, Lord K'arwarasu! Send your *killincho*[8] to watch over me, to shriek at me from on high. I'll kick Rondinel in his ass, damn it, in his stray dog's ribs, in his violin neck! By God, I'm a Lucana[9] Indian, a Lucana miner! *Nakak!*"

I began to feel more cheerful, to get up my courage, by commending myself to the great mountain, just as the Indians of my village put themselves under its protection before rushing into the plaza to fight the brave bulls which had condors bound to their backs.

K'arwarasu is the Apu, the regional god of my native village. It has three snowy peaks towering above a mountain range of black rock. Around it there are many lakes, where pink-plumed cranes live. The kestrel is the symbol of K'arwarasu. The Indians say that during Lent he emerges from the highest peak in the guise of a firebird and pursues the condors, breaking their backs, making them whimper and humiliating them. Flashing like lightning, he flies over the planted fields, across the cattle ranches, and then sinks down into the snow.

The Indians invoke K'arwarasu only in times of great danger. They have only to pronounce his name, and the fear of death vanishes.

As I left the chapel I was unable to control my feelings any longer. As soon as the Father Director and the other priests had gone up to the second floor, I went over to Rondinel and nudged him with the toe of my shoe, by way of warning.

"Hey, Wire," I said. "Right now, right now! On the playground!"

The light was dim there in front of the chapel. Valle jumped in between us.

7. *Apu* means lord or god in Quechua. It is an honorary title meaning "grand seigneur" or "principal judge," and is also given to the mountains of the cordillera, which are worshiped as gods.—Trans.
8. Kestrel.—Author
9. An Andean region where the men are known for their toughness.—Trans.

"The explosion of the sentimentalists!" he said calmly, pulling Skinny aside. "This is a formal challenge, between gentlemen, for Saturday, and not for wrestling and groping around in the dark."

"Yes, yes! Not now!" yelled several boys.

"Oh, let them beat each other up," said Romero.

"My challenge is for Saturday, in the castor-bean field," said Rondinel, springing onto the porch and stopping under an electric light bulb. "I want to see what I'm doing. I'm not an Indian who can spin around like a top in the dark."

I could see he was afraid, that this time he was the one who was frightened.

"Treacherous Indian," said Lleras.

But Skinny corrected him, so that he wouldn't make me angrier, I thought.

"He didn't really kick me," he said. "He was just warning me."

"I think you're the Quixote. You'll be beaten and with even more justification now!" Valle told me, laying his hands on my shoulders. "That 'warning kick' is typical of you. It was an appetizer, for you and for us who shall witness your noble defeat."

This time I was unimpresed by his irony. He was speaking into a vacuum. Skinny sneaked off to the dormitory while Valle was talking to me, and the other boarding students scattered. Little Palacios went off when Rondinel left. And Valle lost his enthusiasm.

I no longer felt ashamed of waiting for Antero to tell him what had happened; I was even able to think about the letters I had written.

At eight-thirty they rang the little bell which announced the hour to go to the dormitory. But those who wanted to could go to bed earlier.

I walked toward the playground. I was sure the feeble-minded woman would go there and that something would happen. It must have been about half an hour before the time to ring the bell.

In one corner of the courtyard, by the toilets, Wig stood guard. He was alone. Nearby, on the playground, Lleras and Añuco were smoking. Since I knew that Lleras had spoken to the feeble-minded woman, I could see that he and Añuco were watching Wig. Quite a bit of light came into the courtyard from the neighboring house; shining across the top of the wall, which was all eroded by the rain, a bright light fell onto the upper part of the playground. The groups of boys who were sitting on the ground along the wall were almost completely concealed. They were telling stories about women and jokes about priests and sextons.

I went off, all alone, to the back of the courtyard, by the wall. I did not want to talk to anyone. I had a strange feeling of pleasure, and felt a sudden impulse to burst out laughing. "That Skinny Rondinel put you into a cold sweat. That Skinny Rondinel made you tremble like a rabbit," I kept saying, almost aloud. But I could not laugh, not even once.

Then I remembered how I had faced Lleras, returning his bullying stare. And I would have kept on thinking about my moments of cowardice and anger if Wig had not just then jumped out into the courtyard and walked over to me.

"What are you doing, hiding here?" he demanded in a menacing tone.

"The idiot is going to come," I told him. "Watch out, brother! I think Lleras is going to do something to you."

"Are you afraid of me?" he asked again, this time not in anger but with great curiosity.

"I don't know," I replied. "I'm not scared of you right now. I'm warning you because I hate Lleras."

Lleras and Añuco hurried over to us.

"What's the stranger telling you? If you don't tell me I'll break your back!" Lleras threatened Wig, even before he had reached us.

Wig kept silent. Lleras looked small beside him; in the twilight Wig's solitary bulk seemed to be looming over Lleras's smaller figure.

"Don't tell him, Wig! Don't tell him. Crush him with your body!" I yelled at him.

The other boarding students ran over to see what was going on. Wig was just about to say something when he heard their approaching footsteps; he sprang away, leaped down over the high step from the playground, sped past the toilets, and entered the passageway. I listened intently; I couldn't hear his footsteps in the passage and realized he was hiding around the corner. The group of boys came up to us.

"What's the matter, k'echas? The stranger is all excited. He's just yelling because he wants to. Get out of here!" ordered Lleras. "Get out!"

I looked for Romero in the group. He wasn't there. They all left. Some of them did not go back to their corner again. They went off toward the main courtyard. I kept still, expecting Lleras to threaten me. I might have answered him boldly, but he went down the path to the toilets with Añuco. The other boarding students settled down in their corners. In a little while they went off in twos and threes. Chauca broke away from the last group and slowly walked over to me, stopping more than once, looking toward Lleras as if he expected him to shout at him and forbid him to continue.

"What's going on?" he asked softly, when he had reached me. "What are you doing here all alone?"

"I'm waiting. Something is going to happen. The idiot is supposed to come."

"The idiot is coming? How do you know?"

"Lleras was speaking with her in the kitchen. Palacios saw them. Afterwards it looked as if Lleras and Añuco were plotting something, against Wig, maybe?"

"The idiot is to come? There's hardly anyone in the courtyard, brother. I shall wait. Maybe I'll get my chance."

"Poor little Chauca! Tonight I don't know what's going to happen. Soon Lleras will come and chase us away from here."

"I'll scream! I'll threaten to call for help if he doesn't leave me alone. It will be now or never." He was panting with impatience.

"Don't get mixed up with Lleras," I warned him. "Go to Huanupata. They say there are other, better *cholas* there. This one is an idiot! Filthy and driveling!"

"I don't know, brother. It has to be her. I think I must be possessed with the devil. I'm damning myself to hell. Why does this driveling idiot drive me crazy? Every night I beg the Christ Child to help me. In vain, in vain! I've had other *cholas*, sure! My allowance is big enough for two. But I come here, at night, and the latrine seizes me, with its smell, I think. I'm still a boy of sixteen. They say the devil gets into one's soul easily at this age. Where, where can my guardian angel be? I think if I could lay her just once I'd rest easy. The loathsomeness of it would cure me . . ."

While Chauca was speaking, the idiot appeared in the courtyard; the short, squat woman stuck close to the wall as she started down the path toward the latrines. She had not walked two yards when Wig jumped on her and knocked her down. Lleras and Añuco came out from behind one of the wooden partitions and went up to Wig.

"We must leave the good little stud alone," we heard Lleras say, in an almost normal tone of voice, not caring if we heard him.

Chauca did not dare run. He took one step at a time, almost as if he were meditating. I followed him. In this way we came to the edge of the playground.

Añuco was fastening something to Wig's shoulder. It looked like the end of a woolen sling, one of those that are finished off with little tassels. Lleras supervised the operation. He paid no attention to us; not even turning his face our way. Añuco stood up and glanced at us, then he looked at Lleras.

"Let's go," he said quietly. "Let the *k'echas* enjoy themselves if they want to."

They tiptoed off, without making the least noise.

I noticed that Chauca was trembling. He placed his right hand on his cheek. A heavy warmth began to rise up through my body, as if it were flowing upward from my feet.

I sprang into the passageway and ran to the courtyard.

Brother Miguel began to ring the bell from the balcony. Clapping their hands, two priests shouted, " Bedtime! It's time for bed, now!"

They went over to the passageway and called out several times from there. We boys who were nearest entered the dormitory. Wig came running in from the playground and took the stairs two at a time. His face was quite pale as he came into the dormitory, and his eyes seemed to have been bathed with some shining liquid. All the boarders stood waiting for the Rector to come in.

The Rector did not inspect the sleeping quarters, as he did almost every other night. This time he stopped two steps from the door by the first cot and recited the Ave Maria. We gave the responses in chorus.

"Good night, my sons. Sleep peacefully," he said, and went out.

In the doorway he met Chauca.

"Oh, it's you, spoiled brat! Rascal!' he said to him.

"I was in the latrine, Padrecito," we heard Chauca answer.

I felt that his weak voice was not only pleading for forgiveness, but also for some greater assistance.

"What's the matter? Is something wrong with you?" asked the Rector, quite kindly. "Come here, son. Come here!"

He brought him into the dormitory and examined him in the light.

Everyone stared at him. He was covered with dirt and there was even dust in his hair. His state of humiliation was so extreme that even Añuco and Lleras did not make fun of him. "Now soon they'll start to laugh," I thought, smoldering with hatred. But they could not laugh.

"I fell, Father!" sobbed Chauca.

"Don't be silly, son. Come to your senses!" the priest told him. And he brushed the dust from him with both hands.

Chauca went to his bed with his head bowed. The priest left, closing the door of the dormitory.

Now Lleras's party will begin, I thought. I believed he would react soon and that he would vent his fury on Chauca. But both he and Añuco were looking at Wig.

One of the boys whose bed was near Wig's suddenly jumped out into the middle of the room and exclaimed, "Jesus! Jesus! Oh my God!"

He was from Pampachiri, a highland town. Horrified, he pointed to Wig's shoulder.

"*Apasankas, apasankas!*" he screamed.

A string of immense, hairy spiders dangled from Wig's jacket. Even the boys who were already lying down got up and went over to Wig's bed.

"So . . . ? What does it matter?" said the latter, seemingly unperturbed.

He carefully removed his jacket, and lifted it up as high as he could, holding it by one of the lapels.

The spiders were kicking. Not with convulsive, rapid movements, but slowly. Tarantulas are heavy; they moved their extremities as if they were asleep. Beneath their downy hair, which was also moving, the dark, reddish black bodies of the spiders looked enormous.

I could not control myself. I have always had a horror of those poisonous tarantulas. In the highland towns they are thought to be sure harbingers of death. I did not cry out; I was able to stifle the scream in my throat, but I leaned against my cot and it was only with great effort that I could fight down my terrible need to scream loudly. Chauca and Romero came over to me.

"What a brute, what a damned scoundrel!" said Romero. "But look, you know they aren't really anything."

Wig had torn off the string of spiders, flung them down on the floor, and was stamping on them with both feet.

"They sure can't scare me with those things; I've been squashing them ever since I was a baby!" he said.

He scraped the sole of his shoe over the crushed bodies of the *apasankas*. Then he did a dance on top of them. There was nothing left but a spot.

Romero helped me to get undressed. He looked into my eyes for a long time, trying to drive away my fear.

"It's nothing, kid. Besides, it's not true that they bite," he told me. "I think here, in the valley, they get tame. Even the little girls play with them; they have wonderful ball games with them. Sure! No one can deny that their bodies are ugly. The boy from Pampachiri, enormous as he is, is just like you—even paler."

Chauca sat down by my bed. No one paid any more attention to him, fortunately. Lleras and Añuco lay down immediately and pretended they were asleep. Chauca placed one of his hands on my forehead.

"This really isn't anything to be frightened of," he told me. "You just wait! Someday we'll do something to Lleras. Something he'll remember all his life!"

"The *apasankas* are nothing to be afraid of!" little Palacios ventured to tell me, from his bed.

This incident was the saving of Chauca. He regained his composure; all mystery, all shadow vanished from his face. And he could remain with me for a while. Romero had already gone.

But still, in my dreams that night I heard, like a recurring refrain, an ancient *huayno*, one I had listened to when I was a child and had long since forgotten:

Apank'orallay, apank'orallay	*Apankora, Apankora,*[10]
apakullawayña,	carry me off at last;
tutay tutay wasillaykipi	in the gloomy darkness of your home,
uywakullawayña.	care for me, I beg of you.
Pelochaykiwan	With your downiness,
yana wañuy pelochaykiwan	with your hair that is death,
kuyaykullawayña.	caress me, caress me.

The next day I got up quite early. After washing at the fountain in the first courtyard to cool my head, I dressed myself, being careful not to awaken the boarding students. Then I went to the playground.

The dawn was fading. The little toads showed their heads through the grass around the water tank. The few trees that could be seen from the inner courtyard and the yellow larks that were singing in their branches made a delicate tracery against the pink clouds in the sky. Some bird feathers were rising on the warm air of the valley.

I wound my beautiful *zumbayllu* and set it spinning. The top leapt harmoniously into the air, descending almost slowly, singing through all of its eyes. A great joy, fresh and pure, illumined my life. I was alone, contemplating and hearing my *zumbayllu* speak with its sweet voice that seemed to bring into the courtyard the song of all the insects that hum musically amid flowering shrubs.

"Oh, *zumbayllu*, *zumbayllu*. I too shall dance with you!"

And I danced, trying to find a step that would be like that of its

---

10. Like *apasanka*, a name for the tarantula spider.—Author

long paw. I had to remember and imitate the professional dancers of my native village.

When the bell rang to awaken the boarders, I was the happiest student in Abancay. I thought about Markask'a, going over in my mind the letter I had written for his princess, for the girl he loved, who, according to him, had cheeks the color of the *zumbayllu*.

"To hell with Wig!" I said. "To hell with Lleras, Valle, Skinny! No one is my enemy! No one, no one!"

7. The Insurrection

That morning, during recess, I gave Antero the draft of Salvinia's letter.

"I'll read it when I'm alone in my room," he told me. "And in the afternoon we'll read it together. I'll wait for you at one o'clock by the school gate."

"Don't you want to read it now?" I asked.

"No. Not now. I'd rather be alone when I think of her. If I wanted to ask you something I couldn't do it here. The boys would bother us."

Then I told him about my adventure with Rondinel.

"But you could surely kill that skinny kid!" he exclaimed. "Everything makes him cry. Poor thing! It would be better if you didn't fight him. He must be trembling by now, crying like a little bird. The poor thing is a wreck. They say his mother is half-crazy and that when Skinny was a little boy she punished him like one of the damned."

"Really! He won't even look at me, nor at anyone else. It's as if he had already been buried."

Then Antero asked me to wait for him at the door of the classroom and went off to look for Rondinel.

"I'll calm him down. I feel sorry for him. His mother is a great friend of my princess's mother. I'll do it for her, I'll tell him you've decided not to accept his challenge."

He came back in a little while, leading Skinny by the arm. Antero was almost dragging him as they ran up to me.

"Here he is," Antero said. "He wants to make peace, too. I'm the referee. Shake hands."

I held out my hand, smiling. In his deep-set eyes, behind those beautiful curling eyelashes, a look of anxiety resisted suppression. I realized that if I did not continue smiling at him, if I did not draw near to him, he would close his eyes and run away.

I gave him a hug.

"I'm a dog. A dog!" he said. And he began to cry.

We took him into my classroom. All the boys were playing in the courtyards and none of the boarding students witnessed our reconciliation. They were the only ones who could have disturbed it.

Skinny sat at a desk and, resting his head on Antero's arms, wept for a moment.

"Don't be stupid," Markask'a told him.

"The others are worse," I told him. "Lleras, Valle, Añuco. Not us, brother."

"God will punish them one of these days!" he exclaimed.

He stood up and shook hands with me again.

"You're a gentleman. I admit you're a man. From now on I'm going to like you."

He was trembling slightly.

"Let's play, little brothers!" he shouted suddenly. "Let's spin our *zumbayllus*. Come on!"

We ran out, Rondinel leading me by the hand.

In the passageway between the courtyards we bumped into Valle. He walked slowly, as stiffly erect as ever. Like a flash of lightning, a look of astonishment interrupted his pompous severity. Rondinel stuck his tongue out at him, yelling, "Sit down and wait for us to fight! Stupid!"

And we went on. Our friendliness was not a bit forced. We wanted to be kind to one another. Skillfully, we set our tops to humming. We cast them all together and one time Skinny's top spun longer than Antero's. How happy it made him! He jumped up and down, glanced at me, and then at Markask'a. He spun around on one foot. The sun was shining for him alone, that morning. He had the round world burning in his hands, like a shiny toy. It was his! And we all shared the joy of feeling he was the owner.

At twelve o'clock when the day-pupils went out into the street, we heard women shouting outside. Standing on the steps that led up to my classroom, Rondinel and I could see the street. Several women ran by; they were all mestizas, dressed like the waitresses and owners of the *chicha* bars. The Rector came out of his office, went to the entryway, and looked up and down the street. He came back immediately and hurried into his office. We thought he looked frightened.

The tumult in the street grew louder. More women ran by. A police officer entered the school.

The Rector appeared in the doorway, summoning the priests in a loud voice.

"Go and call them!" he said to me, clapping his hands.

I ran to the dormitories and the dining hall, calling the priests. There were five of them, and Brother Miguel. They met with the officer in the Rector's office, conferred for a few moments, and then went into the street together. Brother Miguel was left in charge of the school.

"It's nothing," he said. "I'm going to call the boys to lunch."

The gatekeeper kept on watching the street; he had not closed the entry. People kept running down the street. Men, women, and children sped by, as if chasing one another. The boarders all gathered in the entryway.

Just then the bells began to ring out the alarm signal, and the outcries of the women, as loud as the sound of the bells, came to us from the main square. Lleras and Romero dashed out and went off toward the plaza. We all followed them. The gatekeeper began to shout in Quechua, "They're running away, Padrecitos. Help!"

At the first corner we met Antero; he came running up to us. Rondinel was with me.

"Not you, Skinny," said Antero. "Your mother will come to the school looking for you and she'll go crazy if she can't find you. Go on home. Run! The square is seething with angry women. You might get trampled. They might kill you! Go on!"

Rondinel hesitated between fear and curiosity.

"Take me with you, little brothers!" he pleaded.

He seemed to find sufficient protection in Antero's forceful way of speaking.

"I want to go, Markask'a! Take me with you, little brother."

"No!" Antero replied. "There are too many people. It's like a flash flood. Who could take care of you, brother? We'll tell you all about it later. Go up onto the balcony of your house and you'll see the people going by. Hurry now! We're going to run."

We started off and Skinny could not keep up with us. I turned to look for him when we got to the end of the street, and he was still standing hesitantly in the same place.

As we came out into the square, a great crowd of clamoring women extended from the church steps to beyond the center of the square. They wore shawls of Castilian cloth and straw hats. The schoolchildren watched the crowd from the street corners. We made our way toward the middle of the park. Antero opened a path for us, bending over and butting the women in the waist with his head.

There were no men in sight. With their bare feet or high-heeled boots the women crushed the delicate park flowers, breaking off rosebushes, geraniums, lilies, and violets. They shouted in Quechua, "Salt, salt! The robbers, the thieving salt dealers!" [1]

Antero kept getting closer to the tower. I followed him angrily.

I was excited by the women's violence. I felt like rushing at somebody, like fighting.

The women occupying the terrace and the wide sidewalk that ran along the front of the church carried big bags of stones in their left hands.

From the edge of the park we could see the woman who was speaking in the arched entrance to the tower. It was impossible to get any closer. On the sidewalk the crowd pressed tightly together. The women were sweating; earrings made of silver and of gold coins glittered in the sunlight. The woman who occupied the tower archway was a well-known *chicha* bar owner; her stout body completely filled the arch; her blue silk bodice, trimmed with beads and velvet ribbons, shimmered. The ribbon on her hat shone even in the shade; it was satin and stood out in high relief from the extreme whiteness of her hat, which had recently been painted with white lead. The woman had a broad face, pitted all over with smallpox scars. Her plump bosom, rising like a rampart, was moving; its bellows-like rhythm, from her deep breathing, could be seen from afar. She was speaking in Quechua. The soft *c*'s of the sweet Quechua of Abancay now seemed to have been chosen especially as notes of contrast to make the guttural sounds that carried to all the walls of the square harsher.

"*Mánan! Kunankamallam suark'aku . . .* !" she said. "No! No longer shall they steal our salt! Today we're going to throw all the thieves out of Abancay. Shout, women; shout loudly so that the whole world can hear you! Death to the thieves!"

The women shouted, "*Kunanmi suakuna wañunk'aku!* (Today the thieves shall die!)"

---

1. Salt was a government monopoly and was sold only in state shops.—Trans.

When they repeated the cry, I shouted it in chorus with them.
Markask'a looked at me in astonishment.

"Hey, Ernesto, what's the matter with you?" he asked me. "Who
do you hate?"

"The thieving salt dealers, of course," one of the women answered him.

At that moment a wavelike motion of the crowd reached us.
The Rector was moving through the throng of women, escorted
by two friars. His white vestments stood out against the multicolored shawls of the women. They made way for him and he
advanced rapidly to the tower archway and stopped in front of the
chicha bar proprietor. He raised his right arm, as if to give her his
blessing, and then spoke to her. We could not hear the priest's
voice; but from the woman's expression we could see that he was
pleading with her. The woman remained silent; little by little the
silence spread throughout the square. One could hear the sunshine
falling on the women's bodies, on the crushed leaves of the park
lilies. Then we listened to the priest's words. He spoke in Quechua.

"No, my daughter. Do not offend God. The authorities are not
to blame. I tell you this in God's name."

"And who sold the salt to the haciendas for their cows? Do
cows come before people, Padrecito Linares?"

The *chichera*'s question could be heard clearly in the park. The
angle formed by the tower and the church walls acted as a sounding board.

"Don't defy me, my daughter. Obey God!"

"God punishes thieves, Padrecito Linares," said the *chichera* in
a loud tone, bowing to the priest. The priest said something and
the woman shouted, "Do not condemn me, Padrecito! Condemn
the thieves!"

He moved his right arm, as if pulling on a rope. All the bells
took flight, once more ringing out the alarm signal.

"Ready! Let's go, onward!" shouted the *chichera*, in Spanish.

She stepped down from the archway, circled the priests respectfully, and set off for the nearest corner. The crowd made way for
her. The older women, who were also the fattest, like the owners
of the *chicha* bars, formed a sort of front line to the left and right
of the leader. They set off toward the corner.

Some shots were heard.

"Nothing, nothing! Onward, onward!" shouted the leader.

"Onward, onward!" repeated the crowd of women.

"Onward, onward!"

"Onward, onward!"

It was now a single cry that was repeated to the tail end of the mob. The cry ran like an undulation in the body of a snake.

The policemen who were guarding the corner were routed. The women didn't strike them. They were the lowly customers of the *chicha* bars, and they fired into the air, visibly raising their rifle barrels skyward. Their weapons were taken away from them.

Most of the school boys and curiosity seekers fled at the first shots. Markask'a was not frightened. He looked at me doubtfully. "Shall we go on?" he asked.

"Let's see how it ends."

"Shout 'onward,' " the women told us.

We shouted with all our might.

"That's the way! Brave boy! Onward, onward!"

As we turned a corner, the last one before coming to the salt shop, Antero tried to drag me out of the crowd.

"Let's leave!" he told me. "It's ugly to go along in the midst of so many *cholas*.[2] Let's go home! We've gotten into enough trouble for today."

"No," I answered. "Let's stay till the end. Till the end, Markask'a!"

The crowd began to shout more furiously now. A few shots were heard, fainter than before; Antero went off. "I'm leaving. I'm not alone," he shouted in my ear. "I have her to take care of!"

It was true. In all the houses people must have been trembling at that moment. I could see by his eyes that he was not afraid. Quite the contrary, when he spoke of protecting her and broke away from the mob, it was as if he were going off to fight another greater battle.

Bending over, he opened a way through the crowd. I went on. If he really were leaving to take care of his beloved, what would I do? I shouted louder, pushing forward. From the front ranks there came a loud noise. Stones began to crash against the posts, railings, and doors of the salt shop. Windows were broken. There was no more firing.

"Blood! Blood!" I heard people saying in Quechua, by the walls of the store.

They broke down several doors and entered the courtyard of the salt shop. There I managed to reach the front row. The ringleader had a rifle slung across her back. Her hair was dripping with

2. Indian women who wear modern dress and speak Spanish; may be derogatory.—Trans.

sweat. Climbing up onto a high stone bench on the veranda, she looked down sternly at everyone.

"Silence!" she ordered.

A woman standing next to her had a large bloodstain on her side, near her left shoulder. She, too, held a rifle.

"What's this, woman?" she asked. "A salt dealer's bullet! That can't hurt anybody!" Swinging her arm violently, like a windmill, she burst into laughter.

"Warehouse! Twenty to the warehouse!" the ringleader ordered in Quechua.

A group of cholas entered the salt warehouse. After a moment they called out from inside, "Kachi, kachi.[3] Plenty of it."

They began to drag the sacks of salt out into the courtyard.

To the amazement and shrieks of the women, they brought forty sacks of white salt out into the courtyard.

"Padrecito Linares! Come!" exclaimed the chicha bar owner, with a long, drawn-out cry. "Padrecito Linares, here's the salt!" she said in Spanish. "Here's the salt! Here's the salt! This man sure thief! This man sure damned thief!"

The multitude grew quiet, as if a moment of silence were needed for the chichera's words to reach their destination. Once more the woman called out, "Padrecito Linares . . . !"

She got down from the stone bench for a moment, had the doorway of the warehouse cleared, then issued several orders. The women opened a path, pressing tightly against one another.

And the distribution began.

She presided from atop the stone bench. There was no disorder. The designated chicheras opened sacks with knives and filled the women's cloaks. Then they went out through the shop and those who were at the entrance came in.

In the Indian villages women remain silent when the men are holding solemn meetings. At family parties, and even in municipal council meetings, the Indians all speak loudly at the same time. From the outside they look like the meetings of wild people. Who is speaking to whom? There is, however, a certain order; thought reaches its destination, and the meetings end in agreement. The same woman who is quiet when the men participate in council meetings shrieks, shouts, and is unrestrainable in quarrels and riots.

Why didn't they scratch one another, scream and tear each other apart in the courtyard of the salt shop? How was it that they did

3. Salt.—Author

not insult one another and call to those who were still outside on the street? If only one of them could have shouted as they did when they were free, she would have kindled the mob and they would have torn her to pieces.

But there she was, the ringleader, controlling everything from atop the stone bench, even to the heartbeats of each of the angry, triumphant *cholas*. At the slightest attempt to break the silence, she stared, and the women themselves nudged one another, imposing order, trying to calm down. From the broad face of the *chichera*, from her low forehead, from her almost invisible eyes, flowed a regulating force that enveloped, detained, and drove away fear. Her gleaming hat shaded her to the eyebrows. Her forehead, in shadow, contrasted with her round jaw, tightly closed mouth, and black pockmarks, which were exposed to the sunlight.

"For the poor of Patibamba, three sacks," she said in a way that made me shiver.

By this time most of the sacks of salt had been given out and the courtyard looked empty.

In view of this rather unexpected order, several women went to see the corral of the salt shop. There they found forty mules with packsaddles still on them. This news astonished the *cholas*. But the ringleader made no comment except to order three of the mules to be driven out into the courtyard.

While those who were making the distribution continued to fill the women's shawls with large chunks of salt, they merrily began to arrange loads for the *colonos* of Patibamba.

It was quite difficult for them to lift the sacks when they were full. They had to remove a great deal of salt from the bags and then sew them up again. The bags were so heavy the women could not lift them onto the backs of the mules.

The wounded woman wanted to go to Patibamba. The ringleader looked at her doubtfully.

"It's not bleeding anymore," she said. Lifting her blouse, she bared her breast and exposed the wound.

The leader did not give her consent. She appointed ten women, and asked everyone who wished to go along with them to do so. Nearly fifty of them, their shawls laden with salt, followed those who had been chosen.

"Long live Doña Felipa![4] *Patibambapak!*"[5] shouted the women as they left, following the mules.

4. *Doña* is a respectful title of address for women.—Trans.
5. "On to Patibamba!"—Trans.

"Doña Felipa! Doña Felipa!" chorused all of them, in farewell to the leader.

She had not forgotten the poor, the defenseless people of Patibamba. In their sudden success, none of the others had remembered them.

"Distribute it carefully," she told the delegation in Quechua.

Although the distribution continued in the courtyard, I did not hesitate; I followed behind the women who were going to Patibamba. I was as eager to arrive as they were. A great joy and a desire to fight, even if it were against the whole world, sent us running through the streets.

They drove the mules at a trot. In the salt shop district the streets were full of people. The poorer townsmen formed a sort of passive barricade and would not let the gentlemen with neckties go by.

"The women might cut your throat, sir," I heard them say.

"*Patibambapak! Patibambapak!*" shouted the women, as they drove the mules. People made way for them.

From some of the balconies on the central streets bystanders jeered at the *cholas*.

"Thieves! Excommunicates!"

Not only the ladies, but also the few gentlemen who lived in those houses hurled down insults.

"Prostitutes, filthy *cholas!*"

Then one of the mestizas began to sing a carnival *danza*; the group sang the chorus on a higher pitch.

In this way the troop was transformed into a *comparsa*[6] that went through the streets at a run. The voices of the chorus drowned out all insults, and set a special pace, with a rhythm almost of attack, for those who were marching to Patibamba. The mules took up the rhythm of the *danza* and trotted along more gaily. Wild with enthusiasm, the women's singing grew even louder and livelier:

Patibamballay	O *pati*[7] tree
patisachachay	of Patibamba!
sonk'oruruykik'a	No one knew
k'orimantas kask'a	your heart was of gold;
sonk'oruruykik'a	no one knew
k'ollk'emantas kask'a.	your breast was of silver.

6. A group of people in masquerade who parade, singing and dancing, to the music of drums and other instruments at carnival time.—Trans.
7. A tree native to the Andes.—Trans.

K'ocha mayullay	O my pool,
k'ocha remanso	my river pool!
challwachallaykik'a	No one knew
k'orimantas kask'a	your fish were of gold;
patuchallaykik'a	no one knew
k'ollk'emantas kask'a.	your ducklings were of silver.

Near Huanupata many men and women joined the group. People came out of the houses to see us go by; they ran down the side streets to look at us from the corners.

In this way we reached the highway, the wide dusty road to the hacienda. By now it was a whole town that followed the mules, keeping step to the rhythm of the *danza*. The *chicheras* continued the singing, with smiles on their faces.

I had thought that once they were out on the road they would stop singing and that we would keep going at a steady pace. It is more than a mile from Abancay to the Patibamba workers' quarters. Dust was raised by the mules' hoofs, by the feet of the people who were marching rapidly along. In the still air the dust rose to the treetops, covering the highest of the large, red *pisonay* flowers with dirt, extinguishing their glow. In the middle of this tongue of dust the mules and the people marched along gaily. We splashed through irrigation ditches and puddles; we swept passers-by into our midst for a time, incorporating them into the *danza*.

The women reached the stone-paved road that bounded the hacienda mansion. They passed along the iron fence without even looking into the park; they wanted to go directly to the village, to the dusty quarters of the Indian *colonos*. But I looked in at the verandas of the big house as I ran along behind the delegation. The women raised their voices even louder at the gate, but that was the only notice they took of it. At the ends of the veranda two mestizos wearing boots and wide-brimmed hats knelt with rifles in their hands. A man dressed in white was standing on the top step of the stairs; he watched the *cholas* go by without a single gesture, in apparent calm.

We reached the quarters and ran, still singing, down the sweet-sour lane.

All the doors of the huts remained closed.

"Won't they perhaps come out? Won't they come out now? What's going to happen, dear God?" I thought to myself, looking at the frayed, blackened roofs of the little houses.

"Come out, little mothers! We're bringing you salt!" shouted one of the *chicheras* in Quechua.

"*Mamachakuna! Mamachakuna!*"[8] called another.

The silence continued. The women began to look all around, their expressions inquiring and full of hatred, while some of them began unloading the mules.

"*Pim manchachinku merdas?* (Who is frightening them?)," exclaimed the guide. Her almost masculine voice, full of menace, brought the settlement to life.

"*Pim manchachinku merdas?*" she asked again. She charged at a door and broke it in with her shoulder.

"*Au mamacita! Au mamacita!*" whimpered the women and children in the darkened interior of the hut.

"The people's salt, for you, little mother!" exclaimed the *chichera*, pointing to the loads of salt. Her voice grew sweet and tender.

"Come out and get it, little mothers!" one of the Patibamba women then shouted in Quechua.

Doors opened all along the treacly,[9] wasp-infested lane; and the women came out walking quite slowly, hesitantly.

At that moment the *chichera* picked up a large chunk of white salt and dropped it into the skirt of the Patibamba Indian who had called the others. She ordered her to hold out her skirt and tossed her several more chunks of salt. The Indian woman looked at the *chichera* and at the pieces of salt. She turned around and rushed off toward her hut, her little children behind her, and when all were inside she shut the door.

Then all the women went up to the distribution place. The three sacks were opened and the distribution carried out in a rather orderly way in the midst of an unintelligible hubbub. The Indians took the salt, blessed it with their hands, then went back to their huts and shut themselves up inside.

As they gave out the salt I felt my body becoming soaked with a cold sweat. My heart throbbed with great weariness; an intense feeling of emptiness constricted my stomach. I sat down on the molasses-soaked ground of what passed for a street and held my head in my hands. The murmuring of the people died down. I heard some shots. The women from Abancay began to sing again. The sour odor of the damp cane trash, molasses, and human excrement that surrounded the huts swelled within my veins. With an effort I stood and began to walk toward the hacienda park, seeking the stone-paved road.

8. Little mothers.—Author
9. On the sugar plantations the roads are sometimes "oiled" with molasses.
—Trans.

In the sky metallic clouds shone like great fields of honey. I felt as though my head were sailing in a sea of molasses taffy that squeezed me and crackled as it hardened. Overcome with drowsiness, I came to one of the columns of the iron gate. I could still see some butterflies hovering over the lawn and the flowers in the hacienda garden; they came out of the deep corollas of the big lilies and flew off, fluttering their soft, their delicate, wings. I stretched out in the shade of the column and the trees and closed my eyes. The world was swaying. From my heart flowed torrents of blood. It was a joyous blood, shed freely on that beautiful day in which death, if it had come, would have been transfigured, changed into a triumphal star.

The mules must have galloped along the stone-paved road quite close to my feet as the women from Abancay went by in a crowd on their way home. The troop must have withdrawn rapidly into the distance, like a swift wind. I did not see them go. I had sunk into a tenacious, irresistible slumber.

Late in the day, as the sun was setting, a plump lady dressed in pink awakened me. When I opened my eyes she was bathing my forehead with a handkerchief moistened with water.

"You look yellow, my son," she said.

She peeled an orange and gave it to me to eat, a section at a time. I looked at her intently. She wore black stockings and low shoes; her pink skirt reached her feet. The front of her blouse was trimmed with flowerets of ribbons, in mestiza fashion. But she was white, with rosy cheeks and blue eyes. She looked as if she might be a seamstress for an hacienda mansion or some estate manager or clerk's woman.

"Who are you, my son? What has happened to you? Ah, fortunately for you, on this hacienda they even let the oranges and lemons spoil."

Some poplar trees growing by the fence shaded us. The shadows of the leaves played on the lady's hair and forehead. She crouched before me; my head rested on her knees. I felt her hand stroking my head. Then I heard her sobbing, speaking to me in Quechua.

"Who brought you here, my son? Who abandoned you?"

"I came with the *cholas*, bringing salt to the *colonos* of Patibamba."

She remained silent. Beneath the plump hands that caressed me gently, the harshness of the dusty road, of the lofty, scorched sky, and of my memories vanished. Her sobbing, unlike that of other people, did not cause me to weep more desperately. It summoned me to sleep, to the real sleep of a child on his mother's lap. The lady understood this. She sat down comfortably, leaning against the wall that was the base of the railing, and waited while I rested.

It could not have been for very long. People on horseback galloped along the road. The horseshoes clattered on the paving stones. I raised my head and saw several horsemen riding through the dust on their way to Abancay. It seemed as if some of them turned their heads to look at me. At that moment they began to close the iron gates of the hacienda.

"They've gone off with the salt," said the lady.

Getting to my feet, I asked, "What salt, *señora?*"

"The salt they took away from the Indian women."

"From what Indian women?"

"From the hacienda ones. They went into the huts while the horse trainer and his helper were cracking their bullwhips in the quarters, and they took all the salt away from them. With all the whip-cracking, you couldn't even hear how the poor women were crying."

"Are you from here, *señora?*"

"No, I'm from Cuzco. I'm staying here in Patibamba with my mistress. She's come to the manager's house for a visit."

"Did they whip them when they took away the salt?"

"No, they just cracked their whips in the village lane. The workers are still in the cane field. They're holding them back with revolver shots. What's going to happen, my son? The workers say they're corralled and they want to get out and go to their women. They're gradually moving forward. But now that they've taken the salt away from them, they'll let them go by. And you, child. Who are you? Why don't you leave? I'm frightened."

I told her who I was.

Then she accompanied me a long way, almost half the distance to town.

I should have liked to sing, through tears of blood, that Patibamba carnival song to which we had come down this same road, on the way to the hacienda. The lady was almost hugging me as she led me along, but the broad arm she laid round my neck, which touched my shoulders, was not resting on me. I did not feel the slightest weight, only the warmth of her skin. I walked quietly. The world had never been sadder—completely burnt out, without hope, sunken into my entrails like an icy sorrow. "Dear God," I said as I went along, "please let me meet my father at the school gate."

When we parted, the lady kissed me on the eyelids. She turned back. I forgot to ask her name. But like an inextinguishable sun, I shall always see her blue eyes, her kind, immortal eyes.

I walked rapidly. I was obsessed with the idea of finding my father in the town. I could not run because my legs trembled and gave way beneath me.

I reached the Huanupata quarter and found it in an uproar. A festive, holidaylike hubbub could be heard in the dirty street. The ground is hard; they sprinkle it every day; wide damp patches in the dirt alternate with the urine stains from horses and men. Every citizen and every *chicha* bar moistens its own section of the street. The ground is rough. Sometimes the wind blows in toward the city, from the roads, sweeping with it dust, trash, pieces of wool, and dried leaves. Now the dust was coming in from the Huanupata side, carrying rubbish down the street; spinning, whirling, the wind came in like a mantle, seeking the other end of town. In front of the *chicha* bars people were dancing. The chili places were overflowing. The high, jubilant voices of the waitresses traveled a long way, out to the beginning of the highway.

When I had gone a few steps down the street, I saw that there were also men singing inside the *chicha* bars. Entering the quarter, it was as if an early-morning light were raining down on the street; a gray light, moist and wavering. The clouds, so aflame at midday, condensed and darkened now that they covered the weak sun of late afternoon.

Where could so many mestizos and Indians have come from to the *chichería* district? Already drunk, they danced with their eyes closed, tracing almost acrobatic figures with their feet. It was impossible to get into the *chicha* bars. Pitchers of *chicha* were passed from hand to hand over people's heads to those who were outside. Everyone was drinking, as they did on holidays, at someone else's expense, to the point of satiation.

"Want some, boy?" asked a mestizo who seemed to be a market porter.

"Yes, I do," I answered.

He passed me a heavy pitcher; I raised it and, with great difficulty, held it up to drink as the mestizo and the others in his group laughed. The *chicha* was strong, and I felt it warming me.

"It's good, boy! God damn! God damn, you're tough! Inside, inside, consolation," shouted the one who had treated me, hearing me gulp it down.

"And why are they having the fiesta, sir?" I asked him.

"*Ja caraya!*" he said, and laughed loudly. "The woman, well, she's run off the cops. The salt warehouse, well, they've grabbed it. Long live Doña Felipa!"

And he began to sing a comical *huayno* I knew; but the words, which he improvised on the spur of the moment, were an insult to the police and to the salt shop. Everyone in the group made up the chorus. They alternated each verse with outbursts of laughter. The *cholo* would sing the verse slowly, pronouncing each word carefully, and the chorus would repeat it. They'd look at each other and laugh again.

They imposed the song on the *chicha* bar. The people inside began to sing the chorus. Then they all danced to the melody, beating time with their feet. The barefooted ones, those wearing Indian sandals, and those with shoes all stamped the floor violently. The bare heels made a hollow sound, the sandal leather clapped on the hard ground, and the shoe heels hammered. They seemed to be grinding out the words of the *huayno*.

Soldaduchapa riflink'a	The little soldier's rifle
tok'romantas kask'a	must have been made of cactus bones,
chaysi chaysi	that's why, that's why,
yank'a yank'a tok'yan,	it thunders harmlessly,
chaysi chaysi	that's why, that's why,
yank'a yank'a tok'yan.	it thunders harmlessly.
Manas manas wayk'ey,	No, no, brother,
riflinchu tok'ro	it's not the rifle,
alma rurullansi	it's the soul of the little soldier
tok'ro tok'ro kask'a.	that's made of worthless brushwood.
Salineropa revolverchank'a	The salt dealer's revolver
llama akawansi	was loaded
arnask'a kask'a,	with llama turds,
polvorañantak'	and instead of powder,
mula salinerok'	and instead of powder,
asnay asnay supin.	with salt-mule farts.

The song spread to all the groups in the street and to the other *chicha* bars. My host and his group danced with growing enthusiasm. By now they must have forgotten me and everything else.

I stayed outside of their circle, watching them, like one who watches the rising waters of those Andean rivers of unpredictable schedule—so dry, so stony, so humble and empty for years, and then, some overcast summer when the clouds burst, swelling with foaming water and growing deeper, halting travelers and awakening unfamiliar thoughts and fears in their hearts and minds.

I must have been sitting on the ground in front of the *chichería* for almost an hour. Antero found me there, at nightfall.

"I've been hunting for you as if you were Christ, little brother! I came by here several times. Why were you hiding?" he asked me.

He helped me to get up.

"I wasn't hiding. I've been right here, ever since I got back from Patibamba," I told him.

"The Rector is furious. They're not going to let you go out to-morrow. I saw him scolding the boarders."

Shouting to be heard, he led me by the arm toward the center of town.

"You can eat when you get back. They're waiting for you, little brother! They're waiting for you! Salvinia and Alcira! I know it's not right to take you off before you eat something, and the way you look. But she says she likes you because you're crazy, and shy."

"Who? Likes whom?"

"Alcira is a friend of Salvinia's. She wants to see you. If we don't get there in a few minutes it'll be too late."

He made me run a little way. I was sleepy. I could not hear very well and was still quite bewildered. I tried to feel my heart beating and could not. I stopped at a corner.

"Are you sick?" asked Antero.

"No," I replied. "Let's run."

"That way she'll like you even more," said Markask'a, panting. "Your hair's all mussed up, almost standing on end; you're real pale."

I was unable to concentrate on the unknown girl who, according to Antero, was waiting for me at Salvinia's house.

Perhaps on another day, another evening, I would have been delighted with such news, and would have hurried to meet the one who awaited me. What did it matter if she were beautiful or ugly? It was my first news of this kind and I was fourteen years old. I'd been waiting for this moment ever since I was a small boy.

Opposite my native village there is a little river whose edges freeze in the wintertime. The grass at the river's edge, the long branches that trail in the water, are covered with frost until almost midday. The village boys set little paper and reed boats adrift on the stream. The little ships pass rapidly beneath the treelike frost figures. I would wait for them much farther downstream, by a thorn bush whose long spines also seemed to be made of ice. Lying stretched upon the grass, I'd watch the little boats sail by. Many times I imagined that a peerless young girl, the most beautiful of all, would appear aboard one of them. She would be blond. The icy arches would cast their incredible, almost white light on her. For at no time is the sunshine so white as the light that shines from the hoarfrost that has hardened on delicate blades of grass.

But as we neared Salvinia's house another ruder feeling overcame me. Why hadn't I gone into the *chicherías* to find Doña Felipa? Perhaps if I could have seen her dance I would have forgotten the sad image of the Patibamba women giving up the salt to the thundering of the bullwhips. Perhaps I would never see her again. A great impatience seized me. "I'll go to look for her!" I thought. "And I'll also look for the Patibamba lady. I'll ask her her name and kiss her hands!"

"What's the matter?" asked Antero. "Don't you see we've arrived? Look, there's Salvinia!"

How slender and dark she looked! Her short violet-colored skirt and her white blouse shone youthfully beneath the solemn glow of the towering clouds.

"Is she happy?" I asked Antero.

"No one is happier than she. Look! She's calling us."

She ran beneath the mulberry trees, calling us, and stopped at an iron gate in the garden wall.

I realized that at that moment Antero walked quite slowly and stealthily because he was so much afraid. Not daring to look at me, he gripped my arm, not in order to support himself, but to hold me back, to communicate to me his confusion.

"Don't hurry, brother. I'm afraid but I'm also glad."

Was it because of his birthmarks and the sharp profile of his nose, or because of the strange interaction that took place between his eyes and his birthmarks, that Markask'a's face expressed his feelings and his thoughts so powerfully?

I had to nudge him a little.

"Why were you so slow?" she said from the other side of the little gate. "Alcira has already gone."

She had almond eyes, slightly slanted; it was her bangs, carefully cut in a straight line, that revealed the graceful line of her eyes. While neither her face nor her arms were the color of the *zumbayllus*, her eyes were. But they were not the black of the *zumbayllu* when it is still, but rather when it is in full song, spinning rapidly; because then the *zumbayllu* lightens and turns a clear brown color.

I presented myself quite courteously. My father was a model of gentlemanly gestures. If only I had inherited his blue eyes, white hands, and handsome blond beard . . . !

She shook hands with me. Her long fingers produced a lasting sensation of softness.

"I must go now," she said. "My father may come home at any moment. I waited a long time for you, because I had to thank Antero again. How brave he is! Many thanks, Antero. Let me shake your hand."

He did not say a single word.

When Salvinia had closed the gate and waved good-bye to me, Antero was able to speak; quite softly he said, "Farewell, farewell, my princess!"

Perhaps she heard and did not wish to show it. She walked away gracefully.

"She's beautiful, quite beautiful!" I told him.

"Do you know why it is? When they're still, her eyes seem to be slightly crossed; they don't focus the same, one of them looks off to one side. This difference shows there is a doubt in her soul; her beauty seems to be thinking, attracting you. And another thing, Ernestito! When my princess's eyes are still like that they show their color better. Could you tell what color they are?"

"No, Markask'a. I think they are the color of the *zumbayllu*, of the song of the *zumbayllu*."

"Certainly! Certainly! But I'm thinking of another resemblance, a closer one. Someday I'll take you to my father's hacienda. It's way down the Pachachaca, where the jungle begins. No one's ever gone beyond it. I'll show you a pool that lies between yellow cliffs. The sides of the ravine are reflected in the pool. That's the color, brother! The yellow of the cliff with the green of the still water in that pool on the Pachachaca. The ducklings of the river and a little bird that lives along its banks have wings of that color. The Indians say they are the children of the big pool. If I take Salvinia to my hacienda someday, they will say her eyes were made of that water; they'll say she is the daughter of the river. Really, little brother! They'll believe that the river commanded me to bring her. And perhaps they'd be right. Perhaps that's the truth."

"And the *zumbayllu*?"

"Oh, she's like the *zumbayllu* too! But look at this, brother!"

He showed me a little dagger he drew from a sheath that was fastened to his belt. The sheath had silver chasings; the handle of the dagger was of gold.

"I wish someone would try to take it away from me! If only someone would challenge me! I'm eager for a fight, brother!" Markask'a proclaimed. "So that from her window she could watch me beating some rival or someone who had offended her! On horseback! It would be even better on horseback. I'd make the horse paw the air with his front hoofs; I'd bring the other fellow down with a single stab in the chest. I've galloped over roads that ran along precipices. My mother wept when she found out about it. She'll weep again and I will be happy. Did you hear her say how brave I was? Because of some foolishness. Because of some mestizos who stopped on the avenue and looked at Salvinia's house. I frightened them away by showing them the dagger. I have promised her to stand guard tonight on the avenue, near her house. The Indians and mestizos are drunk and gangs of them will be singing on all the streets. The little soldiers have gone into hiding. And even though she disagrees, I'll take my dagger and protect her house. If she gets curious and comes to the window, she'll see me . . ."

Under the street light I could see his face more clearly. I could almost see the bony edge of his nose; his eyes were still smoldering with impatience.

"That's nothing. It's no test of courage to be on guard against drunken Indians. I wish there were some other danger! That I could go on an excursion to an island in the river and a flash flood would come and surround the island. Through the torrent I'd swim all alone, on my horse. I'd go to her rescue, little brother. I'd bring her back and take her home. I know these wild rivers, these treacherous rivers; I know how they flow, how they grow, what strength they have within them, where their currents run. Just to frighten the Indians on my hacienda I used to dive into the Pachachaca in the rainy season. The Indian women would scream as I let the river carry me away. You must not try to cut straight across them; you must escape by letting it carry you along; the current trembles, and you stretch out in the same direction as the flow, and suddenly, with a swift motion of the body you escape; the force of the water casts you out. That's a real challenge, something for your darling to see. Let her weep, and then see you reach the bank! And if you save her? If you go to the island through a storm on your horse and save her? Great Pachachaca, wicked river, I should like that! My horse knows the wiles of this river better than I do. Because it's deep, because it flows through ravines, because in those ravines the prickly cactus plants, all ugly and tangled with Spanish moss, reach out like snakes—that's why the Indians fear them. My horse laughs at them. I've taught him, and he's taught me. Sometimes we have crossed the river opposite a precipice, just to touch the rocks that faced us. The Indians say that I store up strength in my birthmarks, that I'm bewitched. How beautiful, brother, how beautiful! I sometimes think even my mother is doubtful about me. She looks at me thoughtfully, examining my birthmarks . . . But my father just laughs, and is happy and gives me horses . . ."

Markask'a was better than I; he had explored a river, an awesome river, and not just as a traveler explores it. Pachachaca! "Bridge over the world" is the meaning of this name. I could not have said which it was that I loved more—the real river, or the author of my thoughts.

Markask'a's voice was like that of the angry Pachachaca. When he conquered his early shyness, he would speak to Salvinia in that same language. "Either he'll frighten her or he'll subdue her," I thought.

"They say it's not possible to love one girl after another," he went on to say. "No! Her alone! I do not intend to study very long. I shall carry her off, and if the devil takes her away from me, I shall dedicate myself to the *chola* women. I shall have twenty or thirty."

He no longer looked like a schoolboy; as he talked his face hardened and grew more mature. "I didn't know him, I didn't really know him," I thought, meanwhile. He could have been dressed in riding clothes, with those leather-patched pants, carrying a whip in his hand and wearing a wide-brimmed straw hat on his head. He had the look of a small landowner, generous, full of ambition, and loved by his Indians. Where was the happy, skillful champion *zumbayllu* spinner of the school? His eyes that had watched the dance of the *zumbayllu*, mingling his soul with the dancing toy, now stared like those of a rapist, of a grown cub impatient to begin its life of freedom.

We had reached the school gate. He hugged me.

"You've made me talk," he said. "All the things I think of when I'm alone, I've sung to you. I don't know why, when I'm with you I open my thoughts, my tongue is unloosened. It's because you're not from here; you can't trust the people from Abancay. Except for Romero and Lleras, the rest seem to have been born sissies. I'll look for you tomorrow, early. I'll bring you your *zumbayllu*! The one that's a *winku*, brother, a magic *winku*! I'll make it right now!"

He ran off. I entered the school through the little door.

8. Deep Canyon

The Rector took me to the school chapel. Before a little altar decorated with artificial flowers he whipped me.

"It's my sacred duty. You followed the Indian mob that was led astray by the devil. What did they do? What did they do? Tell it all to God, here at this altar."

It was a small, braided whip. I was almost glad to be beaten and to feel the pain. I remembered the thundering of the bullwhips in the village of Patibamba. I knelt on the carpeted altar steps.

"You were seen running through Huanupata, behind the mules the Indian women stole. Did you sing with those outlaws? Did you sing? Speak up!"

"Yes, I sang. They were taking salt to the poor people of the hacienda. We were singing."

My chest seemed to be flooded with fire.

"Did Felipa curse me? Confess! We are alone in the chapel. Alone with God! Did she curse me?"

"No, Father. She just called for you loudly, that's all, when they discovered the forty sacks of salt."

The priest laid his hands on my shoulders.

"Your eyes look innocent. Is it you, really you, or the devil in sheep's clothing? Why did you go, child?" he asked.

"You would have gone, Father!"

"I didn't know the salt had arrived. The tax collector is an imbecile. But anger must not be allowed to enter here. Let us pray, my son. Then you may confess your sins so that you can go to sleep."

I told him about everything—the salt distribution, Doña Felipa's orders, our arrival at the hacienda, my weary walk to the iron park gates. My awakening on the lap of the blue-eyed lady, and how we had seen the horses galloping by, taking back the salt.

"They didn't come in on the highway," said the priest. "Luckily they took a roundabout road to the police station. The farm manager is forceful and shrewd."

"They took the salt away from the poor people by cracking their whips. They tore the hearts out of them," I dared to tell him.

"Not stolen goods, my son. Not even the poor should have stolen goods."

"They didn't steal; they didn't want to take anything. We gave them the salt and they ran away."

"Why do you say 'We gave them the salt'?"

"I did it too, Father. Is that stealing?"

"You are impudent, my boy. If you are innocent, don't pass judgment. I am old, and a son of God."

"They struck my heart, too. I saw them galloping down the road. And the lady cried, tears of blood."

I leaned against the priest's chest.

"Either you're sick, or momentarily confused. The rebellious Indian women have breathed some of their foulness on you. Get down on your knees!"

He prayed over me in Latin. And he struck me again with the whip, across the face, but not so hard.

"I shall have to tell your father about this. You shan't leave the boarding school again, nor wander about on Sundays. You'll go with me to the haciendas. Your soul needs company. Come."

We went out. The punishment and the prayers had made me feel small. I was afraid I might keep on crying until I choked. The boarders had already eaten and were speaking in low tones on the twilit porch. From one of the columns, Lleras and Añuco watched the chapel. Putting his arm around my shoulder as if to protect me, the Rector led me to the dining hall. I did not feel hungry, just sleepy.

The priest went on eating for a long time. Then he drank his wine.

"Your body is empty spiritually, that's why nothing appeals to you. It's better that you fast," he said.

He summoned the boys to recite the rosary.

"Now you've done your duty. You deserve God's mercy. They had better put you to bed."

Old Father Augusto took me to the dormitory. He was the one who had taken in the feeble-minded woman. He always had a kind, persuasive expression on his pudgy face, even though he was a miser, notorious for his stinginess.

"Ah, you little bum; little skunk, little skunk," he kept repeating.

The boys jostled one another on their way up to the dormitory; they crossed themselves, were led in the usual prayers by the priest, and went to bed. But scarcely had they heard the Rector's footfalls on the stairway when they ran over to my bedside. I could not see their faces very well in the twilight.

"What did he say to you? He threatened to whip you until you bled."

"He was never like that before. He wasn't any saint this time; he was more like an avenger. Why?"

"What did the *cholas* do?"

"They saw you running after the mules. You looked crazy."

"Let him tell about it tomorrow!" exclaimed Romero.

"Tomorrow," echoed Chauca.

"He's a hero! Let him tell about it right now," said Valle.

"Leave him alone, leave him alone, you hornets!" said Chipro, going off to bed. "Hornets, *akatank'as!*"

I covered my head with the blankets. They went on talking for a long time.

"If you want him to talk, pull his blankets off. Either throw water on him or shut up!" yelled Lleras.

The voices of the boys, the voice of the Rector, the voices of Antero and Salvinia, the song of the women, and the song of the birds in the poplar grove of Condebamba echoed and commingled in my mind, falling upon my dreams like an uneven rain. Sunlight often appears between scattered showers; it shines through an opening in the clouds and the fields stand out, water sparkles, trees and grass are illumined and shimmer, birds begin to sing. Man contemplates such a disputed world uncertainly, deeply moved by the sun and the dark clouds that cast down their rain.

The next day the Rector came into the dormitory quite early, almost at daybreak. The bell had not yet been rung. He opened the door and came right over to my bedside.

"Get up," he told me. "We're going to Patibamba."

Some of the boys sat up and said good morning to the priest.

"Sleep some more. It's not time to get up yet. I must go on a mission with Ernesto."

He waited for me to dress. Then he went down to the court-yard, where an automobile waited by the school door. It was from the hacienda.

Not even the dawn is penetrating in the hot valleys. At that hour in the highlands, the sun's rays traverse the elements; man dominates the horizon; his eyes drink in the light, and with it the universe. On the Pachachaca the dawn light is soft; inviting sleep, it drifts across the world like a rose-colored mist.

It was the same atrocious road as the evening before. But now I was going along it in a car, sitting beside the Saint of Abancay. The Rector prayed as he went. Immense *pisonay* flowers passed by rapidly overhead, like a wide, red border. You did not see them one by one or tree by tree as you would if you were on foot. I recognized a tall cedar tree by the roadside.

"Here's where I said good-bye to her," I said aloud.

"To whom?" asked the priest.

"To the lady with the blue eyes."

The automobile did not stop at the mansion gate. It kept right on toward the Indian quarter.

Gathered in the sugar mill yard were the people of the hacienda, all the *colonos* or *runas* of Patibamba. Around the edges of the field were the women, dressed in blue or black. The men wore a kind of homespun flannel with corduroy jackets.

When the Rector appeared, they all cried out in unison.

Near the arched entrance to the factory they had built a sort of platform and decorated it with palm leaves.

The Rector went up the steps onto the stage. I followed him.

There, before the platform, were the men I had sought in vain in the town *chicha* bars; and beyond them, near the walls were the women who, terrified and fleeing, had accepted the people's salt from us the day before. What was the priest going to do with them and with me? I looked around questioningly.

The odor of cane trash rose up more sourly from the ground with the coming of the day.

The Rector sat down on a chair that was on the stage. The hacienda manager's footfalls clattered loudly as he went up onto the platform. He wore the highest of boots, with steel buttons. Standing at the edge of the platform, he spoke in Quechua of how the Holy Father of Abancay had come early in the morning to preach to the hacienda people because he was greatly worried about the *colonos* of Patibamba; they were the people he loved the most. Then the manager jumped to the ground; he did not go down the steps.

When the Rector arose and walked over to the edge of the platform, the Indians cried out again. They wrung their hands, contemplating him with shining eyes, holding back their tears. The wind had begun to rustle the priest's white cassock.

The priest spoke in Quechua, in his high reedy voice:

"I am your brother, humble, like you; like you, kind and worthy of love, Patibamba peasant, little brother. The powerful people do not see the little flowers that dance on the banks of the canals that water the earth. They do not see them, but they give them their sustenance. Who is stronger, who has more need of my love? You, little brother of Patibamba, little brother; you alone are in my eyes, in the eyes of God, our Lord. I come to comfort you, because the flowers of the field do not need consolation; for them the water, the air, and the earth suffice. But people have hearts and need to be comforted. We all suffer, brothers. But some more than others. You suffer for your children, for your father and brother; your master feels deeply for all of you; I, for all of Abancay; and God, our Father, for the suffering people of the whole world. We have come here to weep, to grieve, to suffer that the thorns may pierce our hearts as they did the heart of Our Lady! Who has suffered more than she? You, perhaps, Patibamba peasant, whose heart is as beautiful as that of the bird who sings in the *pisonay*? Do you suffer more? Do you weep more . . . ?"

As the women began to cry, the priest bowed and went on speaking.

"Weep, weep," he cried. "The world is a vale of tears for the poor little children, the Indians of Patibamba."

It was as if everyone had become infected. The priest's body was trembling. I looked into the peasants' eyes. Tears streamed down their dirty cheeks, falling onto their chests, their shirts, running down their necks. The manager got to his knees. The Indians followed his example; some had to kneel on muddy ground.

By now the mountain peaks were glowing in the sunlight. I did not kneel; I wanted to run away, although I did not know where to go.

"Get down on your knees!" the priest ordered me. "Get down on your knees!"

I crossed the stage, leapt far out, and landed at the feet of an old cane worker. The priest's voice began again:

"Stealing is the damnation of the soul; he who steals or receives stolen goods becomes a lost soul—a lost soul who never finds rest, who drags his chains, who falls from the snowy mountain peaks into the abysses, and climbs up like an accursed donkey out of the gorges into the high mountains. . . . My little daughters, little sisters of Patibamba, fortunately you have given back the salt the drunken *chicheras* stole from the salt shop. Now, immediately, you are going to receive much more salt, which your master has had brought for his infants, his poor little children, the *runas* of the hacienda . . ."

I arose to look at him. From the dark ground beneath the platform the chief manager's assistants were dragging out full sacks.

The Rector gave the *colonos* his blessing. They all crossed themselves, and then began to seek out one another. They were happy. They milled about, murmuring confusedly, like bumblebees burrowing into old wood, circling around and buzzing.

I went out on the road. From the top of a wall I saw the salt being given out. The sunlight was nearing the courtyard; it had already reached the plumes of the sugar cane fields. At that moment I decided to run down to the river. The Rector saw me and called me. I looked at him fearfully; but he, too, was smiling.

"Go back to school," he told me. "I'm going to say mass in the chapel. You're a confused child. I shall decide what to do about you. One of the foremen will go with you."

"Couldn't I go to see the lady, Father?" I asked.

"No, the foreman will take you to the school door on horseback. You may not go out again, nor the other boys either."

And I rode back to Abancay on the shanks of a Patibamba horse. For the fourth time I was fleeing down the same road.

"Do you know a lady with blue eyes who has come to the hacienda with her mistress, sir?" I asked the foreman.

"Yes."

"Is she leaving soon?"

"Tomorrow."

"Why?"

"The army troops still haven't gotten here from Cuzco. They're frightened. That's why they're leaving."

"Troops?"

"So they say. The owners got scared. The troops are coming, by truck as far as Limatambo. The lady is just visiting here."

"Tell her that the boy from the school says good-bye to her, that he kisses her hands!"

"Kisses her hands? Why?"

"Couldn't you just give her that message?"

"All right. She's very kind, that lady."

"And the owner of the hacienda?"

"He hardly ever comes. He lives in Cuzco and doesn't speak Spanish very well."

"Who got scared, then?"

"The chief manager. And the owners of the haciendas down below here."

"What are the troops going to do?"

"I don't know, son. They'll come to scare the *cholas,* and the Indians, too. Maybe they'll kill someone, as a deterrent."

"Deterrent?"

"Well, Doña Felipa has the police corralled. She made them run."

Deterrent? It was an old word I had been hearing ever since I was a child in the villages. It made my blood run cold.

"And the salt? Is it the same they took away from them yesterday?" I asked.

"I don't know, boy. We took the sacks out of the hacienda warehouse just now, at dawn. The *padrecito* is a saint."

"He must be. He makes the Indians weep."

"Well, they're going to be real happy, now."

"How many Indians does the hacienda have?"

"There must be three hundred belonging to it. They also have day laborers for the more responsible jobs."

We reached the town. There were very few people on the streets. I did not see any policemen.

We dismounted at the school gate. The foreman rapped sharply on the little door set into the huge wooden gate.

Brother Miguel opened the door.

"You didn't stay?" he asked me.

"No, Brother, the Rector sent me away from the factory yard."

The foreman greeted Brother Miguel and galloped off on his horse.

"How strange! Something must be happening," said the friar. "You must have breakfast in my cell and tell me about it."

He took me to his cell.

Brother Miguel was black, but he had a sharp, almost hawk-nosed profile.

"Don't be afraid of the Rector," he told me. "He guides people's souls like a saint. But the *cholas* upset him yesterday."

"The Rector is strange, also, Brother Miguel," I answered. "I don't understand him! Why did he whip me yesterday? He said it was because he loved me. And now, he preached to the Indians and made them weep. I didn't want to kneel while he was making the Indians cry. I think he was threatening me . . ."

"You're only a boy, in the care of the school. You need to be playing, and not doing anything else. Now I'll get out the volley-ball net. We'll play all morning. The boarding students are out on the playground. The Rector will have to forgive you for every-thing."

He had them serve me cocoa and muffins, the priests' breakfast.

"Did Antero come, Brother?" I asked him, suddenly remem-bering Markask'a's promise.

"No, perhaps he'll come later."

"Will you let him in, Brother?"

"I'll let him in, I promise."

I arose, went over to him, and embraced him.

"When the Rector comes you should give him a hug too, as you did me."

"I will, if he doesn't reject me."

"You'll see, he'll accept you, that he'll hug you."

Suddenly I asked him, "Do you like the *zumbayllu*, Brother?"

"It's a beautiful toy. There are others like it in Lima, but they're rainbow-colored and bigger. They spin with an automatic cord. But they're not so unusual; I'd say they are quite ordinary com-pared to the little Abancay tops, even though they are colored and hum more loudly."

"What are the Lima ones made of?"

"Of painted tin."

"I didn't know! Then they don't just come from Abancay?"

"From Abancay. You wouldn't like the Lima tops."

Someone knocked on the door, just as I was beginning to dread having to face the boarding students.

"It's the boy Antero, Brother," said the gatekeeper.

We went out with the friar.

"Let him in quickly," he ordered.

Antero ran in and met us at the foot of the stairs.

"The *winko*, brother!" he shouted. "*Winko* and *layk'a*;[1] some-thing that's never been seen before."

He showed us a dark gray *zumbayllu* with reddish streaks.

"Brother Miguel, it's the best one I ever made. I worked almost all night on it. Shall I spin it?"

1. *Layk'a*, "sorcerer"; *winko, winku*, "a deformity in objects that should be round."—Author

"On the stones, child?"

"One that's bewitched can dance on the tip of a needle. Look how sharp its tip is!" He wound it. The cord was also black, with yellow.

"It won't spin," said the friar. "I bet it won't spin."

Antero cast it high. The top came down spinning. It perched on one of the round paving stones, singing with a high voice; its hum became more and more intense, piercing the ear like a cry issuing from the very blood of the listener.

"There won't be any deterrent! There won't be any deterrent! Doña Felipa will live!" I exclaimed, talking to myself as the top whirled in the dirt.

"You devilish boy! What have you done to it?" exclaimed the friar. "I feel as if the toy had got inside of me."

Antero did not laugh. He squatted with his eyes fixed on the *zumbayllu*.

"It's flying over the river," he said. "Now it's getting close . . . close to the bend where the Pachachaca winds round the mountain."

The humming sound deepened. All three of us were squatting now. The top's spots began to appear separately. Its voice sounded like that of a slow bumblebee.

"Now it's a widower. But don't die! I'll stop you with my hands."

He picked it up. The reddish sphere made a few turns on Antero's fingers.

"Brother Miguel, this isn't an everyday *zumbayllu*. It's under a spell. It has to be taken good care of! Ernesto should only spin it when he's alone. If the other boys see it they'll either take it away from him or crush it with their feet, or with stones. *Winko* and *layk'a*!

"I want to see if you can make it go," he said, handing me the top.

"Sure, I know all about *layk'as*. I've seen Saint George struggling with the tarantulas."

I wound the top reverently, praying to it. Fortunately the playground was still deserted.

I threw the *zumbayllu* into the air. The cord snaked through my hands. I thought it was going off to one side and would hit the wall, but the sphere paused in midair, straightened its tip, and came down slowly. It fell among some rough stones and began to scrabble about.

"Get up, *winku*!" cried Antero.

The top dug its tip into a shelf on the biggest stone, on a milli-
meter of space; there it balanced, spinning, settling with its tip
fast. The stone was round, and the tip did not slide across it.

"It's not going to the mountain now, it's just going upwards,"
exclaimed Antero. "Straight up to the sun. Now up the waterfall,
winko, up over the falls!"

The *zumbayllu* came to rest, as if it were sprouting from the
stone, a mobile toadstool on the surface of the boulder. And its
voice changed.

"Do you hear?" asked Antero. "It's going up to the sky, it's
going up to the sky! It's going to merge with the sun . . . ! The *pisonay* is singing! The *pisonay* is singing!" he exclaimed.

Pisonay flowers grow better on the sun than on the earth, according to the Pachachaca Indians. When the humming sound
began to deepen in tone, Antero picked up the top.

"Now what do you have to say, Brother?" asked Antero.

"I say you're either a little devil, or a big one. How could you
fashion a toy to make it change its voice like that?"

"No, Brother, it wasn't me, it was the material it's made of."

"Very well, I'll get out the net and entertain the boarding students. You may keep on playing."

When Brother Miguel had gone, Antero looked at me intently.

"It's a mixture of angel and sorcerer," he told me. "*Layk'a* for
its fire and *winku* for its form—devils; but Salvinia is in it, too.
I sang her name as I fastened on its tip and scorched in its eyes.

"I always keep my word!" he exclaimed, when he realized I
might protest. "It's yours, brother. Keep it. We'll make it weep
in the fields, or on some boulder in the river. It will sing even
better."

I put it away in my pocket. I was afraid that there on the pavement it might strike against the stones and break its tip. I felt it
carefully with my fingers. It was really *winku*, that is to say lop-
sided, in spite of being round; and *layk'a*, or bewitched, because
it was streaked with red. That's why it kept changing its voice and
color, as if it were made of water. It had an orangewood tip.

"If I make it spin and blow its song in the direction of Chalhuanca, will it reach my father's ears?" I asked Markask'a.

"It will, brother! Distance doesn't mean anything to it. A little
while ago it went up to the sun. It's not true that the *pisonay* blossoms on the sun. Indian beliefs! The sun is a red-hot star, isn't it?
What flowers could be up there? But a song can neither burn nor
freeze. A *winku layk'a* that's well wound and has an orangewood
tip! First you speak to it, into one of its eyes, giving it your mes-

sage and telling it which way to go. And then, when it's singing, you blow, you blow it carefully in the direction you want it to go, and keep on giving it your message. And the *zumbayllu* will sing into the ear of whoever is expecting you. Try it, right now!"

"Must I be the one who spins it? Just me?"

"Yes, whoever wants to send the message should do it."

"Here, on the paving stones?"

"Didn't you just see it? Don't try to fool it, nor discourage it."

This time I wound it more carefully than I had before. And I looked at Antero.

"Speak to it softly," he cautioned.

I covered one of its eyes with my lips.

"Tell my father I'm bearing it very well," I said. "Even though my heart is afraid, I can bear it. And you must blow your breath on his forehead. You must sing for his soul."

I pulled the string.

"Upstream on the Pachachaca, upstream!" I cried.

The *zumbayllu* hummed loudly in the air. It came down on one of the porch steps, skipped over the ridges of the old wood, and stopped on a smooth streak on the floor.

"Blow! Blow on it a little!" exclaimed Antero.

I blew toward Chalhuanca in the direction of the great river's high valley.

It sang sweetly.

"Let it die by itself," Markask'a told me.

The *layk'a* wobbled, its voice fading little by little; it scraped its head on the bottom of the step and stretched out in the shade.

"Now let the Padrecito Rector come!" I told Antero. "He has whipped me. He's pushed me. He's made *sanku*[2] of the hearts of the Patibamba *colonos*. But just let him come now! My father is with me. What do you say, Markask'a?"

"Let's go to the playground. We'll spin the *winku* in the middle of it!" he exclaimed. "The two of us will defend it against Añuco, Valle . . ."

"No! You said I should spin it all alone."

"All right, then tell he what happened to you last night. What about the Patibamba *colonos*? Why did the Rector whip you? Did he really whip you?"

"You tell me if you were keeping watch over Salvinia's house . . ."

As we were talking, an automobile stopped at the school gate.

2. Cornmeal cooked in water. A very old kind of porridge in Peru.—Author

We glanced at one another. I was about to say something to Antero when Brother Miguel's voice took us by surprise. From the inner courtyard he shouted, "On your knees, you beast! On your knees!"

We ran through the passageway and leapt onto the playground. Lleras was on his knees, beneath the net. His nose had been broken and blood streamed from his mouth onto his chest. Añuco knelt, when he got there, and covered his face with both hands. Even his bare legs, for he still wore short pants, were pale; the tendons stood out tensely on his neck; his forehead was furrowed with deep wrinkles, from fear. Valle was looking at Brother Miguel rather defiantly; Romero had gone over to the latter with clenched fists.

"Shall I kick him, Brother?" asked Romero. "Shall I kick him to make him go?"

"Walk on your knees!" Brother Miguel shouted at Lleras, nudging him with his foot.

Brother Miguel would have made a stone walk. We thought everyone would kneel. Valle blinked. For Brother Miguel was ashen; he snorted through the nostrils of his aquiline nose like one of the wild puna bulls that attack the shadows of the birds; the whites of his eyes were showing; he would have terrified even the dust, I believe.

Lleras dragged himself along on his knees, and Añuco followed him, weeping.

"To the chapel!" said Brother Miguel.

We boarders followed him; Antero and I, slowly circling the court, came to where the other boys were. Wig and little Palacios looked on from a distance, by the wall.

"How's he going to get down the terrace steps? He'll fall! He'll take advantage of that place to run away," I thought, as Lleras crawled along, scraping his knees on the gravel. Valle followed with us. Chauca stopped, beginning to cry.

Just then we saw the Rector. He was about to cross the courtyard to the steps. When he noticed the turmoil he looked at us in amazement.

"Help, Father!" shrieked Añuco. "Help, Padrecito!"

The Rector came. He would have liked to run, but he held himself back. I saw him clearly. He quickened his pace.

"Don't get up!" ordered Brother Miguel.

But Añuco ran, threw himself upon the priest, and clung to him.

"The nigger, Father, the black bully!" he shouted angrily.

We stepped forward, almost forming a line, to see the priest.

Antero stayed behind and retreated to the door of the toilets. Brother Miguel calmed down and stayed with Lleras. He would not let him get up. The Rector could not walk very fast because Añuco held onto his arm.

"The nigger! The nigger!" he repeated dazedly, choking with tears. The priest covered his mouth and shook him.

The Rector came up to us. Lleras looked as if his throat had been cut, by the quantity of blood. It had soaked his shirt and dripped from his waist. And the blood that was still oozing from his nose glistened in the strong sunlight of the valley.

"What's this?" exclaimed the Rector, looking at Brother Miguel.

Antero and I should have liked to ask the same question.

"He offended me, Reverend Father," answered Brother Miguel. "For nothing, for almost no reason at all he insulted me, struck me on the chest, and knocked me down. Then I couldn't take any more and by God, with the hand of God, I punished him."

"With whose hand? With whose hand did you say?" asked the Rector.

"I punished him because he insulted me. I wear the habit of God."

"Get up, Lleras, and come here," ordered the priest. "Let's go to the chapel. Brother Miguel, go to your cell and wait for me."

Lleras got to his feet with difficulty, and as he straightened up, we students heard him say in a strained voice, "He's a damned nigger!"

He had meant to say this under his breath.

The Rector had already turned his back on us. We never knew if he heard Lleras. Brother Miguel folded his hands and went down the embankment like that, behind Lleras. Only Añuco walked with the priest. It seemed as if his legs were giving way beneath him, that he was going to collapse. He was staggering. The boarding students began to talk.

"That k'anra was bound to come to such an end," said Romero.

"He's a lost soul," said Chauca.

"He pushed Brother Miguel!" exclaimed Palacios. "He knocked him down, little brother! Just because he called a foul on him, he grabbed him by the shoulder and yelled 'Nigger, shitty nigger!' at him. Brother Miguel—I don't know how—got up, punched him, and blood spattered all over his face. What will happen now! What will happen! Maybe it'll rain ashes! Maybe frost will kill the little plants! Heaven will take vengeance, little brothers!"

Palacios embraced Romero and only then began to weep despairingly.

"I think the sun will die! *Ay papacito!*"

Romero picked him up, clasping him to his chest, and carried him off to the dormitory.

"But Brother Miguel went too far. What's black is black," Valle said aloud.

"And that you're a dunghill chicken is also true," said Ismodes, the *chipro*.[3]

"What?" exclaimed Valle, perplexed.

"A yellow-footed chicken."

And Ismodes went over to him.

"I don't fight. Ever. I wouldn't stoop to that," said Valle disdainfully.

"There's the proof, don't you see? Chickens never fight, they just get stepped on."

Chipro burst out laughing. We all looked at one another. Even Wig came over to look at Valle more closely. Antero did not dare to come out.

"Imbeciles!" said Valle, hurrying off down over the bank.

"That's the way it is when you see blood, little brothers," Chipro told us. "Some turn chicken—the sissies, those *k'echas*. And it makes the rest of us want to defend somebody. You can't just stay still. The brother, hell, Brother Miguel! Who says he's not good, that he's not kind? What dog could say so?"

"Only some lost soul, one of the damned!" I said, hugging him.

"And who says that Lleras is not a whore-lover, a bully, and a lost soul as well? Valle? Look at him, waiting for some rooster to peck him on the head."

"To the chapel!" exclaimed the Rector.

Antero stayed behind in the playground, hiding behind the wooden partitions. We boarders rushed off together.

"To the chapel!" cried the Rector.

Romero came down from the dormitory with Palacitos. Valle appeared on the porch; he had withdrawn into one of the classrooms. He was pale; he stepped down into the stone-paved courtyard and came along like a sleepwalker. I stared at him as he walked, stumbling to the chapel door. "Something, something is wrong with him!" I thought.

We entered the chapel. Lleras was not there. The Rector reached the altar and stood before us. He gazed at us for a long time, observing us one by one. I felt the expression on his face calming

---

3. Quechua nickname for a person whose face is pitted with smallpox scars.—Author

me. We looked at one another in a special way; it was not only the Lleras affair that needed to be settled between us, between him and me, but also the memory of the morning, of the *colonos'* tears which I didn't know if he still remembered, but which continued to blaze within me like the sun that had shown down so unexpectedly on the hacienda cane fields. The Rector looked at me calmly.

"My sons! My beloved children!" he said. "Whoever sees a great sin committed should also ask God to pardon him; a great sin spatters all around it; all of us witnesses should kneel down and beg God to leave nothing, not a trace of a stain either in the hearts of those who have sinned or in the thoughts of those who were so unfortunate as to be witnesses . . ."

This time the priest spoke in a different manner, not the way he had on the platform at the hacienda, facing the muddy yard that had been trampled into mire by the Patibamba *colonos.* Perhaps it was only an idea, a notion of mine. The Quechua he had used to speak to the Indians had left me with a feeling of bitterness. "Could he possibly have several spirits?" I asked myself as I listened to him in the chapel. "He doesn't try to make us weep in torrents; he doesn't wish to humble our hearts, to make us fall down into the mire where the cane-trash worms are crawling. He illumines us and lifts us up until we become one with his soul . . ."

"My children! Our Lord blesses you every morning with his mercy; a guardian angel keeps watch over each one of you . . . but we are also free, that is the good and the evil of the world. But there is nothing more infinite than the heart that God has granted us, that he has set into the human infant . . . you shall soon see the proof of this! . . ."

Afterwards, at that hour of the morning, we recited the whole rosary. But I could see that Valle was not praying. As usual, he was two seats away from me, across the aisle. He shifted from one knee to the other on the wooden bench. He rested his head on his hands, and moved it every little while, showing signs of impatience. Añuco prayed aloud, at the foot of the altar, on the stone steps.

The Rector blessed us and told us we could go. Añuco stayed behind with him.

Valle was the last to leave. Most of the boarders remained in the main courtyard. They did not speak to one another. I went to the playground, looking for Antero. He was no longer there. I saw Chipro and Chauca together, entering the passageway. The Rector and Añuco crossed the courtyard and began to go up the steps. Chipro and Chauca reached the playground. The boy from Pampachiri also came into the inner courtyard, alone. Behind him came Valle, walking rapidly. He did not look at us but went to the back wall on the side that faced the street.

"Ismodes!" he called. "Come, Ismodes!"

Chipro went, walking slowly. I reached Valle first.

"You wouldn't disobey the Rector," I told him.

He did not answer.

"What's the matter? What do you want?" Chipro asked him.

I don't know why, but all the pockmarked people I knew when I was a boy were dark-skinned and inscrutable looking, always easily angered, energetic and small-eyed, like Ismodes. They had a certain fixed expression on their faces that emphasized the look in their eyes.

Valle was taller; beside Ismodes he looked like a young land-holder standing before some clerk or messenger. Chipro's shirt was dirty at the waist; I think all his shirts were too short and he was always tucking them into his pants with his hands and getting them dirty. He gestured as he answered Valle.

"There aren't many people on the playground now. I'll answer your challenge and your dirty insults by wrestling," Valle told him.

"Right now! So that the Rector will expel me, so he'll see I'm an Antichrist. Sissy, sissy!" shouted Chipro.

Valle grasped his jacket. Pressing his thin lips together, he grew pale.

"Funeral candle!"[4] exclaimed Chipro, staring at him, still without reacting.

Valle butted him with his head, at the same time kneeing him in the stomach. Then he let go of him.

"You sneaky *k'echa*," yelled Ismodes. "Not in the face! The Rector must not see it!"

Suddenly he bent over and grabbed Valle by the testicles with both hands.

"Now, sissy!" he said, almost laughing. "Yes, he had them, brothers, he sure did!"

Valle slumped over against Chipro, without crying out. Chipro moved aside and let him fall, headlong; then he straightened up and asked us, "Is there a lump on my nose? Am I black and blue?"

His jaw was beginning to swell a little. Chauca pressed a coin against the swelling.

The Pampachiri boy lifted up Valle. Supporting him with one

---

4. Tall, decorated candles are put at the four corners of the bier. This insult implies that Valle is tall, waxy, and deathlike.—Trans.

hand, he quickly brushed the dust from his clothing. Valle was paler than ever. His lips were quivering. I went over to him.

"You're brave," I told him. "You're brave. Didn't you know that pockmarked people are strange, that you should be afraid of them?"

"Only the Indians!" he said. "Or the sons of Indians."

I did not answer him. The Pampachiri boy and the rest of us accompanied him to the steps leading down to the toilets where there was shade. There he sat down, completely exhausted. The Pampachiri boy looked at him pityingly, quite moved, unable to understand him.

Some frail weed stalks protruded through the cracks in the board fence around the toilets. I knew that on the other side, near the wall, was a yellow flower that reached up to the sunlight that filtered down through the roof. In that corner the boys could not crush it. I thought of that velvety lobe—in Quechua it is called *ayak'zapatilla*, "corpse-slipper." Seeing Valle exhausted, and with my burning memories of all that had happened during the day and the evening before, I found that no other thought could capture my attention. The *ayak'zapatilla* blooms gaily in great profusion on the damp retaining walls of the planted terraces, and on top of the walls by the roadsides; and the *huayronk'os*, the big black bumblebees, seek it out; they come down heavily onto the little opening of its corolla and fly off later, their wings and belly spotted with the flower's yellow dust.

The next day was Monday, and the day-pupils did not come to school. We learned that the main streets were empty, and the stores closed.

We boarders spent the day all scattered about, as we had Sunday afternoon. Antero did not come back. Rondinel stayed at his mother's house. The boarders were reading or writing. Valle passed the time in his classroom, apparently reading. Romero walked about wearily, accompanied by Palacitos. The boy from Pampachiri often went up to the door of the room where Valle was, but did not look inside. Chipro and Chauca conversed or read aloud to one another. They were classmates.

"That vine Valle is done for," Chauca told me, in the morning, when I went over to the stairs where they were sitting. "The hero!"

"No," I told him. "He came to life again yesterday after he thought things over."

"Keep moving," Chipro told me.

I stroked the *zumbayllu*, but was afraid to show it to anyone. Chipro had not spoken to me angrily. "What if I told the two of them that I had a *winko layk'a?*" I thought. I trusted both of them; but still I remembered Antero's warning: "It's a *layk'a*, it's bewitched; and it has Salvinia in its soul, too; I kept saying her name as I was opening its eyes with fire . . . !" I did not dare. Chipro was from Andahuaylas, the son of a mestizo; he might disapprove of *layk'as*; if he did he would gladly trample a *zumbayllu winko* underfoot as if it were something to be rejected, no matter how beautiful its song.

At noon Romero decided to play his mouth organ. Romero swayed back and forth, keeping time to the music with his tall, supple body. He began the first measures of the introduction to his favorite carnival song: "*Apurímac mayu . . .*" Like all true harmonica masters, he would put the instrument well inside his mouth and puff out the accompaniment with his lips in slow rhythm on the bass; then he would slide it over and play the melody on the very highest notes . . .

Romero had never played in the daytime before. He began rather listlessly, becoming livelier as he played. Perhaps he realized that the innocence of the music was needed in that courtyard. Lleras did not put in an appearance, nor did Brother Miguel; Añuco remained secluded in old Father Augusto's room. The Rector had presided over the lunch and dinner tables on Sunday; we knew that at that hour of the morning he was out on the street. The boys began to come out onto the gallery. They did not go right over to the fountain where Romero was playing. I went first, then the boy from Pampachiri, then Chipro, Chauca, Wig, Saturnino, Iño Villegas . . .

"Don't change tunes," I begged him.

The song ended with a *fuga*, for the feet-stamping part of the dance. Romero nodded in time to the music. The rhythm grew more rapid at the end. Romero threw back his head, as if to send the music up to the frosty mountain peaks, where it would be carried off by the wind; we felt that through the music the world was coming back to us once more, its happiness restored. But when all of us had gathered round Romero in a circle, we suddenly heard Añuco's voice, as if from the other side of the valley.

"Be quiet, Romero! Little brother Romero, don't play!"

He was leaning over the balcony railing, weeping. He was pale and wan, with circles under his eyes.

Romero stopped playing.

"What's the matter with Abancay, these days?" I said to myself in bewilderment. I squeezed the *zumbayllu* in the bottom of my pocket.

Añuco disappeared back into Father Augusto's room.

As we were dispersing, the porter came into the courtyard through the entryway and ran toward us, saying, "The troops are coming down now; they say they've already crossed the Sok'llak'asa pass! The *chicheras* are going into hiding. The police have gone and taken back their rifles. All but Doña Felipa's; she's still got two Mausers. They say they're going to break down the door of her *chicha* bar when the troops get here. In Huanupata the people are running all around. The people are coming out of the *chicha* bar; they're leaving. They say a colonel is coming who was in Huanta and who decimated the Indians in the cemetery. The men are leaving. In Huanupata everybody's trembling . . . The police are scared, too . . . The colonel might shoot them because they let the *chicheras* beat them . . . Some of them, they say, are running down the hill to hide in the Pachachaca . . . Christians, Abancay has fallen under a curse . . . ! They might kill anybody now . . ."

"And you, what are you scared about?" asked Romero.

"The people are running away. Because the troops are coming! They say this time they're going to crush Huanupata. They aren't going to shoot bullets. It might burn down. So many thatched roofs. There might be a fire. Now then, get going! Run away, there's the gate."

He motioned toward the entry with his outstretched arm and continued, "*Jajayllas!* I've seen skirmishes. In a skirmish I don't think they aim; the stray bullets fly overhead, too; they hit windows, posts, the tower. In Huanta they even fell in the cane fields; they say they blazed up and lit up the whole valley in the night. That's how they decimated the Indians in the graveyard."

"That was in 1910, you beast!" Romero shouted at him.

But the damage was already done. The gatekeeper had managed to awaken the worst forebodings in the boys who surrounded him in the courtyard. We stared at one another. Wig rolled his eyes, as if he were looking for someone, or hunting a place to hide.

"They're not going to kill anyone now! Maybe they'll just beat the *cholas*," said Iño Villegas. But his voice was quavering.

The porter heard the little door in the gate opening and ran off toward the kitchen. We saw the Rector come in. He was smiling, and walked rapidly. He clapped his hands as he entered the courtyard.

"To the dining hall," he cried. "Why haven't they called you? It's already past time."

"Padrecito, what do you know about the troops coming into Abancay and shooting the *chicheras?*" Wig ventured to ask.

"What criminal idiot said that? The army is coming to restore order. The storekeepers are already opening their shops."

"What about Huanupata?" I asked him.

"The *chola* women are running away. Only the ones who are responsible, that's all! Come, let's go to the dining hall."

He was unable to transmit his happiness to the boys. We ate lunch in silence. Valle, who was alone, stole a glance at Chipro. Those who had witnessed Valle's downfall had kept it a secret. Perhaps he was ashamed. Much later Chipro might tell the tale, laughing like an idiot. Now he seemed confused; he returned Valle's look without irony, blushing a little. And Valle kept on looking at him. He could think of nothing else. Then he scrutinized me, Chauca, and the boy from Pampachiri. He studied us. He was struggling to regain his famous elegance. Could he maintain it after the way he had been put down in the playground? But we had heard the gatekeeper, almost crazed by the threats, by the alarms he had picked up in the streets; we'd heard and seen Añuco hanging over the balcony railing, pleading; we knew that Lleras lay on his back, with a herb poultice over his mouth and nose in the Rector's antechamber, and that Brother Miguel would not come out of his room. None of this could make any difference to Valle. Would they tell on Chipro . . . ?

Some great evil had unleashed its fury on the school and on Abancay; perhaps an ancient prophecy was being fulfilled, or the little section of the Patibamba hacienda occupied by the city had been brushed by the last streaks of weak and noxious light from the comet that had appeared in the sky only twenty years before. "It was blue, the light, and it drifted along quite close to the ground, like the early morning mist, and just as transparent," recounted the old people. Perhaps the evil effects of that light were only now beginning to be felt. "They say Abancay is under a curse," the gatekeeper had shouted, wringing his hands. "They might kill anybody now."

The Rector, however, did not seem to share these presentiments; he gazed at us with calm condescension; I even suspected that it did him good to see us upset and anxious.

The troops were due to arrive at five in the afternoon. At three the school bell was rung.

The boarding students left the classrooms and the porches; some came from the playground. The priests came down from their cells. The Rector stood in his office doorway and ordered in a loud voice, "Get in line! As if you were going to mass."

We lined up in order of height, facing the office. Without looking at anyone, Añuco took his place between Palacitos and Iño.

The five priests made up another short line on the porch, by the steps leading down to the courtyard.

Then came Brother Miguel, hatless. He descended the wooden steps slowly, as if afraid. His hair looked even kinkier than usual, and was in a thousand little knots. He was ashen, but he walked with an erect gait, with his head held high, although his eyes looked downward, with a humility that depressed us.

We all watched him; his steps re-echoed in the courtyard and in our hearts. I would have liked to see the expression on Valle's face, to see how he looked then. He did not glance at the friar; perhaps he had seen him come down the steps, but afterwards he did not turn his face toward him; he stared coldly at the Rector.

The Rector came over to our line. Brother Miguel stopped a short distance away from the group of priests, on the gallery.

"Come down now, Lleras," shouted the Rector.

We saw Lleras appear on the balcony opposite us; he came through the door from the Rector's parlor onto the roof of the arched entryway. His jaw was still black and blue. He hesitated, as if he were about to fall.

"Come down!" ordered the Rector.

Lleras made up his mind and walked rapidly to the stairway. Hurrying down the stairs, taking them two at a time, he went right up to Brother Miguel. Suddenly, when he was quite close to him, he stopped and examined him. We could see his eyes studying the friar. He gazed at his bare head.

"Brother! Forgive me! I ask your forgiveness before my friends . . ." he said.

Something—something more he was about to say and do. He bowed—started to bow. The brother had raised his hands.

"No!" cried Lleras. "No! He's black, Padrecito. He's black! *Atatauya!*" [5]

He jumped down into the paved courtyard, dashed across it, and entered the shadow of the archway; we heard him open the entry, one side of the huge gate, and slam it shut immediately from outside.

This hardly disturbed the Rector at all. With a flashing look, he checked Añuco, who was fidgeting about in line.

5. An exclamation of disgust.—Author

"You!" he said to him. "You, the friend of that lost soul!"

"Me, yes, Father. Yes, Padrecito!"

He walked to the gallery rapidly, without running. He went up the steps and knelt before Brother Miguel, unable to speak. He was crying as he kissed both of the friar's hands. Then Palacitos followed. He dashed past us. No one stopped him. Prostrating himself before the friar he began to kiss the hems of his habit.

"Pardon, *perdoncito!*" he pleaded. "The moon is going to weep; the sun is going to make it rain ashes! Forgive me, little Brother! Say you'll forgive me, little Brother!"

Brother Miguel lifted him up, clasped him to his chest, and kissed him on his face and eyelids. Añuco jumped with joy.

"I forgive all of you, and ask you to forgive me!" said the friar.

And he bowed to Añuco. He kissed him on the cheek, almost respectfully.

"Please let me go to the chapel, Father," Añuco said.

His eyes seemed watery; the whites looked large and were also glistening. It was that color, so heightened by the dark skin around his eyes, his ingenuous eyes, which gave him such a tender look. A ray of warmth, seeming to come from the sun or from the ground, permeated my blood, brought joy into our lives. Palacitos and Añuco were dancing by Brother Miguel's side, in the depths of that dread valley, amid so many dire omens. "Now no one will die!" I thought. "A cool shower will fall on the fields. The troops will come in, perhaps playing trumpets, on horseback."

"Go with Brother Miguel," consented the Rector.

"Only those who want to," said the friar.

But we all went.

Chipro went up to Valle. They looked at one another. In his pockmarked face—"Moorish" as we used to call it in the highlands—disfigured and pitted by so many scars, Chipro's eyes glowed with joy. Valle smiled, not so brightly, but Chipro kept looking at him, transmitting to him the strength of his joy. His face was like a *pisonay* flower, his eyes were so small; but despite the immobility of his expression, his whole face was lit up by the fire in his eyes. "Chipro is a devil," I said to myself as I walked along. "He's a devil!" No one else's eyes ever had such a gleam in them. Perhaps a *pejerrey*[6] might flash like that as it darts across a pool in the sunlight. Who wouldn't laugh, who wouldn't dance, in the presence of such joy? Even Valle, the proud, the great gentleman.

6. A small, silvery fish with a blue stripe.—Trans.

Laughing, they entered the chapel, the *chipro* and the Don Juan, the dandy of the boarding school. But Valle was smiling, obviously trying to make a show of his strength. Chipro must have noticed his antagonist's comical gesture; he gave me a look different from the one he had given Valle, and winked his eye.

Once he had reached the altar Brother Miguel did not know what to talk to us about; he looked at us all and smiled. He should have gone to the playground and turned us loose there, or thrown us out into the street.

"It's just that he had to finish the ceremony somehow," I reflected. After a long while, the friar was able to speak.

"Near the town where I was born, San Juan de Mala," I recall him saying, "there are some sea cliffs, I mean to say some very high rocks, where the waves break. At the top of those rocks the figure of a Virgin with her Child was discovered. You know, my boys? That rock is black, blacker than I am . . . Go and play; with my humble hands I give you that Virgin's blessing; may she make you forget the sins you've seen. My only wish is to hear the waves breaking at her feet; their voice would be stronger than that of my guilt. Good-bye, boys . . . ! Go to the playground. I'll stay here for a while."

We went out. How could the brother, being black, pronounce the words so perfectly? Being black?

Palacitos ran out, slapping his thighs loudly, pretending to be a spirited horse. He went round and round in circles. Añuco hesitated in the doorway of the chapel for a few moments.

I went up to him.

"Look!" I said.

I showed him the reddish *winku*.

"A *winku*!" he exclaimed.

"And *layk'a*!" I answered.

"Have you spun it?" he asked.

"It dances better than a *tankayllu*. Like a world it spins. According to Antero its song goes up to the sun. Shall we make it dance, Añuco? Shall we defend it against anyone who wants to step on it?"

"Who'd want to trample it? Who?" he said.

"Come on, then! Come on, brother! Remember it's *layk'a*!"

I dragged him a part of the way. Then he started to run. Palacitos capered about the playground.

I began to wind the top. Almost everyone came over to where I stood.

"A *winko*!" said Romero. Looking at it a while longer, he cried, "*Layk'a*, by God, it's bewitched! Don't throw it!"

Palacitos managed to get close enough to see the top.

"Who says it's *layk'a*? Didn't you have it in the chapel when Brother Miguel blessed us?"

"Yes," I answered.

"Then it's not bewitched anymore, now that it's been blessed. Spin it, stranger!" exclaimed Palacitos energetically.

I felt sad.

"Isn't it *layk'a*?" I asked Añuco.

He looked at me, thinking it over.

"There'll always be some magic left in it. Throw it!"

I cast it angrily. The top came down in almost a straight line. It sang through its eyes, as if through its black holes some strange, unknown insect were whistling and stinging some nerve deep in our chests.

"Candle made it!" exclaimed Chipro. "Honestly!"

"Will you give it to me?" asked Añuco anxiously. "Will you give it to me?"

"Spin it, Añuco," I told him.

He wound it carefully, one turn against another, pressing the string back with his fingernail to make the circles fit tightly together. He cast the top without looking at me.

He spun it skillfully. The *zumbayllu* whirled in the dust, humming as if we were hearing it in our dreams; it stopped, as if paralyzed, spinning invisibly.

"It's sleeping!" said the Pampachiri boy.

Then it toppled over, scrabbling about in the dust with its tip.

"*Layk'a*, not *layk'a*, *layk'a*, not *layk'a*, *layk'a*, not *layk'a* . . . ! Not *layk'a*! Blessed!" yelled Palacitos, picking up the top, when it had stopped spinning and had fallen over on its side in the dirt.

"It must have some of its magic," affirmed Romero. "It must have some left!"

"It's yours, Añuco," I told him gaily.

"Really?"

"What a *zumbayllu* you have!" I repeated, handing him the top. "There's a little of everything in its soul. A beautiful girl, the most beautiful there is; Candle's strength; my memory; what's left of its magic; the blessing of the Virgin of the Coast. And it's *winko*! You must spin it when you are alone."

"What did you say?"

"I'll tell you later."

"Let it dance just one more time," said Valle, surprising me.

"Do you want it to dance?" I asked Añuco.

"Yes," he said. "Beautiful instrument. It's a beautiful instrument."

9. Stone and Lime

By six o'clock we still had heard neither rifle shots nor hoofbeats. We gathered in the main courtyard in order to be near the street. We did not hear the army go by. As darkness fell the sound of applause could be heard in the distance.

"They've come down quietly. They're arriving now," said Romero.

We could not see the troops march in but the cheering sounded louder and louder.

"Death to the *chicheras*!" We heard this cry clearly. And immediately afterwards, another, "Doña Felipa, the virago!"

Just then the electric lights were turned on—some dim, reddish bulbs, good only for outlining the shadows of things.

All of us boarding students were crowded together in the entryway.

But there wasn't any shooting.

"Long live the Colonel!" they shouted.

"The glorious regiment!"

"A regiment, against the *cholas*?" asked Valle.

"The *chicheras* are worse than men, even worse than soldiers," answered Chipro.

"The myth of the race! The *cholas* will die like Indians if they're machine-gunned."

Valle always talked like that; you couldn't tell whether he meant to insult the one who was listening to him or the person, or even the things, that he was talking about.

"Didn't you hear the gatekeeper? Doña Felipa hasn't given back the rifles."

"Two Mausers," he said. "Two Mausers. Great artillery to fight a regiment."

The bells began ringing.

"It's a regiment of *cholos*," said Romero, shouting to make himself heard.

"The myth of the race again. Let them kill one another until the end of time. I'm just an infelicitous spectator."

"Infelicitous? What do you mean by that? A *cholo* could take it out of you."

"He could, sure he could. While the sons of my sons amuse themselves . . . riding on their backs."

"And if the *cholos* tickle you a little?" Chipro asked him.

"Then I would have to laugh."

"Ah, tears, little tears," mocked Chipro.

"Shooting!" yelled Palacitos.

"Can't you tell what they are, *cholo*? Rockets in honor of the troops."

The sounds of explosions came down from somewhere over our heads.

We could no longer hear the cheering. The troops must have reached the prefecture and be marching to the barracks in the Condebamba district. There was an empty old structure there, painted dark gray, with battlements and towers on the corners. People said that on moonlit nights one could hear sentinels' voices counting off. The police took prisoners there on Saturdays, and made them pull the weeds that grew in the courtyards; the city took care of the side streets. Thus the barracks displayed its façade, its towers, and its buttresses; it was the largest edifice in town, and awesome because it was empty. No one dared to soil the lower part of its walls for fear of the toads which abounded there—and of the police. Toads will unexpectedly catch hold of bare human flesh.

The bells kept ringing. We heard the footsteps of a group of people approaching the school gate.

"There wasn't any shooting," said Palacitos happily.

"It must be the Rector coming," observed Romero.

We ran back into the courtyard.

The Rector opened the door and walked rapidly toward us.

"All's quiet, my boys. The Colonel is prefect now. There'll be school tomorrow. Don't pay any attention to the predictions of the *cholos*. They're terrified," he said as he approached us.

"Aren't they going to shoot anybody?" asked Wig.

"You again? To the study hall, all of you," he ordered.

I didn't dare to ask him about Doña Felipa or Lleras just then. The boarders went off to their classroom. The Rector started up to his apartment. I caught up with him at the foot of the stairs, and took shelter behind a porch pillar in the darkness.

"What about Doña Felipa, Padrecito?" I asked.

"They'll arrest her tonight," he answered sharply.

"She's got rifles, Father."

"That's why. If she tries to resist, they'll kill her."

"She will resist, Father."

"God forbid. The soldiers would shoot her full of holes. She's guilty."

"But she can kill too. Maybe I should go. Maybe I could bring back the rifles."

"You? Why?"

He came quite close to me. In the twilight I could easily see his eyes and his face, his cheekbones and his white hair.

"Why you?"

He looked taller. His white vestments sparkled, as if reflecting the great impatience that possessed him; his chest rose and fell before my eyes.

"I know her, Father . . . I could ask her to give me the guns . . . I could tell her . . ."

"What, my son? You just followed her around like a dog. Come, let's go upstairs!"

He hurried up the stairway. By now there was no one left in the courtyard.

"I could go with Brother Miguel," I said loudly, catching up with him on the balcony.

"You know, if your father were still in Chalhuanca, I'd send you off to him tomorrow; but he's already reached Coracora, a hundred leagues from here."

"I can go," I told him. "I can go, Father. I know how to travel through the cordillera. Send me off, Father. Send me off. What's a hundred leagues to me? I'd be in my glory."

"Now I know you really need me to take care of you, by heaven. But why do you want to run after the *cholos* and the Indians? They won't do anything to Felipa. They won't do a thing to her. I'll go. I'll send word to her, son, to give back the rifles."

"I can go with Brother Miguel," I said, coming closer to him.

He took me into his parlor. It was like the Old Man's. The floor was almost completely covered with red carpeting. There was a piano and high-backed, upholstered furniture. I suddenly felt humiliated in there. Two large mirrors with gilded frames were gleaming on the wall. The deep light of those mirrors has always intrigued me, as if by looking through them one could see beyond the end of the world. There are a lot of them in the churches of Cuzco, hanging high up on the columns, out of reach.

The Rector patted my head. He had me sit in a big armchair that was upholstered in silk.

"It doesn't matter that your father has gone so far away; you're with me," he said.

"Why didn't my father tell me about his trip to Coracora? I'll get to know another town. I'll walk a long way. Will you defend Doña Felipa?" I asked him.

"No, son. I've already told you she's guilty. I'll send word to her to run away . . . I'll intercede for her, somehow."

"Then after that I shall leave. You'll let me go. I'll go from one town to another asking for my father until I get to where he is. I'll weep like an angel when I suddenly stand before him! Is that town very far from the Pachachaca? Is it far from the main stream of the river?"

"It's quite far."

"Then the *winko's* song must have got lost!" I exclaimed. "And now it doesn't work anymore; Brother Miguel blessed it."

The priest looked at me intently.

"Are you determined to disobey your father and me? He wants you to continue with your studies. What are you talking about?"

"But didn't you say you were going to send me off?"

"Not now, child. And you don't seem to be making sense. You will remain here. You will be a good son of God, I swear it."

Leaving me, he went to his bedroom and came back with a glass of water.

"Drink it," he said.

It was a bitter drink.

"I drank some, too."

"I'll stay, Father," I told him. "Sure! It must have gone badly for him in Chalhuanca. He must have asked you to tell me that."

"And he's already sent you some money from Coracora. You can buy yourself a new suit."

"And you will let me go out with Antero, Father?"

I took his hand.

"With Antero, Father?"

"Why not, son? You can go out with him Saturday afternoon, and I'll give you some spending money."

I ventured to put my feet on the carpeting and stand up.

"Let's go," said the priest.

As he put his arm around my neck, I could smell the lotion that he used on his hair. We left the room. From the balcony we saw the rockets rising and bursting in the sky.

"Death to the *chicheras*! Down with them!" shouted the people in the streets.

"That's still the way of the world," said the Rector. "While some people are celebrating, others are hiding."

"And Lleras?" I asked.

"He's sure to be lost. He ran away from us. Now, son! Why is it that when I'm with you we always speak of such serious matters? From now on you must just study and play. And that's all!"

"Yes, Father. Maybe Lleras has been turned into a lost soul because of the way he bullied the little boys."

"Run, call the priests," he bade me. "Ring the bell, ring it three times."

I descended the steps and rang the bell. The priests and Brother Miguel went to the upstairs parlor.

Añuco did not come to the dining hall. The Rector sat at the head of the table. I had thought of going to the playground that evening with him to make the *winko* sing, and repeat the message to my father. I'd throw the top up into the air and then, guiding myself by its humming sound, catch it on the palm of my hand. I would have spun it in a corner of the dark courtyard.

None of the boys went to the playground after supper. We saw the priests coming to the dining hall, bringing Añuco, guarding him. I couldn't speak to him as they went out; he walked in the midst of the group of priests, his eyes on the ground. I did not dare to call to him. His face was immobile. He never associated with us again.

I called Romero.

"Romerito," I said. "Could you play the Apurímac carnival song on your harmonica for me, out there on the playground?"

"Why?" he asked.

"Abancay has the weight of the sky on it. Only your harmonica and the *zumbayllu* can reach the mountain peaks. I want to send a message to my father. He's in Coracora now. Have you seen how the clouds get like molasses taffy over the sugar-cane fields? But the *zumbayllu*'s song can go through them. At noontime the *winko* sent its song flying and Antero and I sent it in the direction of Chalhuanca by blowing on it."

"You can do that with water, too," said Romero. "Like the school water over there; it comes from a mountain spring, not from the Mariño River. Put your mouth to the stream of water and speak through it."

"I don't believe that, Romerito. I just can't believe it. The cordillera is worse than steel. If you shout, your voice echoes back to you."

"But water can trickle down even through *alaymosca* rock. Haven't you seen water seeping out of the cliff rocks?"

"But how's the water going to get through into whatever house my father is staying in right now?"

"What a *cholo* you are, stranger! Isn't your blood made of water? It's through the blood that water, which is always there under the ground, speaks to the soul."

"I don't believe it, Romerito. Come, and play your harmonica."

"Harmonica? Don't you see it has tin on it? The *winku* is different. The *winku* hums so loudly that no one can hold it back. It's like a star twinkling. That's how it is, just like that. But Brother Miguel tamed it by blessing it in the chapel; he took away its strength."

Palacitos noticed we were whispering, and came running over to us.

"Don't you think the harmonica's song would go as far as a hundred leagues if someone pleaded with it?" Romero asked him.

"I wanted to send my father a message with the harmonica's song, Palacitos," I told him. "Romero will play 'Apurímac Mayu' . . . I'll beg the song to go through the air, between the mountain peaks, to reach my father's ears so that he may hear it. He'll know it's my voice. Will it reach him, Palacitos? Will the music reach Coracora if I plead with it in Quechua? You know more about these things than I do."

"What about that tin on the harmonica? He has to rip that off first."

"Why?"

"The harmonica's wood must be exposed to the air. Didn't you know that?"

"That's right," said Romero. "I know."

With his teeth he tore off the strip of tin on which the factory trademark appeared. He was an athlete, a good-natured Indian from Andahuaylas.

"Let's go," I said.

We managed to reach the darkened playground alone.

He played the carnival song.

The music would go down through the scattered woodlands to the Pachachaca. It would cross the bridge and climb up through the gorges. Once it had reached the highlands it would be easier; in the snow it would take on new strength, re-echoing and flying with the winds, across the steppe lakes and the dry grass that, in the great silence, transmits every sound.

"If the *winko*'s voice didn't reach you, here comes a carnival song," I said, thinking of my father, as Romero played the harmonica. "Let the whole world try to overcome me. Let it try. It won't succeed," I continued with growing enthusiasm. "Nor shall the sun, nor the choking dust of the valley, nor the Rector, nor the regiment. I will go; I will go in spite of everything."

"That's fighting music," came Chipro's voice from the edge of the courtyard, as he came up onto the playground.

He, too, started to sing.

"Look! The idiot!" exclaimed Palacitos, pointing to the figure of the feeble-minded woman, who was coming out into the courtyard. She stopped.

"Go away!" Chipro yelled at her.

Romero kept on playing.

Wig also appeared. He wanted to hurry the idiot off to the latrine. She resisted.

"Wig's a beast!" said Chipro.

We saw Wig kicking the madwoman and heard him insult her.

Romero stopped playing.

"Get out of here, Wig, or I'll crack your skull."

While Wig stopped to look around and see if Romero had decided to interfere, the idiot escaped. Wig wanted to follow her. Romero stamped his foot. Wig hesitated for a moment, and the madwoman disappeared down the passageway.

"What a beast Wig is," exclaimed Ismodes. "What a damned beast."

In a little while we were called up to the dormitory.

Next day the town boys did not come to school. The gatekeeper opened the entryway at the usual time. Father Augusto had it closed a long while afterwards. The Rector was busy with town affairs.

Añuco did not come down to the courtyard. In the morning his cot, his trunk, and a little chest—in which he kept dried insects, castor beans, *huayruros*,[1] glass marbles, and colored rags—were taken out of the dormitory. He had kept his chest locked, and only a few of us boarders had been able to see, from a distance, the mixture of colors and curious objects he saved. We knew he had a collection of glass marbles that we called *daños*[2] because they were the biggest; all the ones Añuco bought had red streaks, many different shades of red, even yellowish. He played with these, always choosing weaker or less skillful opponents. And he never lost a marble. He kept the *daños* with the insects. We were fascinated by the little glass spheres, by those dark waves of color, some narrow and drawn out into several swirls, and others that widened out in the center of the marble into a single bundle and thinned out smoothly at the ends. There were reddish streaks in Añuco's new marbles, but in the cloudy, chipped ones the bands of color also appeared, strangely and inexplicably. Añuco's things were taken to Father Augusto's cell.

Around twelve o'clock Añuco looked out over the balcony railing. He did not call anyone. It seemed to us that his eyes were even more deep-set in their sockets. His complexion was a pale, almost greenish color. This time his pallor was to his advantage. The boarders respected his privacy. In a little while he disappeared. Valle, reading by the fountain, smiled.

A day-pupil who was a friend of Iño Villegas came in through the little door set into the gate. He ran to the end of the archway, followed by the gatekeeper. There we caught up with him.

"They're flogging the *chicheras* at the jail," he said. "Some of them screamed real loud, as if they wanted to get everybody stirred up. They say that they're flogging them on the rear with their husbands watching. Since they don't have underpants on, they can see everything. A lot of them have insulted the Colonel, in Quechua and in Spanish. Now, you know nobody in the world can be as insolent as they can. They stuffed excrement into their mouths. It's even worse than that, they say! It's a battle of insults against whips . . ."

"Homeric! It's Homeric!" exclaimed Valle.

No one paid any attention to him.

" 'Don't make me swallow the little Colonel's shit! It's shit! It's shit! It must have been shit! Did they bring the shit from Cuzco?

---

1. A kind of red and black colored seed native to Peru.—Author
2. Damages; the name given to animals which stray onto someone else's land and are held by the landowner. Here it refers to winnings in a game of marbles.—Trans.

How well they squeezed it out of him! Hooray for the one who did it! That's the way to make the Colonel give birth, by God!' That's what one of the *chicheras* said, one of the ones who went to Patibamba. People are snickering about it in the street."

"Who are they laughing at?"

"At the *cholas* probably, but there are soldiers with rifles in Huanupata and on all the street corners. The policemen are searching the highland villages and the cane fields for the women who got away."

"What about Doña Felipa?" I asked.

"They say she escaped in the night. But she's been seen. They've gone out after her—a sergeant and a lot of policemen. She went down the Pachachaca. They say she has relatives in Andahuaylas."

"Did they say if she had any rifles?"

"That's why so many of them went after her. She and another woman are on muleback. They were seen trotting downhill with rifles slung over their shoulders. They say that because of their white hats they make good targets, and that they'll surely be able to pick them off on the slope because the police are riding cavalry horses."

"The police or the soldiers?" asked Valle.

"How should I know? But they'll catch up with them."

"Not if they're policemen, they won't; if they're regular troops or *guardias civiles*,[3] they might, they might . . ."

"Why didn't the town boys come to school?"

"Everybody's worried. The *cholas'* screaming has got everybody all excited. They insulted the Colonel like lost souls. They're not frightened a bit, and might start an uprising among the Indians and the *cholos*. There's going to be a proclamation from the prefect today. The town crier is going to read the proclamation. If they kill the two *chicheras* . . ."

"Nobody'll know anything about it," said Valle, laughing. "They'll throw them into the river."

"Indians just die," said Romero. "But a *chichera* with a rifle? Have you already forgotten what happened on Saturday?"

"But this time it's the army. And the women either have their backs turned or their bottoms bare. Nothing's going to happen."

Iño's friend went off. The gatekeeper made him leave. The boarding students did not gather in groups; they dispersed.

The sun was heating up the courtyard. From the shadow of the archway and the porch we looked out onto the blazing paving

3. National rural police.—Trans.

stones. The sun instills silence when it shines into the depths of these rocky, bushy ravines at midday. There are no large trees.

Several bumblebees crossed the porch, from one end of it to the other. The slow flight of these insects, whose black bodies absorb the fiery heat unharmed, caught my eye. I followed them. They burrowed into the wood of the pillars, their wings buzzing. Doña Felipa might perhaps be firing on the troops from the shade of a bush at this very moment. They'd kill her in the end, there were so many of them, and bury her in some secluded spot in the canyon. But it could be that she might fire on them from behind some rocky parapet, or hole up in some labyrinthine passage or archway on the right bank of the river, which becomes steep and rocky near the bridge. The call of the migratory parrots re-echoes there. If this should happen, I thought, watching the slow flight of the bumblebees, she might even now be aiming her rifle, staring until she made out even the ants on the road opposite her. She would take aim with her small eye, which shone like a diamond in her enormous, pockmarked face. Then she could only be wounded in the head and would fall from the top of the cliff into the Pachachaca. Maybe they wouldn't be able to get to her body. That was important, I thought. What mightn't the furious policemen be capable of doing at the sight of such a hated, bullet-ridden, mutilated body?

But we learned later that her pursuers had found one of the mules that had fallen down in the middle of the Pachachaca bridge. Someone had killed it by slitting its throat and had strung its intestines across the bridge, tying the animal's guts to the crosses on either side. Some travelers had stopped there. They had looked at the strands without daring to cut them. From one of the stone crosses a halter dangled down into the river. And a shawl made of Castilian cloth fluttered from the top of the cross.

The *guardias* cut the intestines that were obstructing traffic, and as they were looking at the halter that hung down into the river, they heard a group of women sing out from a hiding place on the Abancay side:

"*Huayruro,*" *ama baleaychu*;	Huayruro,[4] don't shoot
chakapatapi chakaykuy;	on the bridge, on the bridge;
"*huayruro,*" *ama sipiychu*	huayruro, don't kill;
chakapatapi suyaykuy,	sit down on the bridge
tiayaykuy; *ama manchaychu.*	and wait, don't be afraid.

4. Quechua nickname given to the *guardias civiles* because of the color of their uniform.—Author

The *guardias* mounted their horses; they galloped across the bridge and along the narrow stretch of level road that skirted the cliff. They had already gone part of the way up the immense slope when they heard shots; seeing dust rising from the bridge, they halted. A bullet struck quite close to them. They dismounted and observed the mountain opposite them. It was wooded, not stony like the one they were climbing. The sugar-cane fields came down almost to the river's edge and were bordered by guava and *pacae* trees. On the sheerest slopes there were clumps of pepper trees.

"The *cholas* stayed back on the other side where there's brush," said the sergeant.

"The viragos are going to force us to cross the bridge under fire; they've got it all figured."

"They're firing from two places."

The sergeant ordered them to turn back.

"They can't screw us up," he said. "Gallop across one at a time. The *chicheras* can't possibly be good shots."

The firing continued. When the *guardias* reached the precipice on which one end of the bridge rests, they stopped to watch and listen. The Pachachaca roars in the silence; the noise of its waters spreads out like another universe within the universe, and beneath that surface one hears the insects, even a locust hopping about in the brush.

There was no firing so long as the *guardias* were halted in the bend where the level stretch comes out onto the bridge. The sergeant raced along the road and crossed the bridge at a gallop, with the *guardias* following him. They went up the slope at a trot. High up the hill they found the two rifles hanging from a pepper tree.

"They've made fools of us," said one of the *guardias*. "Those weren't the ringleaders. They must be far from here by now; they must have taken the footpaths. They can get to the top of the mountain quicker than a horse."

"Take one man with you and follow them, even if you have to go the whole way to Andahuaylas," the sergeant had ordered Zamalla, who was nicknamed "Machete" and was the oldest of the *guardias*. "I'll take the rifles. There's no danger now; don't forget one of them is wounded."

The tale was told by many people in Abancay. There had been witnesses: the travelers who had been stopped on the bridge and who had seen the *guardias* turn back, the *cholas* who had sung out from the brush while the *guardias* were looking at the river and then fired at them, and the *guardias civiles* themselves.

For a long time, at night, in Abancay and the neighboring villages groups of men and women sang the same *jarahui*, "Don't shoot, *huayruro* . . . ," but they added another verse:

Fusil warkusk'atas tarinku,	They found the rifles hanging,
mana piyta sipisk'anta.	that had done no killing.
Mula yawarllas chakapatapi	From the bridge only mule blood
sutuspa sutusiask'a	seeped, was seeping,
sutuspa sutusiask'a.	seeped, was seeping.

It was said that they sang it all over the city, and one night even came quite close to the main square.

On Saturday afternoon Antero came to see me. We chatted on the playground.

"They kicked the *chicheras'* husbands out of jail and made them sweep the street," he told me. "There were ten of them. Two were Doña Felipa's. They tied tails made from rags on them and, kicking them as they went, made them sweep the pavement. At the end of the block they let them go, and set off rockets as they ran away. It was all done at the jail warden's orders."

"Is it true, Antero, that the *chicheras'* husbands are quite meek?"

"Doña Felipa's are, they say. She had two. They claim she threw the warden out of her *chichería* because he wanted to stay there and sleep. He was drunk and they left him lying in the street. Now he's gotten even with her. But Doña Felipa has promised to return to Abancay. Some people say she went down into the jungle. She's threatened to come back up the river with the Chuncho Indians and set fire to the haciendas. Lleras has run off with a mestiza from Huanupata. They headed for Cuzco on horseback. The mestiza was a seamstress and had a bar in the Huanupata district. Lleras has put a curse on Abancay! He's been saying he knocked down Brother Miguel and trampled him. Everybody knows about it now. All the ladies and pious women [5] are praying for the friar. 'Even though he's black, he wears priest's clothing,' they say. But they want him to leave Abancay. The aunt I live with told me, 'We're going to ask the Rector to send him away—a friar who has been affronted shouldn't stay here in town any longer; he shouldn't even go out in the street.' Rondinel's mother has decided not to send him back to school; they're going to transfer him to a boarding school in Cuzco. 'Where God has been offended, my son shall not go,' she said. And she won't let him out of the house. Skinny was crying; I saw him."

5. *Beatas*—pious, sanctimonious, very religious women.—Trans.

"Where will Lleras go?" I asked Antero. "If he goes along the banks of the Apurímac, when he gets to Deep Canyon the sun will melt him; his body will drip down off the back of his horse onto the road like wax."

"Are you putting a curse on him?"

"No. The sun will melt him. It won't let his body cast a shadow any more. It's his own fault. The town would have had bad luck, but the school might have been spared. Lleras has been hatching out a curse against the school for a long time."

"And Añuco?"

"He's nearly dead. I gave him the *winko* and that revived him a little. When Brother Miguel blessed us, he blessed the *zumbayllu* too and burnt out its magic powers. But it still sings and dances as well as ever. Añuco will tame it, in the end; it was born to be free, and now it's in a cell, the same as its new owner. Mold will grow on its tip and in its eyes, just as Añuco's spirit has already been extinguished. I believe that since he's an orphan, the priests have decided to make him a friar too. That's what they were meeting about. And he's stopped hanging around with us ever since."

"That's the last of the school's bad guys, then," exclaimed Antero. "And what's even better, you're going to see Alcira today. Everything's quiet in Abancay, too. But they say that on all the haciendas people are talking about Doña Felipa; they're afraid. They say that if she comes back with the Chunchos and sets fire to the haciendas, the *colonos* might run away and join the *chicheras*."

"The *colonos*? They won't go, Markask'a; they won't!"

"There aren't many on my hacienda," he told me. "And they're always being flogged. My mother suffers for them; but my father has to do his duty. On the big haciendas they tie them to the *pisonay* trees in the courtyards or string them up by the hands to a tree limb and beat them. They have to be beaten. Then they start to weep, along with their wives and children. They don't weep as if they were being punished, but more like orphans do. It's sad. And when you hear them you feel like crying too, the way they do; I used to, brother, when I was a little boy. I don't know what I needed to be consoled about, but I wept as if I were seeking consolation, and not even my mother's arms could comfort me. Every year the Franciscan priests go to those haciendas to preach. You should see them, Ernesto! They speak in Quechua, bringing consolation to the Indians and making them sing mournful hymns. The *colonos* crawl around the hacienda chapels on their knees; moaning and groaning, they touch their faces to the ground and weep, day and night. And when the priests leave, you should see them!

The Indians follow them. The priests ride off rapidly and the Indians run after them, calling out to them, leaping over fences, bushes, and ditches, taking short cuts; shouting, they fall down, only to stumble to their feet again to climb the hills. They come back at night, and go on sobbing in the chapel doorways. My mother used to wear herself out trying to comfort me on such days, and never succeeded."

"I've heard the *colonos* in Patibamba, Markask'a!"

"When you're a child and hear something like that, a whole crowd of grownups weeping, it makes your heart feel faint like a night that never ends; it makes it feel faint and oppresses it forever after," said Antero excitedly.

"Markask'a," said I, "in the towns where I used to live with my father the Indians aren't *erk'es*.[6] Here it's as if they wouldn't let them grow up. They're always frightened, like little children. That feeling of faintness you were speaking about—I've only had it on bullfight days, when the bulls would gore the chests and bellies of the drunken Indians, and when, at dusk, on the edge of town, they would set free the condors that had been tied to the backs of the brave bulls. Then everyone would sing bitterly, men and women, suffering as the condors rose. But that song doesn't oppress you; it sweeps you along with it, as though you were looking for someone to fight, some damned scoundrel. Feelings like that seize hold of you; they clutch your insides."

"Ernesto," exclaimed Antero, "what if the Chunchos do come back with Doña Felipa? Where will the *colonos* rush off to when they see the sugar-cane fields ablaze? Maybe they'll go on to set fire to more barracks and more cane fields, and then run down the hill like stampeding cattle, seeking the river and the Chunchos. I know them, Ernesto, they can get awfully angry. What do you think?"

"Yes, Markask'a," I shouted. "I hope Doña Felipa comes. A man who weeps because they've been slapping his face for years for no reason at all can become angrier than a bull that hears a dynamite explosion, that feels the condor's beak on his neck. Let's go, Markask'a! Let's go to Huanupata!"

Antero stared at me. His birthmarks had a sort of glow to them. He gave me a piercing look with his jet-black eyes.

"As for me, brother, if the Indians rebelled, I could go and kill them easy," he said.

"I don't understand you, Antero," I answered in astonishment. "After what you said about having wept for them."

6. Crying children under five years of age.—Author

"I used to weep. Who wouldn't? But the Indians must be kept down. You can't understand because you're not a landowner. Let's go to Condebamba; that's the best thing to do."

It was Saturday. We could leave the school. The Rector had bought me a new suit.

"To Condebamba? What for?"

"Alcira and Salvinia are waiting for us, under the poplar trees. With your new clothing even I am jealous of you. Alcira will be envious."

"Is it far, is your hacienda very far from the bridge?"

"From what bridge?"

"From the Pachachaca."

"It's a long way, two days."

"And the Chunchos?"

"They're three days from my hacienda."

"Down the Apurímac?"

"You must go upstream if you're coming to Abancay."

"Whom do you think the Pachachaca takes sides with?"

"Are you talking about us? About you and me, and about Salvinia and Alcira?"

"No, Candle, I'm talking about the *colonos*, the Chunchos and Doña Felipa, against you and the *guardias*."

"Probably the Pachachaca's on Doña Felipa's side. He stopped the *guardias civiles*. Doña Felipa's shawl is still hanging on the cross on the bridge. They say the river and the bridge frighten away anyone who tries to take it down. The wind will carry it off."

"You just go on to Condebamba alone, Candle."

"Why did you call me 'Candle'?"

"Don't we all call you 'Candle'?"

"Not you. You've been calling me 'Markask'a' ever since I gave you my *zumbayllu* in front of Lleras."

"You go to Condebamba, Antero. I still have time to get to the river."

"To the river?"

"I'll speak to him about you, about Salvinia, about Doña Felipa. I'll tell him you are capable of shooting at the *colonos*; that you're going to string them up to the *pisonayes* on your hacienda and beat them, like your father."

"What?"

"Isn't that the truth?"

"You're sick, Ernesto. What about the *winko*? Why did you give it to Añuco?"

"I still have the other one. The first one! I'll make it dance on some boulder in the Pachachaca. In the sky its voice will merge with the voice of the river; it'll reach your hacienda and the ears and innocent hearts of your *colonos,* the ones that your father flogs every once in a while so they'll never grow up, so they'll always be like little children. Now I know. You've taught me. I'll call her to come and set the cane fields afire on both sides of the river. The Pachachaca will help her! You said yourself he was on her side; maybe he'll reverse his current and come back, bringing the Chunchos' rafts."

"You're sick, you're raving mad, little brother, only the *winkos* can carry messages. Just *winkos,* that's all! And you've told me how Brother Miguel ruined your *winko* in the chapel! Let's go to Condebamba! What would Salvinia say if she knew you'd been begging the Pachachaca to bring the Chunchos to burn up the valley? So that everyone would die, Christians and animals! Everything burning while you celebrate! You must be delirious. Alcira will calm you. Just the sight of her . . ."

He put his arm around my neck and led me out of the school. My new rubber shoes were gleaming; I felt awkward in the new suit I was wearing for the first time.

"Let's go to the river, Markask'a!" I begged him in Quechua. "The Pachachaca knows the spirit in which the little children come to him, and why they come to him."

"Sure. We have all day Sunday. I'll swim across under the bridge. You'll see how Lord Pachachaca respects me. I'll dedicate that crossing to you; I'll dive into the swiftest rapids. You can tell Salvinia about it afterwards."

"I'll follow you, Markask'a. The river knows me."

"Not if you get into him. Not if you go against the current. He'll want to sweep you along and break your bones on the boulders. It's not the same at all as when you speak to him humbly from the bank or look down at him from the bridge."

"I'll cross it, wherever you do!"

"Maybe."

"But out in the middle of the stream is scarier; what I mean is that the Pachachaca's like an evil spirit there. He's not the Lord you imagine him to be when you're just watching him. He's a demon; when you feel his full strength, you're in the clutches of all the spirits that peer out from the cliff tops, from the caves, from the mine shafts, from the Spanish moss that dangles from the trees, swaying in the wind. You must not go in; you must not! As for me, I'm like a son to him."

All the same, Markask'a took me with him to the poplar grove.

The *calandrias* were singing in the mulberry bushes as if they had been trained. Usually they perch on the highest branches. They were also singing and swinging in the tops of the few weeping willows that grew among the mulberries. The native word for the *calandria* is *tuya*. A flashy, strong-beaked bird, it flies to the highest part of the trees. In the tops of the darkest ones—the *lúcumo*, the *lambra*, the avocado (but especially the *lúcumo*, which is straight trunked and crowned with a whorl of branches)—the *tuya* sings. Its tiny, yellow, black-winged body may easily be seen against the sky and the coloring of the tree. The bird flies from one branch to another higher one, or to another neighboring tree, to sing, changing its melody. It does not go up into the cold regions. Its song transmits the secrets of the deep valleys. From the beginning, the men of Peru have composed music on hearing it and seeing it wing across space, beneath the mountains and the clouds, which in no other part of the world are so extreme. *Tuya, tuya!* As I listened to its song, which is surely the stuff of which I am made, that nebulous region from which I was torn to be cast in among men, we saw the two girls appear in the poplar grove.

Alcira was an almost identical portrait of another girl I had loved when I was ten years old. I had met her in Saisa, a dry, waterless village of goatherds, that produced nothing but gourds. The young girl from Saisa had hair the color and texture of thrashed barley straw. Her eyes were blue, like my father's, but were restless, like those of a highland bird; and they could not possibly have been any larger; they were like mountain pools. Her dress was made of calico, and she wore high-buttoned shoes. Her sweetheart was a brandy smuggler, a bristly-haired man; the palms of his enormous, calloused hands were the color of death. She was called Clorinda. I had only two days to contemplate her, and then we went on with our journey. I repeated her name as I crossed the great desert that separates Saisa from a southern port.

Alcira's face was so much like that of Clorinda's that for a few moments I thought she was the young girl of my childhood and that she must have run away from her sweetheart and her village.

In the girls' presence I was unable to overcome my embarrassment. I decided to leave. I had to go to the river, even though it meant coming back at night. Salvinia stared at me in surprise; I realized she was looking me over as if she had never met me before. Alcira raised her eyes only twice. She seemed to be afraid of Salvinia. We were in the shade of a leafy mulberry bush, which sheltered us. I stole a brief glance at Alcira and discovered that her calves were very thick and short and that she was quite short-legged. When I looked at her face again I felt relieved.

"I must go to Patibamba," I said.

"From here? Now?" asked Salvinia.

"I must go. So long. Where do you live, Alcira?" I asked her.

"On the road from the Plaza de Armas to the electric plant."

I shook hands with Alcira and then with Salvinia, without looking at Antero. I began to run. Antero took a few steps after me. I didn't hear him say anything.

I fled down the poplar-lined avenue, returning to town. I went to see the barracks. They were being painted. Ten men were slapping paint on them with some swabs made of skins tied to the ends of long century-plant stalks. At the gate two soldiers stood guard; a sergeant leaned against the wall in the shade, watching the field. Through the large gateway I could see some enormous horses, and several officers crossing the courtyard. They had cut down the bushes around the barracks. I stopped in front of the gate for a few moments. Then I took off toward Huanupata.

"Alcira, Alcira!" I said as I ran along. "Clorinda!"

The *chicha* bars were open. I went into two of them. Several soldiers were eating chili peppers and had huge glasses of *chicha* on the table before them. The waitresses were serving them.

"Soon there'll be music," I thought, "and the soldiers will dance. It's Saturday."

The soldiers were speaking Quechua, telling dirty jokes and puns and laughing. The waitresses were enjoying themselves.

The neighborhood was not quiet. There were people about. I hurried over to the *chicha* bar in front of which I had stopped on my return from Patibamba the day the *chicheras* rioted, and found it open. It was Doña Felipa's. I went in. There were more soldiers inside. I didn't stop at the tables, but proceeded straight through and out into the back yard. I found a dog there tied to a stake. He was stretched out on the filthy ground, amid the refuse. Clouds of flies were buzzing around; the air was black with them. The dog did not growl at me. I approached him. A soldier came out and urinated against the wall. Then he looked at me intently.

"Your dog?" he asked.

"It's Doña Felipa's," I said.

"Fuck it! We'll give it one shot. One little shot, that's all."

"They say Doña Felipa's certain to come back with the Chunchos," I told him.

The soldier began to laugh.

"It'll have to be her ghost, then. By now she's all fucked up in San Miguel. For sure!"

He was drunk.

"None for the army, damn it. For us, me, boss, chief. Woman here, cry and cry, but screw her anyhow. Nice, damn it, Abancay woman. Beautiful weeping, damn it."

I went out of the yard. I asked one of the mestizas who it was that had opened up the *chicha* bar.

"Doña Felipa's husband," she answered, pointing to him.

He was sitting at one of the tables, with two *cholas*.

He had the florid complexion of a hot-pepper addict. He cut up a large, yellow green chili pepper, slicing it carefully. His forehead was beaded with sweat.

"Is it true they've killed Doña Felipa?" I asked the mestiza, looking her in the eye.

"*Jajayllas! Jajayllas!*" she shrieked with laughter. "Drunken soldier sure dreaming. Drunk is drunk! Get out of here, kid!" She gave me a push.

I went out into the street. The soldier who had spoken to me in the yard was approaching, staggering to a table.

The river road started there, quite nearby. One of the little varicolored crosses which mark the beginning of the long roads appeared, fastened to a stone at the street corner; the white cloth that shrouded it fluttered in the breeze.

I began to run. I had to go down to the Pachachaca, to the bridge. To see the ringleader's shawl and the blood spots left by the animal whose throat had been cut, to see the river and speak to him, to give him my messages and to ask him about Clorinda.

I saw Father Augusto coming down the hill on the other side. He was riding a mule and was already quite close to the river. I remembered then that he had been called to Raurabamba to say mass in the hacienda chapel. I had to conceal myself before he reached the bridge, and let him go by. I hid behind a guava tree that was held prisoner by vines. The little vine leaves spread out over the wall that bordered the road and climbed up over the tree, enveloping it. It bore some silvery pods with a sweet, silky pulp. I picked some and chewed them as I watched the priest near the bridge. He crossed it at the slow pace of the animal. Then I spied the idiot, the feeble-minded woman from the school, running, half-hidden by the bushes, a short distance behind the priest. At that moment I spotted Doña Felipa's shawl on the stone cross of the bridge; it was fluttering in the wind. It was orange colored.

The idiot reached the bridge; still running she went out onto the roadway and stopped in front of the cross. She stared at the Castilian cloth of which the shawl was made. She stood by the cross for a while, looking at the road on my side of the river, and then bellowed loudly. She wasn't mute, but that was the only way she could shout. She bellowed several times. I went on down, then, until I came to a high rock that was near the river, on the edge of a cane field. From the top of the rock I saw that Father Augusto had stopped on the road and was beckoning for the feeble-minded woman to come; she was calling to him, too. The priest spurred his mule on, and left the idiot behind. I was afraid for her. The bridge is very high and the water alluring as it swirls along, splashing against the abutments; and the damp, rocky precipice that rises sheerly from the bridge toward the sky oppresses the heart; there on the floor of the bridge one could hear a sort of hum, a deep metallic sound coming from inside the cliff, of rough water, of the sky itself, so remote, shut out by the rocks. I knew that skittish animals sometimes buck on the bridge, and that then the riders jump off, because if the frightened beasts run near the sides they can throw their riders into the river.

The idiot climbed up onto the side of the bridge. Unable to reach the shawl from there, she grasped the cross and began to climb it, like a bear. She got up to one arm of the cross, hung onto it, and managed to pull her chest up onto the outstretched stone. I started to run, then; the priest had already gone. I went down through the bushes, tearing the creepers. The idiot tore the cloth loose and tied it around her neck. I was at the approach to the bridge. She was hugging the crosspiece with her back to the river, not to the roadway. How could she get her hands down from the arms of the cross? She'd fall into the Pachachaca. Perhaps she deserved it. But she went circling round the vertical stone with her chest and belly to it and put both feet down on the side of the bridge. There she rested a moment. Presently she jumped down into the roadway. She shook out the shawl jubilantly and draped it around her shoulders. "I'll go," I thought, "I'll take the shawl away from her and throw it into the river. I'll bring her right back to the woods." But she started to run off, bellowing, bellowing like a lost soul. She passed by without looking at me. Her face shone with joy. She was calling Father Augusto, or perhaps Lleras. She disappeared, zigzagging up the slope, still running, so short and squat. She bellowed in the tone of voice that is typical of short-necked, fat people.

I went up onto the bridge. My first thoughts, the desires with which I had come down to the Pachachaca, had been upset. Several swallows were amusing themselves by darting through the eyes of the bridge, skimming over the water and the stone parapet, flying off and returning. They passed over the crosses, always on an erratic course; never pausing nor slowing their flight, they paid delicate homage to the great bridge, to the current that roared along in a hurtling cavalcade, splashing through the bottom of the gorge where, for an instant, I felt like a fragile worm, even lowlier than the winged crickets that passers-by crushed underfoot in the streets of Abancay.

Then I remembered Doña Felipa, Clorinda, and the mestiza from the *chicha* bar.

"You're like the river, *señora*," I said, thinking of the ringleader and watching the stream flow round a sharp bend in the distance and lose itself in the flowering gorse. "They'll never catch you. *Jajayllas!* And you'll return. I will see your face, powerful as the noonday sun. We'll set fires. We'll burn everything down! We'll put the idiot in a convent. Lleras must have melted away by now. Añuco must be dying, I think. And you, Pachachaca River, give me the strength to go up the slope like a swallow! I must guard Alcira's house. And if I come tomorrow with Markask'a, don't kill him; just frighten him and let me cross quickly, like the *zumbayllu*'s song. Like the *zumbayllu*'s song!"

I set off up the hill at a run, certain I would reach Abancay before Father Augusto. I stopped for a moment on the edge of the path to contemplate the river. The swallows sheared through the air soundlessly, came up to me in their circling, and, like black stars, darted down through the arches of the bridge.

"I shan't be any slower than you, swallow!" I exclaimed.

But on the outskirts of Patibamba I had to stop and rest. I had left Father Augusto and the idiot behind. They were coming up on the main road while I had taken a short cut along the footpaths.

"What impudence," I said to myself. "To even think of the daughters of the bridge. They're swifter than the clouds and the water. But no Abancay schoolboy is faster than I. Not even Markask'a!"

I came into town just as it was growing dark. The soldiers were leaving Huanupata in groups. A sergeant was herding them along, watching them. The clouds were aflame, blazing up from the west toward the center of the sky.

"Me, *patroncito!*" said a soldier sobbing and mixing barbarous Spanish with his Rukana Quechua. "Me . . . chief, *aguila, waman-*

challay, patu rialchallay.[7] That makes four screwed now; sure, pregnant by me, in a strange town! Me . . . ! *Runapa llak'tampi ñok'achallay . . ."*[8]

He was weeping. The sergeant kicked him. The soldier's face froze; his expression grew rigid. He attempted to march, but instead began to sing again, softly, *"Aguila, wamanchallay, patu rialchallay."* And he said, "Pregnant by me, in a strange town, all fucked up."

"If he were to see the bridge," I said to myself, "if he should see the bridge, this Rukana Indian might stop weeping, or, roaring, he might throw himself headlong from the cross into the river."

I should have gone down toward the electric plant, to guard Alcira's house. I should have hurried, but I couldn't. I followed the soldier to the Plaza de Armas. He closed his eyes and felt his way along. He spoke the same kind of Quechua as I did. At the corner of the square the sergeant made the troops turn off to the left.

It was late; dusk was falling and it was growing dark. I went back to school. Inside I kept singing the soldier's unfinished *huayno*: "When I saw you from the heights, you were all alone, weeping, royal eagle . . . ."

Most of the boarding students had already returned to the school. They seemed to be content. Romero was playing his mouth organ on the porch steps. Palacios was sitting beside him.

The gatekeeper came over and told us, "Father Miguel is leaving for Cuzco early tomorrow morning, with the boy, Añuco. The horses are already here."

---

7. First words of a *huayno*: "O eagle, O kestrel, O royal duck."—Author
8. "All alone, all alone in a strange town."—Author

10. Yawar Mayu

Brother Miguel did not come down to say the rosary with us, nor did the Rector preside over the dining hall. We ate in silence. Palacitos approached Father Cárpena in the passageway and inquired loudly, "Is Brother Miguel leaving, Father? Is Añuco leaving?"

"I don't know anything about it," answered the priest curtly. Palacitos returned to the dining hall doorway.

"They're leaving," he said in Quechua. "This time Lleras will really be turned into a lost soul; growing bristles on his body, he will sweat and frighten the animals in the cordillera. He'll shriek from the mountaintops in the night, cause rocky crags to tumble down, and rattle his chains. No one, no one, not even his mother, will ever forgive him. Oh dear God!"

He glanced at Valle, who was staring at him.

"Go to confession tomorrow, Valle," he told him in Spanish, with unexpected energy. "Confess your sins to the Rector, so you may have a heart."

Chipro was with us.

"I'll confess," said Valle, smiling, and walked off toward the courtyard.

"I'd like to beat him up in a *real* fight," said Chipro.

"Tomorrow, before Brother Miguel leaves," said Chauca. "Challenge him now. And we'll get up early in the morning."

NOTE: The title of this chapter, "Yawar Mayu," means "bloody river," as has already been explained by the author.—Trans.

"Not tomorrow," said Palacitos.

"Tomorrow," insisted Chauca. "I've heard the regimental band is going to give a concert in the plaza after mass, in the afternoon. If you give Valle a black eye, he won't be able to strut around like a peacock with his *k'ompo*. Beat him up!"

Chipro went off to the courtyard, calling, "Valle! Valle! Hey, you weak reed! Hey turkey!"

We followed him.

Valle was waiting for him in the courtyard, by the first pillar.

"Is there going to be a concert tomorrow?" Chipro asked him.

All of us had reached the courtyard.

"Why tomorrow?"

"Because tomorrow I'm going to beat you up; not like the other day, not in the tender parts; tomorrow we fight until we cut each other's faces open. Don't you want to get revenge? At dawn, on the playground."

Valle hesitated before answering, "Tomorrow! All right, you're a sneaky Indian. Wake me up."

And he went off down the porch.

"Not if Brother Miguel stays, Chipro," said Palacios. "If Brother Miguel stays we'll go to the concert with Valle."

"Valle? You think he'd go with you?" asked Chipro.

"No, he'll go with his young ladies. But if Brother Miguel and Añuco leave, beat him up. I'll pray for you. You'll beat the shit out of him. That will really make him confess."

"All right," said Chipro.

It was a dark night; Wig disappeared. In a little while the older boarders also disappeared. They went to the inner courtyard.

"Lost souls can never find rest," Palacitos informed us on the porch. "They can't even find anyone to burn them. Because if someone tricks them and corrals them in a field with high walls, or in a store, then he can burn them up by building a fire of brushwood or kerosene round and round them. But you've got to be a saint to corral a lost soul. They burn like hogs, squealing, calling for help, trembling; even the stones, they say, split asunder when the groans of the damned go through them. And if they hear anyone playing the *quena*[1] then, when they're blazing up like that, they dance mournfully. But when they're all burnt up a dove arises from their ashes. How many lost souls must there be who are suffering eternal punishment! On all fours they gallop across the cor-

[1]. A reed flute with a slot in one end which the musician blows across.—Trans.

dillera, through the snow-clad mountains, and enter the lakes; they go down into the valleys, too, but not very often. Lleras must already feel his skin hardening, and feel the fat growing under his hide. Poor thing!"

"And his woman?"

"She'll be the first one he'll devour, dear God!"

The older boys came back from the inner courtyard. Wig went upstairs to the balcony.

At that instant the idiot must have been laughing as she contemplated her shawl, or perhaps she might have hidden it in some drawer in the pantry. She had practically danced up the hill, with the shawl over her shoulders. She hadn't gone to the playground.

In the middle of the night we heard the sound of horses' hoofs in the courtyard. I was awake. Palacitos got to his knees in his bed. Chipro heard it, then Chauca and Iño. We got dressed.

"Wake up Valle," said Chauca, as Chipro came tiptoeing over to my bed.

"No, we'll say good-bye to Añuco first," I told him.

We went out onto the balcony together.

The waning moon shone down on the courtyard. Two saddled horses waited at the foot of the stairs. A man was holding them by the reins. A loaded mule stamped the paving stones near the fountain. Father Augusto's bedroom was open. Brother Miguel came out of there, and the moonlight illumined his white vestments; his felt hat cast a shadow on his face. We were barefooted. Then Añuco came out. I had never seen him look so small as he did in that light and in the stillness. The roof peak was clearly visible; the moonlight made a halo over the housetops. The shadow of the walls, of the crosses on the roofs, of the weeds that grew between the roof tiles, seemed somehow blacker, sadder, and more lugubrious than all other nocturnal things. The friar and Añuco walked quite slowly. They looked at us without speaking. I reached the stairway first. The moon shone full on Brother Miguel's face; he laid his hands on my head and kissed me, then bent over Palacitos and kissed him on the forehead. When Añuco came nearer and the moonlight illumined his sunken eyes, I could no longer hold back my sobs. But he was determined not to cry. "Good-bye," he said, and shook my hand. His face had grown longer; he wore a gleaming white starched shirt. "I'm leaving, I'm going away," he told me. And as I did not move, he held out his hand to Palacitos. "I'm leaving you my *daño* marbles," he said. "Don't let anyone take them away; Father Augusto is going to give them to you." I stepped aside. Palacitos hugged him. "No, I won't let anyone see them, just the people from my home town," he answered. He did not cry. He was confused by his happiness at receiving the gift. Bathed in moonlight, Añuco descended the steps. They mounted their horses. Brother Miguel rode in the lead as they went out. Añuco looked back at us from the arched entryway, reined in his horse, and waved his arm in farewell. Not only did he seem terribly small on horseback, but he looked thin and frail as well, as if he might soon die.

The courtyard was empty. Palacitos hugged me and burst into a flood of tears.

"Little brother, little brother, *papacito*," he wailed.

The night held him in its clutches—the night made even more unfathomable and suffocating by the leave-taking, a night in which life itself seemed to run the risk of vanishing into thin air.

Chipro, Iño, and Chauca emerged from the darkness, where they had been waiting.

Together we led Palacios away, holding him gently.

"Don't wake up Valle," he begged. "He must be respected. He must be loved."

"We won't wake him up! Let's not fight any more," I told Chipro.

Chipro nodded his head.

"No. Not any more," he said.

For a while we heard, through the windows, the sound of hoof-beats on the cobbled street. We went to bed and slept soundly.

In the morning, Valle looked over at Chipro.

"You didn't wake me up."

"What do you say we postpone it?" Chipro answered. "The band concert and the girls come first; there'll always be time for fighting. The regiment might leave."

Valle did not answer. There was a questioning look in his eyes.

"Forgive me, Valle, it's not that I'm afraid. Now that Brother Miguel is gone, I don't want to fight any more."

"That's reasonable, quite reasonable." Valle opened his wardrobe and busied himself with inspecting his neckties and suits.

Chipro came up to Palacitos and asked him, "Will you give me one of Añuco's *daños*?"

Iño, Chauca, and I gathered around Palacitos, without asking for anything. But he must have understood.

Palacitos hesitated, looking at us intently for a moment, before answering, almost solemnly, "I'll give Romero one, too. But don't play with them. They're to remember him by."

The city was transformed by the concert. During mass the Rector preached a long sermon, in Spanish. He never spoke Quechua in the Abancay church. Eulogizing the Colonel, who had been named prefect, he praised the regimental chief's generosity, judgment, and honesty. He said he had wisely punished each of the guilty people in accordance with their condition in life and brought peace to the city. "Those who fled because they were frightened by their guilt will return," he said. "Perhaps their only punishment will be the mortification and hardship they have undergone. There's been a bloodless deterrent. It was the women themselves who barbarously sacrificed a noble animal and used the victim's entrails to try to hold up traffic on the bridge." He announced that a detachment of *guardias civiles*, made up of police well trained to maintain order, would be installed permanently in the barracks. "The rabble is conjuring up a specter to frighten the Christians," he said. "And that is a ridiculous farce. The *colonos* on all the haciendas have innocent souls, they're better Christians than we are; and the Chunchos are savages who will never leave the bounds of the jungle. And if, by the devil's handiwork, they should come, their arrows would be powerless against cannons. We must remember Cajamarca . . . !" he exclaimed, and turning his eyes toward the Virgin he begged, in his high metallic voice, for forgiveness for the fugitives, for those who had gone astray. "You, dearly beloved Mother, will know how to cast out the devil from their bodies," he said. He knelt down in the pulpit and began to say the Hail Mary. Kneeling, the ladies and gentlemen, the mestizos and the schoolchildren, and some men from the Indian communities who had come to town with their women, chorused the prayer. "Doña Felipa, the idiot from the school has your shawl; dancing, dancing, she came up the hill with your shawl around her shoulders and now she doesn't go to the courtyard at night. She doesn't go any more!" I murmured in Quechua as the others prayed. "A soldier said they killed you, but it's not true! What little soldier could have killed you! Sighting along your rifle from a great distance, from the other side of the river, you could hit him in the hand, maybe in the heart. For the Pachachaca, the Apu, is with you. *Jajayllas!*"

"You're laughing," Chauca whispered to me.

Joining the chorus, I repeated the closing words of the Hail Mary and then said, "There isn't any more mule blood on the bridge; the dogs must have lapped it up by now."

As we left the church, in bright sunlight, the musicians played a march. It was a big band; they paraded, four abreast, to the center of the park. The last soldiers were illumined, almost dwarfed, by the huge, metallic instruments they carried.

"Little soldiers, little soldiers," yelled some boys, and we all followed them.

Most of us Abancay children had never heard a big army band. The little soldiers who carried those immense instruments in the last rows made us all happy; we leaped for joy. The bandleader wore the gold chevrons of a sergeant; he was quite tall; a handsome paunch lent solemnity to his great height.

The musicians formed rows in the park bandstand. I was with Palacitos and Chipro. We were intrigued by the black clarinets with their intricate metal parts; I watched the functioning of the thin silver arms that moved the stops, how they opened and closed the holes of the instrument, how they let out the air to make such unusual sounds. The saxophones were shiny all over; the soldiers raised them and turned them toward us. They sang with the voices of human beings, those silvery instruments on which not a single piece of wood or yellow metal could be seen. They held a single note sweetly for a long time; their deep voices flooded my soul. They weren't like the voice of the large southern *pinkuyllu*, nor like that of the Chanka *wak'rapuku*. In that scorching plaza, the brightly silver-plated saxophone sang as if it were the herald of the sun; truly, because none of the instruments I had ever seen in the Andean towns, no instrument manufactured by mestizos or Indians, has any relation to the sun. They are like the snow, like nocturnal light, like the voice of the water, of the wind, or of human beings. But the song of the saxophones and of the metal trumpets that the soldiers raised jubilantly seemed to go up to the sun and come back from it. One of the musicians, who played the trombone, worked the slide like a circus star. The drummers and the cymbalists seemed to be sorcerers, or good elves; we would see a drumstick twirling in the air. At times the bass instruments would grow still and we would hear the melody on the clarinets and saxophones; and then, like a resounding, tamed river, whose main current suddenly flows into a forest where larks are singing, the brass instruments, the trombones and the cymbals that marked the rhythm, would suddenly raise their voices, making the railings and roof of the bandstand tremble. A soldier with gold uniform buttons standing out on his chest played the cymbals. I hadn't known that they had such an inadequate name—"little plates." Sometimes he smashed them together furiously making them explode, and I wondered why those blows didn't make little snakes of fire fly from the edges of the disks. Every little while I'd look at them, intently and expectantly.

Not only the plaza, but also the whitewashed church façade, the towers, the balconies, the mountains, and the scattered woodlands that climbed the slopes of the cordillera almost to the snow line—even the clear sky in which the sun was shining—all were delighted with the music of the regimental band, with the harmony that had been imposed on so many mysterious instruments. The leader never glanced at us. With every passing moment he seemed more powerful and taller; his majestic paunch seemed to play some indispensable role in the way he silenced some of the musicians, damping down the sound with his hands or suddenly setting the trumpets in motion.

When they played a *huayno*, an outcry went up from around the bandstand.

"Hey, Chipro, wait for me," I told him. "I'm going to go and declare my love to Alcira."

Just then Palacitos, who had been standing in awe before the bandstand, shouted, "Chipro, Iño, Ernesto! Look! Prudencio, from K'ak'epa, from my home town; Prudencio is playing the clarinet. Prudenciucha! Hey, handsome! *Papacito!*"

He pointed him out to us. When the Indian saw Palacitos pointing his finger at him, he winked and nodded his head at us.

"*Jajayllas! Jajayllas!*"

Palacitos began to jump up and down, waving his arms. He hugged us.

"Prudencio! From my home town! He was an Indian, little brothers! They caught him, handcuffed him, and dragged him off to the army; we sang farewell *jarahuis* for him. There he is playing! What a handsome fellow! What a prince!"

I left him with Chipro and Iño.

"Wait for me. I'll be right back," I told them.

I wanted to see Salvinia, Alcira, and Antero. And then to become a falcon and to soar over the towns where I had once been happy; to descend to the level of the rooftops, following the course of the streams that bring water to the settlements, hovering for a moment over the familiar trees and stones that mark the boundaries of the tilled fields and, later, calling down from the depths of the sky.

I saw Valle pompously promenading around the plaza, escorting a row of young ladies. The big *k'ompo* knot in his red silk necktie was comical; it was too big and bulky for his scrawny neck, or even for his ceremonious appearance and courtly way of speaking, his way of moving his lips as if they didn't belong to him. Posturing, he made the girls laugh. Where could all of these elegant young men and these ladies and gentlemen have come from? They must have been called in from the haciendas. They were the only ones who strolled on the sidewalk around the outside of the park, with the soldiers; the common people did not promenade on the inner walks and in the stone-paved street; they were seated or stood about in groups. The older schoolboys circled the park in long rows, behind the students from the girls' school.

Salvinia and Alcira were with a group of girls. They looked more babyish in their school uniforms. Alcira's thick legs were even more evident in her black stockings. They were unpleasant-looking. But her hair was lovely; it shone like ripe barley on the threshing floor, although it seemed slightly darker, perhaps the hue of *capuli* grass, which ripens inside of a lobe that yellows with age. A fine down covered her skin. Her eyes were like Clorinda's —sorrowful. Why? In Clorinda's case it was understandable. She had been born and brought up in a desolate, windy town, surrounded by dry hills that flowered only briefly in the winter— when it was cold and the fog would settle in for weeks at a time, or drift along in low-hanging layers, almost without rising, descending into the hollows and climbing slowly up the mountain sides. "What are you? The brow of the coast," they'd say to the people from Saisa, Clorinda's town. Neither coastal plain nor Andes. Neither sea nor river water. Only the soft rains and mists of wintertime. It was not in the desert; nor were there tilled fields or permanent pastures; in Saisa there were only seasonal grasslands, a scanty spring to which foxes and larger beasts came to drink from great distances, and gourds that the *comuneros* planted in the bottom of the ravines, wherever there might be a little moisture. And besides, Clorinda's sweetheart had bristly hair and calloused hands. She was the only perennial flower in Saisa, as rare as her native region, unforgettable; her voice was a bit husky, perhaps as a result of the dampness and beauty of the winters. It was impossible for me be near Alcira while thinking of the girl from Saisa. Her thick calves and stocky body annoyed me. I had to leave.

I did not see Antero. For a while I walked behind Salvinia. She and her friends tried not to look directly at the young men. I felt more sure of myself than ever before. My patent leather shoes were elegant; I was wearing a tie, and my shirt cuffs were rather long. I was no longer embarrassed by my new suit. I held my head high, and when the colonel and a group of gentlemen who wore gold chains across their vests passed me, I moved aside without my usual feelings of bashfulness and indignation. "Go ahead, please!" I said. Two young men I had never seen before approached Salvinia's group of girls. They introduced themselves politely. And the tallest one went over to Salvinia.

"I am the son of the commanding officer of the Guardia," I heard him say.

Inviting the other girls to continue with their walk, he took Salvinia by the arm, drawing her aside so that he could walk with her alone. The other girls permitted this, blushing and bewildered but radiant with joy, I thought.

I became furious. Perplexed, I followed along behind the group although I didn't know the people. But on the corner I saw Antero standing on the brick curbing. His eyes had reddened; they were murky like those of a fierce dog who has been struck on the muzzle with a cane.

I stopped near him.

"I'm going to beat his brains out," he told me. "Right now."

The band played a *marinera*. It was nearly twelve o'clock.

He waited until they had gone a few steps beyond us. We heard Salvinia laugh. Antero strode after them. I followed him.

He tapped the young man on the shoulder. "He's the son of the Comandante," I warned him.

"Hey," said Antero. "Hey, turn around!"

The boy stopped. The others turned to face us. As more rows of strollers were approaching, we all withdrew to the edge of the sidewalk nearest the street. Salvinia turned pale. I could see that she wanted to come over to where the four of us were; she looked at us wonderingly.

"Move over this way more," Antero instructed the youth. "You keep walking," he told the girls. They obeyed him and walked away rapidly.

Antero led the way to the castor-bean field. Taken by surprise, the two boys came along. It wasn't very far to the field—about twenty yards. I thought the Comandante's son would do something to stop us. Antero had intimidated them. He dominated all of us. Perhaps my anger had helped to arouse him. Markask'a spoke in the same tone he had used Saturday night, the day of the insurrection, on our way back from Condebamba.

"Listen," he told the boy once we had reached the field, "that girl, the one you held by the arm, is my sweetheart. I'm Antero Samanez. If you want to court her, you'll either have to get rid of me or break me like a wild horse. I'm from Apurímac."

And once again I saw him as if he already had leather leggings and a whip. Of course! He could kill the *colonos* on his hacienda, "easy," as he had confessed to me the day before.

"Don't you know I'm the son of the Comandante?" said the youth, incredibly nervous. His lips trembled a little.

"That's your father," Antero replied. "Maybe your mother's a bitch!"

The other boy, the witness, made a rush for Antero, who ducked in time, grabbed him by the legs, and hurled him against the old wall that shielded us from the gaze of those strolling by. Antero's birthmarks grew darker, as if they were throbbing, I thought.

"I don't give a shit about that *cholita*," shouted the officer's son. And he ran off toward the park. Antero could not stop him.

The other boy got to his feet.

"Let's go farther off," he said. "One of us must kneel down and beg the other's pardon. I am also a son of the Comandante. No one shall pull us apart!"

The band played a march; it was already leaving. I had to follow the musicians. Palacitos was to introduce me to Prudencio.

"I have nothing against you. There was no offense intended. I'll get down on my knees. I'll get down on my knees, boy! But like a man!" Antero said.

Markask'a really knelt down; he put one knee on the ground where there was human excrement because many passers-by went behind the old wall to leave their filth.

The other boy looked at him in surprise; I saw the amazement in his eyes, and then the flame of his courage being rekindled.

"I'm from Piura," he said. "I didn't think that in Abancay, in Abancay . . ."

He helped Markask'a up, giving him his hand.

"I'm going to follow the musicians," I said.

I started to run, leaving them behind; the speed at which I ran was nothing—less than nothing—compared to the impulse I felt within me.

"Prudencio! Markask'a! It's me," I shouted. "Palacitos!"

I found the plaza deserted; the march could no longer be heard. I kept on running, and caught up with the soldiers near the barracks. Palacitos stood by the side of the road. The band passed through the massive arched gateway to the barracks. The musicians marched in, making a right-angled turn onto the stone walk that ran across the field to the barracks.

"I'm going to wait here for Prudencio in the afternoon," Palacitos told me.

"I'll come with you."

"No. In Doña Felipa's *chicha* bar you wait for me. I'm going to talk with him about my home town first."

"Can't I listen, Palacitos?"

"Well, it's about my home town that we're going to talk. I have things to tell him. Afterwards we'll go to the *picantería*[2] for sure."

"What if they don't turn Prudencio loose in the afternoon?"

"The evening call is at six o'clock. He'll get out after mess. I'd better wait; you go back to school. Ask the Rector to excuse me; tell him I'm waiting for someone from my home town. You'd better run."

"And what if they don't turn him loose?"

"I'll stand at the gate and beg them to do it. Really! I'll beg the sergeant," he told me, seeing me hesitate.

I left him on the edge of the wide dirt road to the barracks. There were still some town boys and mestizos going by on their way from the barracks to the center of town; other people were climbing up to the villages on the footpaths that snaked along the great mountain, disappearing at intervals into the grass and trees.

"They'll want to be alone when they talk to one another about their home town, the way I would if I had found among the musicians a *comunero* from the village where I was born. A son of Kokchi or of Felipe Maywa!" I thought, on my way back to the school. I was obsessed by the idea of such an unexpected discovery and meeting between the Indian from K'ak'epa and Palacios. He'd ask Prudencio about all of his relatives, about the marriageable girls and the bachelors, about the old men and women, and about the village musicians—some harpist, or well-known *quena*, mandolin, or *quirquincho* player; then he'd inquire about the craftsmen who make those musical instruments, and about the weavers. Which girl had woven the best poncho or belt? And for whom? They'd laugh together. Prudencio would make jokes about some personage or other; perhaps about some one-eyed grouch or the village miser, or even about the priest and the pious women, or about some lame but still serviceable donkey, who bounced his owner about in the air when he trotted. If the rider were a girl they'd find the story even funnier. Palacitos would double up with laughter. The clarinet player would also inquire about the best-

2. Another word for *chicha* bar, alluding to the fact that food highly seasoned with chili peppers (*picantes*) is served there.—Trans.

known animals in the village, perhaps about a powerful team of plow oxen, the envy of everyone, that some small landowner was lucky enough to own; about the mother cows, adored by their owners; and about the dogs and the roosters—but especially about the dogs. The region from which Palacitos came is puma and fox country; there would be some brave, strong dog in the town that would be famous and made much of for his fox-hunting ability, or for having been seriously injured chasing pumas. And later Palacitos would weary the musician by questioning him about his life as a soldier. How had he managed to learn to play that instrument that is found only in the big towns? How, oh how, had he done it? What was a colonel? Had he ever seen a general? And did he, Prudencio, shoot a machine-gun? What was that weapon like? And how far did its bullets travel? And was it true that a cannonball could open up a hole as big as a mine shaft, disembowel a whole herd of oxen, and decapitate a million men standing in line? And that the blood of those million men would flow and splash and foam like a river? And that the generals or captains were so conditioned that they could toast one another with brandy while standing on the banks of rivers of blood? And that a sergeant could never become that cold-blooded, although they became even more furious than colonels in wartime, and disemboweled Christians with the knives they carried on the ends of their Mausers in parades? "They say they become so enraged in battle that they even lap up blood like dogs; and that they rear up then, like cutthroats,[3] with their jaws and even their chests all smeared with blood, and charge forward, screaming; neither thunder nor the souls in torment will scare you the way they do, they say. Christians, Christians, little brothers!" Palacitos would tell us, nights, as he sat on the porch steps. He instilled in me his horror of war. When we were with him, we often thought it would be better to die before reaching the age of twenty-one. "Not even the mother moon feels sorry for the war dead. She doesn't mourn for them, they say. Her light won't even shine on a dead man's teeth; it's the other way around, dead men's teeth turn black, they say, in the moonlight. On the battlefields their bones must go on suffering until Judgment Day. Buzzards vomit when they eat one of those corpses."

Palacitos could never stop talking when he started in on the

3. The reference is to *nakaks*, mythological characters who slit people's throats at night and eat their flesh.—Trans.

dead and the lost souls. After listening to him, we'd go to bed shivering, as if we were descending into an icy abyss.

Now he'd talk with Prudencio about his fears, about the soldiers who frightened him, about the equipment they used while being trained to kill; later he would tell us of his discoveries. His meeting with the musician had even made him forget the *daño* marbles that Father Augusto was supposed to have given him at the very moment he stood there fasting, fasting by the side of the road, waiting for the clarinet player, with the whole sky blazing overhead. For not a single cloud had arisen; it was a clear day, and like me, he was not a valley dweller.

I thought of all these things as I went through the streets. I must have been walking quite slowly.

Near the school a *kimichu*[4] of Our Lady of Cocharcas appeared before me. He had come out of the Cuzco road onto a street corner, and I met him near the school gate. He was calling people together by playing his *chirimía*.[5] A little parrot rode along on the top of the box which held the Madonna. Looking well feathered and happy, he watched the people go by. But more than by the song of the *chirimía*—which I had heard in the highlands, where the voice of a single instrument sounds as clear as crystal—my attention was drawn by the pilgrim's accompanist. Like Indians from Andahuaylas, both wore white homespun flannel that was flecked with gray. The accompanist had a beard that was almost blond; his jacket was quite short. Around his neck he wore a thick scarf with a dark background on which a design of big flowers stood out in bright contrast to the wavy lines, resembling the yellow stems of water plants, that surrounded them. The man walked with his head bowed; his matted hair fell down over his scarf. He glanced at me. His light-colored eyes conveyed a feeling of deep anxiety. Perhaps he was a madman. I followed him for a few steps. He began to sing in Quechua, in an extremely high tone. Like his eyes, his voice was penetrating. The hymn he sang was a slow one. The boys, and the other people who followed him, remained silent, so that they could hear the hymn better. The *kimichu* began to walk more slowly. I could not follow them any farther. The singer's lips were stained with coca leaf juice. I saw that he carried a pear-

4. An Indian musician who journeys from one town to another as a pilgrim, carrying a case of glass and wood containing a portrait of the Virgin Mary and begging for alms.—Author
5. A wooden instrument similar to a recorder or flageolet.—Trans.

shaped gourd with a metal mouthpiece for the *llipta*.[6] "Where is
he from, I wonder where?" I asked myself in amazement. Perhaps
in my early childhood I had seen and heard him in some village, or
seen him coming down out of the mountains, or crossing some
large and bare plaza. His face, the tormented look in his eyes that
intrigued me so, his high-pitched voice, that blond beard, maybe
even the scarf, were not his alone; they seemed to emanate from
somewhere inside me, from my memory. They left, followed by a
small group of people. "I'll look for him," I promised myself.
"He'll be easy to find in Abancay," and I entered the school.

A solitary harpist was playing in Doña Felipa's *chicha* bar. I
was surprised that he was not accompanied by a violinist. That is
the usual orchestra in the small towns—violin and harp. I knew of
only a few quite popular harpists who were hired to play alone for
fiestas, and could do an adequate job. Someone would beat time on
the delicate wooden box of the harp to mark the rhythm and liven
up the dancing. The voice of a good harp has a clear, sweet tone.
At midnight, depending on the fiesta, the participants all would go
out and dance in the streets and in the plaza. The harpist carries
his instrument over his chest and shoulder, with the wide part up
and the steel strings close to his jaw. In the open air the instrument's voice does not grow weaker. It can be heard more than a
block away in any direction from all the corners of a square. By
their style of playing, the most famous harpists are known and
they are sometimes hired to play in far-off towns. Maybe this man
is one of the great harp players, I thought, when I saw him sitting
in the back of the chili place with his instrument before him.

Boys my age would go to the *picanterías*, but they seldom went
alone. I did not sit down but remained standing near the harpist,
leaning against the wall. Customers were already beginning to arrive. I wished that I had worn my old suit, but that was not possible on Sunday. Many people cast inquiring glances at me. The
waitress recognized and smiled at me in a way that was both good-
natured and scoffing. The one who had spoken to me about Doña
Felipa brought me a big glass of *chicha*. Just then the harpist began
to tune the strings of his instrument.

How was I going to drink so much *chicha* without sitting at a
table? She looked at me triumphantly.

"Well, drink up, kid!" she told me. But she wasn't making fun
of me. She was laughing.

---

6. Lime or *quinua* ashes.—Author. (See glossary.)

"Well, drink up, kid. Enough for a man I brought you."

I looked one way and then the other. The harpist turned toward me and began to laugh, too.

I took the glass in both hands, and, pausing once or twice, emptied all the *chicha* down my throat. I finished awkwardly.

"Damn, you're a tough kid!" said the waitress. She had a dirty face; her high, round breasts showed jubilantly through her pink blouse.

I felt a violent desire to go out into the street, and wait for Palacitos there.

"You must sure listen to Papacha[7] Oblitas," the waitress told me, pointing at the harpist. "About Doña Felipa he's also going to sing."

She took my glass and went off the kitchen. Her handsome hips swayed rhythmically; her bare legs and feet looked youthful against the dusty ground. She walked rapidly with small steps, her head bent to one side over her little purple shawl. The harpist had noticed my restlessness; I surprised him looking at me ironically.

"She's good, kid," he said to me.

I realized he must be a musician of vast experience. He must have attended a thousand fiestas of mestizos, gentry and Indians; and if they called him "Papacha," it could only be because he was a maestro, a musician famous in hundreds of towns. I must either leave or else sit at a table. My rubber shoes, my long shirt cuffs, my necktie embarrassed and upset me. I couldn't feel at home. Where to sit, and with whom? Just then four soldiers entered the *chicha* bar. One of them was a corporal. They sat at a table near the harp player. The corporal called for service.

"Hey, come here, beautiful-haired girl," he said in Cuzco Quechua.[8]

When the waitress came, the corporal said something sensual and coarse to her. The soldiers laughed. The corporal noticed me.

"Joking with the girl, that's all. Not insulting her. Really, kid," he said in Spanish.

"Jackass, jackass!" said the girl.

"Not jackass, lovesick, like little donkey," answered the corporal, and we all laughed.

The harpist continued to tune his instrument. Surely he was a *papacha*. He tuned rapidly, drawing resonant scales and arpeggios from the strings. The notes did not remain at ground level as they

---

7. This may be translated "Great Father"; it is a term of respect.—Author
8. *"Yau suni chujcha, hamuy."*—Author

do when a harpist is timid or mediocre. The wisps of black soot that hung down from the ceiling of the *chicheria* swayed back and forth. More soldiers arrived, but Prudencio and Palacitos did not come. I would have to leave.

The harpist began to play a *huayno*. It did not have a pure Abancay beat. I recognized it. It was from Ayacucho or Huancavelica. But there was something of the Apurímac style in the cadence of the *huayno*. He sang. The image of the highland towns, of their transparent air, came into my mind.

Utari pampapi	On Utari Plain,
muru pillpintucha	spotted butterfly,
amarak wak'aychu	do not weep any longer,
k'ausak'rak'mi kani	I am still alive,
kutipamusk'aykin	I must return to you,
vueltamusk'aykin.	I must surely return.
Nok'a wañuptiyña	When I come to die,
nok'a ripuptiyña	when I disappear,
lutuyta apaspa	then you shall wear mourning,
wak'ayta yachanki.	then you shall learn to weep.

Why did Maestro Oblitas choose this song to begin his music that Saturday? Those were the most sorrowful words and melody I had ever heard in Abancay.

Just as he was beginning the third verse, the singer who accompanied the *kimichu* of Our Lady of Cocharcas entered the *chicha* bar. Stooping slightly, he walked through the crowd toward the harpist. He still wore his scarf loosely, and its design was just as impressive in that dark hole as it had been in the full light of the street. The yellow of the wavy lines seemed to glow; the flowers stood out as if they had substance and were not just woven designs. They were enormous flowers and took up almost the whole width of the cloth—a rose and a red carnation on a soot black background. In none of the towns had I ever seen such a thick weave— neither in the stockings the Morochucos wore, nor in the *chullos*[9] from the south. When I looked at it more closely, I was surprised to find that the scarf was dirty.

Maestro Oblitas went on singing:

Kausarak'mi kani	I am still alive,
alconchas nisunki	the hawk will tell you about me,
luceros nisunki,	the star in the sky will tell you about me,

9. A cap that covers the head and part of the face.—Author

kutimusak'rak'mi	and yet I must come back to you,
vueltamusak'rak'mi.	still I must return.
Amarak' wak'aychu	This is not a time for weeping,
muru pillpintucha,	spotted butterfly.
saywacha churusk'ay	The *saywa*[10] I built on the mountaintop
manaras tuninchu	has not tumbled down,
tapurikamullay.	ask it about me.

The harpist kept on playing the melody. The verses of the *huayno* were finished.

The *kimichu's* companion called for *chicha*. He watched the harpist as he sang. His light-colored eyes gleamed like a hawk's in the twilight; they gazed at me. "I've seen him! But where?" I asked myself again. He drained a large glass, a "corporal" of *chicha*. Then he approached the maestro. The harpist was playing the melody on the steel strings. The man came and stood with me, behind the harp. He was short, quite short, practically a dwarf, and fat. Out in the street, when he had chanted the solemn hymn to Our Lady, I had not been able to judge his true height. He must have realized that I was obsessed with watching him. "Harpist's good," he said to me in his high voice, pointing to the musician. When the melody ended, he took it up again, singing:

Paraisancos mayu	River Paraisancos,
río caudaloso	strong-flowing stream,
aman pallk'ankichu	you must not fork
kutimunaykama	until I return,
vueltamunaykama.	until I come back.
Pall'ark'optikik'a	Because if you divide,
ramark'optikik'a	if you branch out,
challwacha sak'esk'aypin	someone will prey upon
pipas challwayk'ospa	the little fish I have bred
usuchipuwanman.	and they will die, scattered on the shore.

The rhythm was even slower now, and sadder, much sadder the words and tone. The high voice fell upon my already heavy heart like an icy river. Enthusiastically, Papacha Oblitas repeated the chorus, playing it like a native of Parasaincos. The harp sweetened the song; it didn't have in it the steely sorrow of the man's voice. Why, in the deep river beds, in those abysses of rocks,

10. A heap of stones which travelers pile up in the mountain passes.—Author

bushes, and sun, did the songs have such a sweet tone, when the powerful torrent of the waters was so wild and the precipices looked so terrifying? Perhaps because on those rocks the most delicate of tiny flowers frolicked with the wind, and because the thundering current of the great river flows through flowers and vines, where the birds are fortunate and joyous, more so than in any other part of the world. As he played on, the singer accentuated the lament in the other verses:

Kutimuk', kaptiyña	When it is the traveler who returns to you
pallkanki ramanki.	you will fork, you will branch out.
Kikiy, challwaykuspay	Then I myself will care for the little fish,
uywakunallaypak'.	and raise them.
Yaku faltaptinpas,	And if they need more of the water
ak'o faltaptinpas	and the sand you give them
ñokacha uywakusak'i	I shall care for them
warma wek'eywanpas,	with my tears alone,
ñawi ruruywanpas.	with the pools of my eyes.

Who is capable of setting the bounds between the heroism and the iciness of a great sorrow? With music such as this a man could weep until he was completely consumed, until he vanished, or could just as easily do battle with a legion of condors and pumas, or with the monsters that are said to inhabit the depths of the highland lakes and the shadowy mountain slopes. I felt myself more disposed to fight the devil as I listened to this song. If he should appear wearing a puma- or condor-skin mask, waving immense plumes, or baring his fangs, I would take him on, certain of victory.

The customers stopped drinking and talking. No one tried to dance. When the *kimichu*'s companion stopped singing, the corporal came up to him with a glass of *chicha*; he offered him some and wanted to take him back to his own table. The singer refused and sat on the floor behind the harp. I crouched and asked him loudly in Quechua, "Weren't you in Aucará, at the festival of the Lord of Untuna, with another *kimichu*, years ago?"

"I've been there."

"Did you sing beside the lake in a big field where they say the Lord appeared?"

"Yes."

"And you got an *anku* thorn in your foot when you were walking; and my father, a blue-eyed gentleman, gave you a gold coin."

"Sure; you were a little kid, like this, just like this," and he measured my height from the ground with his hand.

We continued talking in Quechua.

I sat down beside him. The waitress brought us *chicha*. She laughed outright when she saw me on the ground with the singer. By now the *chicha* bar was full of regular customers and strangers.

"Is that song from Paraisancos?"

"No. From Lucanamarca. A boy coming back from the Coast sang it. He made it up, with music from that town. I heard it here, outside in the street, and came in. Me, I'm a singer."

"What became of the boy?"

"He went back to the Coast—Don Luis Gilberto."

"Don?"

"Yes, Don. He's a gentleman now. He's my cousin, has a tailor shop."

"And you?"

"Wandering, wandering, with Our Lady of Cocharcas, such a long time! I never sing in *chicha* bars. But that song of my brother's,[11] it's strong. By the time he got back to his village all the girls he loved already belonged to someone else. They were suffering. Women suffer."

"And the scarf?"

"From Paraisancos. For sure!"

"From your woman?"

"Woman? I wander, I walk all over the world with Our Lady. A little one-eyed girl knitted it for me."

"A little one-eyed girl?"

"Real quick she made it. You think it fades? It always keeps its color."

"But isn't Our Lady from Cocharcas? Paraisancos is a long way off."

"I'm a pilgrim. Wandering I live. I don't go back to Lucanamarca since I was a boy."

"And the girl with one eye?"

"She's from Paraisancos, well, she serves Our Lady. For sure!"

"And the glass case?"

"It's old; it belongs to Our Lady."

I named off twenty different towns to him, and he knew all of them.

"What about you, boy, why do you wander?"

11. In Quechua the same word, *wawqey*, is used for both "brother" and "cousin."—Trans.

"My father's also a pilgrim."

Much of the air of mystery had vanished from the singer's eyes. They gazed at me familiarly, with a tenderness that strengthened me. I took one end of his scarf in my hands.

The singer reeked of sweat and of unwashed woolen cloth, but I was used to those kinds of human odor; not only did they not bother me, but they awakened in me fond memories of my childhood. He was an Indian like the men from my home village. Not from an hacienda. He had come into the tavern and had sung; the corporal had paid him homage, and so had the tavern; now we were sitting together. I did not see Doña Felipa's husband.

"Let's eat some *picantes*. I'll invite you," I told the singer. "What's your name?"

"Jesús Warank'a Gabriel."

"Gabriel?"

"Jesús Warank'a Gabriel."

"Jesús, did you have a dark red *chullu*, all one color, when you were in Aucará?"

"Sure, kid! It was currant color."

"That's why we could see you so clearly on the plain, when we were going around the lake. You were the only one with a *chullu* of that color. Hundreds of doves were flying from one end of the lake to the thorn scrub at the other end. The ducklings zigzagged back and forth, leaving a wake in the water."

"That's how it was, boy! So many thorn bushes on the plain! In the water the thorn scrub showed up too."

"Shall we go and eat *picantes*? My father sent me some money from Coracora."

"Ah, Coracora! Beautiful little *charango* they play there."

By now there were no more empty tables. Maestro Oblitas was playing the sweet *huaynos* of Abancay. The corporal and the other soldiers were dancing with each other. They had let one of the *chichería* waitresses, the same one who had treated me to the glass of *chicha*, get away from them. She served some tables and went right back to the soldiers. She danced with her head tilted to one side, moving her plump arms gracefully in time to the music; she often stamped her feet, tapping her right one, or weaved back and forth between the soldiers, carried along by the gay rhythm. I felt happy. We stood watching the waitress as we waited to go into the kitchen.

The other mestizo customers did not dance; they watched the soldiers. I was intrigued by the absence of Doña Felipa's husband.

"Abancay *huayno* beautiful; watching them dance, listening, warms the heart," said Don Jesús, still in Quechua.

Maestro Oblitas sang:

Jilgueroy, jilgueroy, mañoso;	Goldfinch, sneak-thieving goldfinch.
abaschallaytas suwanki, jilgueroy;	You rob my bean fields, goldfinch.
sarachallaytas suwanki jilgueroy.	You rob my corn fields, goldfinch.
Abaschallayta suwaspas jilgueroy,	Pretending to rob my bean field, goldfinch,
sarachallayta suwaspas, jilgueroy,	pretending to rob my corn field, goldfinch,
sonk'ochallayta suwanki, jilgueroy.	you stole my little heart, goldfinch.

The dance ended with a *fuga* with a lively rhythm. The soldiers stamped their feet energetically. By now they were sweating.

There was a pause. I went into the kitchen and asked for *picantes*. A fat young mestiza with several rings on her fingers was in charge of the kitchen. Gold earrings dangled from her ears.

"You friends with Doña Felipa?" I asked her in Quechua. She nodded.

"In Patibamba I distributed salt to the women," I told her, and she smiled.

"Well, she's my *comadre*,[12] Doña Felipa. We threw Don Paredes out."

"Don Paredes?"

"He's lazy. He must have gone to another chili place." And she smiled again.

"Serve us, and make the singer's portion bigger."

She served us on platters, by the stove. Standing, we tasted the peppery food. It burned like the devil itself, but the singer was delighted with it. "How good it is!" he said.

The *chichera* did not pay much attention to us, not even when I spoke to her of Doña Felipa. She was watching the harpist.

Another waitress—not the one who had been dancing, but an older one—went up to the musician. We saw that she was humming a tune to him.

"Now I've got it," said Maestro Oblitas.

He played a *danza*, a sort of Christmas *jaylli*. The rhythm was

12. *Comadres* are women connected by a religious tie by which they promise to help each other's children and also, in effect, each other.— Trans.

quite similar to the final counterpoint of a *jaylli*. The customers were startled. Don Jesús and I waited, watching the musician. The mestiza began to sing:

"Huayruros," "huayruros,"	They say the *huayruro, huayruro,*
mana atinchu	cannot do it
mana atinchu,	cannot do it,
maytak'atinchu	how could he!
Imanallautas atinman	Why could he? Hey!
way! atinman	What could the frightened
manchak' wayruro	*huayruro* do
Doña Felipa makinwan	against Doña Felipa's hand?
Doña Felipa kallpanwan.	Against Doña Felipa's might?
"Huayruroy" "huayruro,"	*Huayruro, huayruro,*
maytas atiwak'	whatever could you do?
maytas chinkanki	Where could you escape to?
Doña Felipa mulallan	When Doña Felipa's mule
chunchul mulallan	when the mule's guts
chinkachiyta chinkachin	were lost, you were lost
huayruroy huayruroy.	*huayruro,* my *huayruro.*

The soldiers were puzzled. The corporal's face seemed to freeze; despite his befuddlement, I could see from his eyes that he was disturbed by mixed emotions.

One of the soldiers attempted to stand up. Although his eyes did not reflect indignation, they flashed like those of a dancer who hears an unexpected quickening of tempo. Perhaps he had been a *jaylli-* or scissors-dancer in his home village, and wanted to challenge someone, because the *fugas* of the *jaylli* or the scissors dance are competitive dances. But I thought I recognized the most characteristic feature of the dance.

"*Piruchan,*" I said to the singer. "I believe that's the dance they used in my hometown to celebrate the coming of the irrigation water, in Chaupi, in the *ayllu* of Chaupi. *Piruchan*!"

The singer shook his head.

"*Imachá,*"[13] he said. "*Piruchan* is faster."

The waitress began to sing again. And three women followed her out of the kitchen. I continued to watch the corporal and the other soldiers as I listened to that hymnlike song which seemed to have come all the way from the waters of the Pachachaca. What would happen there next? At that moment I noticed that the waitress was also pockmarked; her face was pitted with scars.

13. "What can it be?"—Trans.

The soldier, who had finally succeeded in standing up, made his way into the small cleared space in front of the harpist. The corporal hesitated again. He was sweating.

The soldier did not silence the mestiza; he raised his arms and began to dance skillfully.

"Beautiful! Damn, it's beautiful," exclaimed the singer, Don Jesús. Once more his eyes held that transparent, deep, unfathomable light. I realized that at that moment I no longer existed for him. He gazed at the soldier as if it were not the soldier who danced, but instead his own disembodied soul, that of the singer of Our Lady of Cocharcas.

"K'atiy!" [14] he shouted to the soldier. "K'atiy."

The soldier whirled through the air, landed with his legs wide apart, and leaped again; then he shuffled, shifting legs in a complicated step; he stood on one foot and stamped the other, lifting it as high as his knee. Maestro Oblitas was speeding up the tempo of the *danza*, it seemed. He did not look at the man dancing; but I knew that even with his head bent forward not only did he follow the dancer, but it was even as if he were somehow attached to him, as if his hands were guided by the soldier's leaps and by movements of his body, that both were propelled by the same force. By now the girl was improvising new words to the song; like the dancer and the musician, she was equally launched forth into the unknown.

Huayruruy huayruruy	Huayruro, huayruro,
imallamantas kaswanki?	Of what, of what were you made?
Way! titillamantas	Hey! of lead, of lead alone
Kask'anki,	you were made;
Way! karkallamantas	Hey! of cow manure
kask'anki.	you were made.

It was the last verse. Now only the harpist and the soldier were left. Maestro Oblitas began to vary the tune and the rhythm. We could not tell where the change originated, whether it was the soldier or the harpist who first changed the rhythm. But surely whoever had done it was not from Abancay! Not from that narrow valley which began in fire and went on up into the snow, and which, in its lower depth, was hot, reeked of fermented cane trash, and was full of wasps and mute, constantly weeping *colonos*.

---

14. Untranslatable in this case. Literally it means "keep going, push, or plow."—Author

As we all stood watching the soldier, a *huayruro*—a *guardia civil*—silenced the music and terminated the dancing.

"Everybody out!' he shouted from the doorway.

Probably no one had seen him enter. He must have heard the music from the street and come in.

"I know Quechua, I'm from Pausa. I'm going to arrest the harpist and the soldier," he said.

Behind him appeared a second *guardia*. Both wore hats with wide, stiff brims, pointed crowns, and leather bands. The red cloth stripes on their long jackets stood out clearly in the semidarkness. They were clean-shaven. They were tall. Despite the dusty streets of Abancay their shoes and leggings looked polished.

The singer of Our Lady of Cocharcas gazed at the *huayruros* calmly, his deep-set eyes reaching them as if from a great distance.

The two rural policemen wore pistols in their belts. One of them took out his gun and covered everyone from the doorway; the other approached the musician. The fat mestiza came in from the kitchen. She did not seem frightened. Some of the men tried to escape by crawling out of the *chicha* bar on all fours. The *guardia* made them return.

When the other *huayruro* reached the soldier, the corporal stood up at his table.

"I corporal; I command," he said.

The *guardia* blinked.

"You're on leave; I'm on duty," he answered.

"I command; corporal," repeated the corporal in his barbaric Spanish. "Come, Condemayta," he ordered the soldier.

The corporal was short of stature. He was able to stay on his feet pretty well, but his eyes were glazed with drunkenness. He stood with his legs wide apart, staring at the policeman. The soldier headed for the corporal's table; the *guardia* let him go.

"But you're under arrest," he said to Maestro Oblitas, seizing his jacket and dragging him to his feet.

"Me? I'm a professional musician, sir," said the maestro. "Arrest the proprietress of the tavern."

The Spanish he spoke was quite correct.

"Go and get her!" yelled the other *guardia* from the doorway.

The *chicha* bar owner threw herself at the policeman, screaming.

"Take me, then. Shoot, if you want to! Go ahead and shoot! He's innocent!" she said in Quechua. The three waitresses surrounded the *guardia*.

At my side, the singer as loudly as he could began singing the first line of a religious hymn.

By now the *guardia* was hobbled by the *cholas*, who clung tight-ly to his arms and legs. They were about to pull him to the ground. The other policeman fired his gun.

"*Jajayllas*, little bullets!" screamed the big *chichera*, clutching the *guardia* even more tightly by the legs. Don Jesús continued with the hymn, as if he were in a church or in the midst of the debris of some village that had been washed away by a flood.

The corporal told the singer to be quiet, saying, "*Upallay*, broth-er." And he walked slowly over to the immobilized *guardia* with all of the soldiers following him.

"Let go! Let go of him, *mamitay*! Let go!" he ordered the fat barmaid.

She released the *guardia* and the other women did likewise, tak-ing a few steps backward.

"Come on, *guardia*," the corporal told the *huayruro*.

"With the harp player!"

"Yeah, with the harp player. Marching!" ordered the corporal. The soldiers dragged the harpist out. The soldier who had danced went on behind.

The women were stunned.

"There's nobody for me," said the corporal loudly. "I, army!"

He walked stiffly at the head of the group.

The stout *chichera* could not decide what to do. Her mind was working. She looked at her customers, who had stood up anxious-ly, as if she were looking at a herd of pigs. She looked at the singer. She looked at the harp, leaned against the wall. She looked at me. Meanwhile the soldiers went out into the street.

The Madonna's singer leaped for the harp.

"I! *Papacha*!" he said.

He ran his hands over the strings, tuning them. His fingers plucked the strings, making them explode. Then he played the same piece to which the soldier had danced. He wasn't very good on the bass; his right hand could not manage to strike such a vari-ety of chords on the low notes, but the melody flowed from the steel strings like a fountain of fire. The pilgrim's face and forehead were red; his beard seemed to be alight; his eyes were as deep as a hawk's. But no innocent creature is capable of putting such con-tagious rapture into his look, more intricate and penetrating than all the lights and shadows of the world. I should have danced to the beat of that music. I was on the point of doing it. I had seen the scissors-dancers making diabolical leaps on the terraces in front of the churches, moving their legs as if they were cats, springing into the air, crossing the tiled porches of the villages with tiny

steps, with the steps of a centipede; at daybreak, in the light of
the rising sun, I had seen them dancing on the cemetery walls,
clicking their steel scissors blades in such a way that the dawn
seemed to be born from their tips. A thousand times I had wished
to imitate them; I had done it at school, among the children. I
could have done it then and there, to my friend's music, before a
frightened audience who needed something startling to shake them
up, to restore their souls that they might go out and rescue Papacha Oblitas. But all the customers fled, overturning tables and
benches as they went. The *chichera* insulted them in Quechua,
"*K'anras, wiswis,* motherless people, born of the wind."

We had to sneak out with the singer, after the chili place had
grown still. I accompanied Don Jesús for a long while, through
some narrow streets and out into the country.

He was staying in a straw-thatched hut near the aqueduct that
runs along the mountain above Abancay. On a porch dozed the
kimichu. The little parrot was inspecting himself for fleas, as he
stood atop the case that held the Madonna. It was late. The sunshine warmed the porch, which was in the full light of the sun
that fell on the jagged mountains opposite, on the road to Andahuaylas. We were tired when we arrived.

"*Tatallay tayta!*" [15] said the singer.

Then I thought of that ingrate, Palacitos. He must have spent
the afternoon with the clarinet player, in some *chicha* bar or out in
the country, talking.

"Will you go begging tonight?" I asked Don Jesús.

"No," he replied. "We're leaving tomorrow. Abancay's no
good."

Of course not! Borne by her *kimichu,* Our Lady of Cocharcas
travels along through villages of Indians and mestizos, ladies and
gentlemen, people who believe in her. Those who serve her speak
only Quechua. In the cities she passes through all the neighborhoods; she enters the cathedral or largest church or pauses on the
terrace before it for a moment, to pay her respects to the temple,
then leaves. Hundreds of leagues she travels. The *kimichu* plays
the *chirimía;* the little parrot looks out over the fields from the top
of the case or from the pilgrim's shoulder. Her entrance into the
villages is soon transformed into a fiesta. The *kimichu* and his accompanist, if he has one, are highly esteemed. But there, in Abancay—full of soldiers, and those *guardias* with spurs and polished

15. "O father, my father!", an expression commonly used in difficult or
distressing situations.—Author

leather leggings, and the newly arrived gentlemen who stared at the people from the poorer neighborhoods with the scornful expression of a large landholder's overseer—what, what indeed could Our Lady of Cocharcas, her little parrot, her *kimichu,* and her singer do? Farewell! I took leave of Don Jesús on the porch.

"*Papay,* Don Jesús, you must sing on the Pachachaca bridge, before the cross. For me, so that I may leave here soon."

"Sure," he answered. "Sure! We'll make a station there with Our Lady."

"You must pray to the river for me too, Don Jesús."

"Sure! To Apu Pachachaca I shall pray."

"You must tell our Father that I shall come to take leave of him."

"Sure!"

I hugged him. The sun shone on the great cordillera opposite us, which was all rocky and full of abysses.

I returned to Abancay, in confusion, with mixed feelings of fear and joy.

"What, what are people, then?" I asked myself as I went along.

I met the army band marching toward the plaza, followed by a crowd of boys, "young gentlemen," and mestizos. Some small children scampered about, their ragged clothes flapping; they slipped on the stones and got up again without complaining. They ran round and round the musicians, looking at them closely and inspecting their instruments. One group lined up behind the band and marched, swinging their arms in an exaggerated fashion because of the effort they were making to take big steps; they were obliged to run when they fell behind or else risk having the empty space taken by others. The children who were alone watched the instruments, especially the big brass ones, so huge and spectacular. They laughed because the instruments dwarfed the soldiers, making them look like picturesque insects. The children shrieked with laughter. They listened to the march, watched each other, and played tag. A rather solemn little crowd of mestizos and a few members of the Indian communities followed the band on the sidewalks and on the edge of the paved road. The children, who were chasing one another, hid behind the mestizos and the women, grabbed them by the legs, and stared at the adults, no matter who they were, with shining eyes in which jubilation reigned as if in a sea, or in a forest in which the rain had left myriad patches of frost that sparkled in the sunlight.

I could not, I just could not be infected with that pure joy of the innocents; I marched alongside the band, near the grownups. I recognized Palacitos; he was walking almost at Prudencio's side. He was not a part of any of the groups of little boys who scampered about in the streets; he went along by himself; you could see how important he felt; his expression was noticeably serious; in a way he seemed to be a member of the band, although it was impossible to determine just what function he performed. Did he control some invisible thread that had a secret and indispensable connection with the marching of the band and the synchronization of the instruments? Watching him closely, I realized that he was the only really solemn spectator or follower the band had.

We reached the park and the children burst into jubilant shouting. The little ones invaded the garden, trampling the roses and other flowers to get to the bandstand first. A plaza! Entering it, a man is somehow transformed, either by the sudden change of scene or by his memories. I tried to find Palacitos, but he, too, had run ahead and must have been in the first row at the bandstand by then, clinging to the iron railing. I stopped on one of the inner paths of the park.

Weeds grew in the wide, paved street that separated the park from the sidewalks and houses around it. At night winged crickets, indigenous to the coastal valleys and the deep, warm gorges in the mountains nearest the jungle, sang there. Despite the loud band music, the crickets glided through the air and some were chirping in seemingly remote places. These insects intrigued me. Crickets with wings? If anyone in the towns where I had formerly lived had told me that crickets could fly, I would have thought him strange. Delicate and lively, like those that inhabit the temperate or cold regions, they moved their long antennae, trying to divine their way or recognize the unfamiliar spaces into which they fell. They ventured into lighted rooms. And people killed them, just as they did on the Coast, with no consideration for their sweet voices, for their inoffensive, graceful figures. They killed a messenger, a visitor from the enchanted surface of the earth, when they could have let it fly away, having felt the fluttering of its tiny, cold little body in their hands. That night I devoted myself to removing the crickets from the sidewalks where they were in such danger. The crickets of my home region have not been endowed with cruel wings; at night their crystalline chirping comes from all the fields around, delighting human beings. They had to be defended in Abancay. It was hard work to trap them and very carefully carry them far away; moreover, because their fragile bodies are weakly joined, their limbs come off easily and to see them with

an arm or leg missing, or without their wings, is as horrible as it is
to come upon the smear, a sort of shadow, that is all that is left of
them when they are squashed on the floor of a room, or on the paving stones. Fortunately that night few of them came to the park,
which is near the open fields. And the music was a splendid help to
me.

When I finally noticed the strollers, I saw that I had almost
reached the corner and that some of them were watching me with
great curiosity. I was almost a young man. I decided to go back to
the school and study or read. Then I spied Antero coming along
with the Comandante's son. They were the same height, but the
boy from the Coast walked more gracefully; he was thin, but not
frail. He watched the strollers avidly, especially the girls. The
schoolgirls were not wearing their uniforms now; I recognized
some of them; they looked more presentable this way, like real *señoritas*. Antero waved to me and walked on. But they returned almost immediately. They both came up to me.

"You probably haven't said anything about what happened!
You mustn't tell anybody," Antero told me. "I'd like you to meet
Gerardo."

The Comandante's son gravely offered me his hand.

"I know you're a man," he said. "That you like Antero, and
that you're brave, like few other people, or maybe no one else."

I shook his hand. He spoke with a coastal accent, pronouncing
the words with incredible rapidity. But there was a lilt to his
speech.

"I'm not going to say anything; I haven't told anybody. Just go
on by. I'm glad to have met you, Gerardo."

Despite the dim lighting in the plaza that night, I could discern
a strange difference in the way the coastal boy's eyes shone; the left
one had a rather opaque look, nevertheless it was more striking
and, I should say, better conveyed what was different about the
boy. In the villages deep in the Andes, where we all speak Quechua, someone from the Coast is always strange, is different from
everyone else. But in addition to this, Gerardo, because of that
eye, because of the kind of shadow on it, gazed at me as mildly as
if he were looking at me with the large eye of a horse that had
been imbued with the intelligence and blood of a human being.
The street lamp shone full on his face. During the fight at noontime I had not noticed this aspect of his features. I had not noticed
it; but this time the young man had really stared at me. I realized
that both he and Antero addressed me as if I were younger than
they. I was; but instead of emphasizing the difference between us,

Antero and I had forgotten it, erased it. He had become closer to me, and friendlier, since he had given me the *zumbayllu*, since we had defied Lleras together, just as we had gone together to meet Salvinia in the poplar grove and together had spun the *winku* on the school playground. But now, in the park, he looked more than ever like a half-grown pup, a *maltón*, as we used to say in the highlands, even more so than the youth who had spoken to me on the way back from the Alameda, threatening to keep a dozen Indian women as concubines if Salvinia should prefer someone else or he should lose her.

They went on; overtaking a row of girls, they began to walk more slowly. Antero appeared rough and clumsy beside the Comandante's son. I could see the schoolgirls looking at him in surprise, and perhaps rather admiringly. I waited at the corner for the band to finish the waltz they were playing.

Neither Salvinia nor Alcira passed me. There was perfume in the air. Elegant ladies and gentlemen strolled by, and groups of officers and *señoritas* who walked slowly, in rows. The officers surrounded them and accompanied them. The jewelry with which the ladies had adorned themselves glittered. Some of the earrings were long; they dangled from the young girls' ears, reflecting the light prodigiously, emphasizing the loveliness of their faces. I didn't know them, but I would have strewn mantles of flowers in their path; I would have liked to go up into the heavens and bring down a star for each of them as a token of my respect. I was shocked by the way the boys and young men who followed them shouted at them; by the impertinence with which, even if only a few times, they forced them out of their way so that they could pass by; and even more by the insolent glances the boys gave them. But some boys looked at them and made way for them as was proper, standing aside quite respectfully to let them pass. I thought it my duty, by flogging or in any other way, to humble those brutes who did not bow to the girls in joyful silence. But I doubted if these jewel-bedecked girls could give happiness without dishonoring themselves in the process. How could they? If they were at such an unattainable height? Although they were here, walking the earth, listening to the waltz, they were at a distance which I found so remote and hazardous that no falcon could soar across it; nor could any strong-winged insect such as the *huayronk'o*, or even the "San Jorge," cross it in its magical flight. Or was it necessary to wear a uniform and carry a shiny crop, or walk gracefully and with a certain air of petulance, as Gerardo did, in order to

live near them and hold their hands? No, I could never manage to
become so corrupted.

The waltz ended. Valle came up to me, escorting a row of beautiful girls. But this man exaggerated, dissembled, and ridiculed
other people; he thought he knew more than he really knew and
that he had gone a lot farther than he really had. He gestured,
moving his hands and fingers affectedly, putting them, and even
his mouth, right up to the girls' faces. They must have felt his
breath. Why didn't they push him out into the street, I wondered.
But they did not seem to be very much disgusted by him.

I left the plaza. And I made a decision I thought was foolish,
even though it intrigued me—to go to the jail and inquire about
Papacha Oblitas.

The jail was near the plaza, half a block away. By now it would
be closed. But in the center of the door there was a little barred
window, level with the warder's head. The guard wouldn't be able
to see me very well from there.

"*Señor*," I said to him. "*Señor guardia*, I'm the godchild of
Papacha Oblitas, of the harp player they arrested this afternoon.
Have they let him out yet?"

"I don't know anything," he answered.

From the way he spoke I could tell he was from Apurímac or
Ayacucho. I spoke to him in Quechua.

"*Papacito*," I said. "Ask about him, then. I want to bring him
something, even if it's only his dinner."

"They brought him enough dinner for a bishop. He didn't want
to eat. He'll get out tomorrow, for sure."

"Is he crying?"

"Don't be silly. Why should he cry?" said the guard in a very
low voice. "He's more likely got his hands all fucked up banging
them on the wall. Now get out of here!"

"Thank you, *papacito*. Will you tell him his godson came, the
student who was with him in the *chicha* bar?"

"Of course. Get out of here, now, get out!"

I heard footsteps on the other side of the door, and left, running.

Then I decided to go to Alcilla the notary's house. I still had
half an hour. I had to pass by the school gate. I found the little
door to the entryway open.

Alcilla must have already gone to bed, and his children were
probably shut up in the house; his meek and pallid woman would
be saying her prayers by now. I was afraid of that family. Sickness,
isolation and complaints walled them in. To enter there was to

suffer uncomprehendingly. I would not go there now. The Rector was my guardian, and had been for a long time.

The school courtyard, dusky and silent, tempted me. I gave up my visit to the notary and chose the school instead.

It was the first time I had ever been alone in the main courtyard. I sat down on the edge of the fountain. The music the band was playing could be heard plainly, in spite of the distance and the walls. The toads were jumping about near the fountain, croaking vigorously. I noticed, then, that they had deeper voices than the highland ones, although in the background of a chorus of crickets, the voices of the toads from the colder regions reverberate like the slow tolling of bells. Those from Abancay croak with a certain joy and tenderness. In these deep valleys the crickets do not sing in chorus; they fly and chirp almost singly. There are other insects that buzz in swarms, with uncertain voices that blend in a droning that confuses the stranger, fascinating and bewildering him and making him drowsy.

Toads and crickets would hide on the playground and even behind the wooden partitions, although not very often. There were spiders there; they spun their webs on the ceilings and boldly enveloped the little yellow flowers that grew in the crevices.

For the first time I felt protected by the school walls, and understood what the shadow of a home meant. Up till then I had changed my residence many times, and had, in the village with which I identified myself in my mind, lived in a hostile, alien house (the village was mine, to be sure, but not one house, not one bedroom, not one courtyard, not one porch belonged to me; the cats I'd had were torn apart by the landlord's dogs; he would egg the beasts on with his shouts and his bulgy eyes). The school sheltered me that night; it received me with its familiar places, with its singing bullfrogs and with its fountain where the water fell in the stillness, with its balcony where I had seen pale, bewildered Añuco weeping, where I had heard the vibrant voice of the Rector, angry and uncertain. And now sure of myself, and hoping the inner courtyard would also receive me, I went there, walking slowly; a sort of tremendous weariness and longing for affection made my eyes burn.

I met Wig, pacing back and forth near the toilets.

"She didn't come, the Indian whore," he exclaimed loudly when he recognized me. "She doesn't want to come. And now I'd give her to you, really, for sure. It's time you learned to be a man."

He went on pacing in front of the wooden partitions.

I picked up a handful of dirt and flung it into his face. He yelled and covered his eyes. Hearing him chasing me, I stepped aside, and he kept right on going toward the courtyard. I went into the kitchen.

The cook was my friend, mine and Palacito's. She heard us running and began to laugh. A dim electric bulb barely cast a light on the soot-blackened kitchen walls.

"She's in the tower!" she said to me in Quechua. "*Jajayllas!*"

"In the tower?"

"That's right, in the tower."

"With her new shawl?"

"Sure. You think she'd leave that behind? Hiding, hiding, she went off wearing it."

"Did you see her go up there?"

"Of course I did! The little lock is just as much of a fake as the drunken sacristan. Better than a bear she walks, quietly. I saw her go in."

It didn't seem possible to me that she could have slipped across the plaza without being discovered; it was such a long way. Although no one walked more stealthily than she; it was as if she were a little round shadow. That's how she would suddenly appear on the playground, when all the while the impatient boarding students had been watching for her in the passageway.

"I'll go—I'll go to see her!" I said.

The cook looked at me in amazement.

"Why didn't she sit down in a corner of the park, to listen to the band? By a door, or an entryway, or in front of a store?" I asked.

"Well, they might kick her. They might do anything to her; she's an idiot. Idiots are 'different'! If she wants to, she can leave this world, easy, by leaping into a *quijllu* in the cliffs, or by entering the shadows of the caves. But she must still suffer, they say. That's what she's here for."

"Do they suffer?"

"She's people; why wouldn't she suffer? You think maybe her body is a dead callus?"

"But why must she always do nothing but suffer?"

"That's why God sent her to this town."

"Maybe she's enjoying herself now in the tower. Even more than you do in the kitchen, night and day. And more than I."

"Ha, child, ha!"

"I'm leaving," I told her. "But when I go out into the courtyard, Wig will get me."

"We'll see!" she said.

She took a big flaming stick from the fire.

"We'll see. This'll sure scare him."

We went out. Wig heard our footsteps and tried to catch up with us. The cook drove him a long way back with the firebrand and cornered him at the foot of the stairs.

"*Papacito* stud!" she said. "Be still, now!"

I ran down the street. The band was still playing in the bandstand in the plaza. The park was resplendent with ladies, officers, and gentlemen strolling in a circle, and mestizos and *comuneros* standing on the paved street, on the sidewalks, and crowded around the bandstand. I managed to run to the church corner without being noticed.

The little lock had disappeared from the tower door; the latch hung down against the wood. The door was closed. I went over to it through the shadow of the tower. Although I was frightened, I opened one side of the door with great care, went in, and closed it. The darkness grew denser, but in it I lost all my fear. I felt hope, a hope that made my pulse beat rapidly. Taking off my shoes, I began to climb the stairs. I was quite good at climbing in my bare feet. When I was small I had successfully imitated cats. She would not hear me!

Little by little I neared the light in the tower. It wasn't the electric light alone but its reflection that I saw, and the glow from the sky, which was full of stars that night. I had tucked my shoes under my belt, in order to have my hands free.

I came quite close to her, to the idiot. I saw her plainly. She had lain down in the archway on the side towards the square. Her tangled locks, so uneven and filthy, showed against the light. She wiggled her feet, one at a time, as a sign of happiness, like a puma switching its tail. I heard her laughing unrestrainedly, far from the people. She laughed loudly, in short bursts. She gestured toward the park with outstretched arm, and laughed again. She would point to people she knew or to those she thought deserved to be applauded or to those who looked ridiculous. Her laughter was uneven but not incoherent.

She had untied Doña Felipa's shawl from the top of the cross on the Pachachaca bridge the day before; this evening's exploit was an even greater one. She was listening to the band of musicians from the highest, most solemn lookout point of the city and observing and inspecting the notables of Abancay. She pointed them out and passed judgment on them. She was enjoying herself completely, perhaps more so than anyone else. But her laughter, the motions of her body, and her hair left a horribly sad echo inside of me. Why? Perhaps because I remembered seeing her white and naked, with her dress over her head, being fought over in blind struggle by the boarders. Her figure itself, the dazed look on her face. How I trembled on those evenings when she would fall to the ground, and heaven and earth were unable to swallow me up despite my supplications!

Stunned, I remained a moment longer. I felt I was committing a sin watching her, a great sin that I would have to atone for.

I descended the stairs more carefully, because it requires more skill to go downhill and down difficult steps, and because an emotion contrary to that which had driven me to climb the tower oppressed me.

Only my father's blue eyes could have soothed me that night and freed me from all the evil I had seen during the day. As I had done many times before, I hurried back to school with the illusion of finding him, smiling, in the doorway.

I thought of Wig and waited for the other boarders to return. I heard the band playing the march they used for their return to quarters.

"The harmonica's song must have reached you!" I thought. "Maybe the song of the *winku*! When it didn't find you in Chalhuanca it must have veered round toward Coracora; it was powerful enough to do that, to go round the world," I exclaimed. And once more I felt alone and secure in that city from which my father had been right to flee.

And what of Añuco? By then he must have been weeping as he rode his horse along the feverish banks of the Apurímac. As for Lleras, I knew that his flesh and bones, by now transformed into a putrid mass, must have been cast up by the great river ("God-who-speaks" is its name) on some bank where it must be crawling with devilish, varicolored worms which would devour it.

11. The Colonos

For many days the police hunting Doña Felipa were led astray in the villages. Some people claimed they had just seen the *chicha* bar owner go by at a slow pace on muleback. In the same places others declared they knew nothing of her arrival and did not even know her name. Acting on false or well-meant leads, the *guardias* climbed the long slopes, descended into the bottoms of the gorges, and rode along the mountainsides for hours on end. They often returned to the towns and punished the local authorities. In this manner they came to Andahuaylas. Half of the people in town agreed that Doña Felipa had passed through on her way to Talavera; the other half asserted that she still had not arrived, but that they knew she was getting nearer.

They could not find her. At the prefect's orders the *guardias* remained in Andahuaylas and set up an outpost there. Every day they would receive more news of the movements of Doña Felipa and her companions, and of her flight toward Huamanga. Still other people contended she had started a *chicha* bar in San Miguel, which is so close to the edge of the jungle that flocks of immense blue parrots come there.

In Abancay they did not close down the rebel leader's tavern, not even after the incident with the *guardias*. With police backing, Don Paredes once more became the owner and dismissed the plump young waitress. She was given notice to leave Abancay and go back

to her home town, Curahuasi. She went off with the harpist, Papacha Oblitas, who was also from Curahuasi.

A week later the regiment departed. The Guardia Civil remained, installed in the barracks. The police said that the regiment
had marched on Abancay not only because of the insurrection but
also to carry out their annual maneuvers; that the troops had been
inactive for a long time; and that the lightning march on the Apurímac and the Pachachaca reflected honor on the Cuzco command.

The day-pupils said that the city seemed deserted. Officers no
longer dazzled passers-by on the streets, in the bars, and in the
parlors of the hacienda mansions. I could not understand why
many of the haughtiest young ladies felt so sad, even to the point
of weeping for the officers, nor how some of them could have become engaged to be married to them. I heard that two of the girls
in the city had attempted suicide. They had gone on excursions
with the soldiers to remote places on the banks of the Mariño and
were said to have been "dishonored" there, although voluntarily
so.

The uniforms lent the officers an air of unreality. Never before
had I seen so many of them together, taking over a city, settling
down in it like a flock of ornamented birds, strutting around like
the owners of heaven and earth. The provincial army chiefs I had
known in the small towns were braggarts, almost always slovenly
and drunken; seeing these regimental officers all together like this
aroused unfamiliar fears in my mind. The rifles, the bayonets, the
crimson plumes, the handsome band of musicians—all got mixed
together in my mind; they tormented my imagination with the
fear of death.

The youngest officers carried glossy leather whips. Wearing fine,
high boots, they strode about in an elegant, authoritarian manner.
On the few occasions they entered the Huanupata district they
caused considerable excitement and were shown immense respect
and admiration. The "mature" officers, on the other hand, enjoyed
no special consideration; the majority of them were fat and
paunchy. The *cholas* became frightened when they passed by.

I was told the Colonel had gone only once to Huanupata. He
was from Trujillo, had a historical surname, and his solemnity and
sternness, a well as his gestures, seemed affected. In church, however, he wore a severe expression that impressed everybody. We
thought he looked imposing, with his gold braid and epaulets, beneath the lofty church dome, amid the incense, alone, seated in a
great high-backed chair. We looked upon him as somewhat more

important than a large landholder. I was told that when he visited the *picantería* district he went through the streets quite rapidly. Several officers and gentlemen would escort him, and he would end his visit deploring the disgusting stench that arose from the *chicha* bars and the huts.

People raised a lot of pigs in that district. The flies swarmed contentedly there, pursuing one another, buzzing around the heads of passers-by. The water in the puddles became foul in the heat, turning different colors, all of them murky. But it was here too that the limbs of some royal lemon trees hung down over the tops of the very high mud walls that abounded in Abancay. The trees displayed their green and ripe fruit on high, and the children coveted them. When one of the little boys from Huanupata brought down one of those royal lemons with a stone, he would take it up almost ecstatically in his hands, and run off as fast as he could. Hidden away somewhere inside of his clothing, perhaps in a knot in his shirttail, he was almost certain to have a chunk of the cheapest kind of brown loaf sugar made in the haciendas of the valleys. The Abancay lemon, large, thick-skinned, edible within and easy to peel, contains a juice which, when mixed with brown sugar, makes the most delicious and potent food in the world. It is burning and sweet. It instills happiness. It is as if one were drinking sunlight.

I could not understand how many of the beautiful young ladies I had seen at the band concerts in the park could weep for the soldiers. I did not understand it; it troubled me. I have already explained how gallant and rather unreal almost all of them seemed with their glossy, pointed whips. But I was suspicious of them. Dressed in strange, long, tight jackets, and with those high, multi-hued hats and very special boots, they appeared condescending to me, as if they might be looking down on people from another planet. They were polite, exaggeratedly so, with their gentlemanly gestures; but all of this impressed me as unnatural, an act, the result of rehearsals, perhaps of secret and exacting training sessions held in cellars or in secret caverns. They were not like the other human beings I had known, either remotely or closely. And in the officers who had reached the age of maturity I could observe—in the short time I had been watching them in Abancay—only the slightest trace of that meticulous bowing and scraping courtesy of the young ones. They stood about everywhere with the greatest self-importance, as if they were not of this earth, but instead had given birth to it, no matter where they might be. And they looked at other people with a different expression on their faces—I should say with a kind of lewdness, peculiar to them alone. When I heard that they had left Abancay, and was told the city was deserted, I could not stop thinking about them.

I remember that one evening on the playground, I came to believe that they were also like ritual dancers or apparitions. "They are wearing costumes!" I told myself. Costumed people were always wanting to carry us off somewhere. The scissors-*danzak'* came from hell, according to the pious women and the Indians themselves; he came to dazzle us with his leaps and his costume full of mirrors. Clicking his steel shears, he would walk across a rope stretched between the church tower and the trees in the plaza. He came as a messenger from another hell, one different from that described by the priests when they were impassioned and angry. But the *ukukus*, who dressed in whole Peruvian bearskins, with the little ears standing up, with the slits in their masks that let the gleam in the dancers' eyes shine through—the *ukukus* would try to carry us off to the "*montaña*," to the region on the edge of the great jungle, toward the dread slopes of the Andes,[1] where the forests and the ferocious vines begin. And what of these costumed beings? The Colonel, and the *huayruros*, with their spurs and leggings, so different from the humble gendarmes they had replaced, and the fat majors who bedecked themselves with plumes to escort the Colonel in the parade? Where did they want to carry us off to? What vein deep in the earth did they represent? At what moment would they begin their dance, during which we might be able to recognize them, and to communicate with them?

What had they told the beautiful girls who went with them to the banks of the Mariño, and what had they done to them? Why were those girls weeping? Could Salvinia have given them one of her bright smiles? This last suspicion horrified me. And the horror itself took me a bit further; perhaps Clorinda, the delicate flower of the dry fields that grew green again only in wintertime, had also gazed upon one of these costumed men; perhaps she might even have preferred him to her sweetheart, the sneaky smuggler, and might have given in to him, even if only to the extent of putting her hand on his epaulets.

I clung to my memory of the Pachachaca bridge, of the idiot, content in the church tower, with Doña Felipa's shawl by her side, in order to keep from hurling myself against the wall in blind despair. And then I thought of Prudencio, and of the soldier I had

---

1. In some places there are sheer cliffs 3,000 feet high.—Trans.

accompanied through the streets, because as he went along he had sung, through tears, a song from my home town. "Not them!" I said aloud. "They're just like me! Not them!"

Overhearing me, Palacitos came up to speak to me.

"Is your mind wandering?" he asked.

"What are soldiers good for?" I inquired, without thinking.

"Good for?" he answered, smiling. "For killing, stupid. You're talking nonsense."

"Even him? Even Prudencio?"

"Even more so!" he told me. "I know. Why do you ask?"

"Because I'm dumb," I answered with conviction. "It's because I don't have my father nearby like you do. That's why I only say silly things."

"My father's coming!" he exclaimed. "He's coming!" And he hugged me as hard as he could.

He immediately made me forget all my past presentiments. This was the first time he had ever looked forward to his father's visit. On the contrary, usually when he heard his father was about to arrive he would get all upset; he'd try to study, to review his books. He'd ask for some definitions, become panicky, and spend his time, in the afternoons, lying on some sheepskins the cook had spread out for him behind the door in the darkest part of the kitchen. He'd come out of there to make more inquiries and to jot a few things down in his notebook. He would become quite meek with the priests, especially with the Rector. The Rector understood very well what was happening, and sometimes tried to cheer him up.

"Take heart, Palacitos!" he'd say. "Take heart, child!"

Taking the boy's chin in his hand, he would force Palacitos to look at him. And the boy would manage a smile.

Now, for the first time, he was eager for his father to arrive.

"The *daños*, little brother!" he told me. "I'm going to give them to him. I'm going to tell him about Lleras, about Brother Miguel, about Prudencio!"

He had examined the marbles, one by one. They were all different, like the eyes of unknown animals. The sight of those little glass spheres, streaked with colored lights, excited him into isolating himself once more, but with another kind of isolation. He had shown the *daños* to his friends—to Romero, Chipro and me. For a moment he had wondered whether he should call Valle especially to look at them, but then he muttered a sarcastic insult in Quechua and closed the box. He paced around the dormitory for two or three days, almost always alone, singing, sometimes whistling, and coming up to us.

"Añuco likes me! Doesn't he?" he'd ask us, all of a sudden.

And he began to study, to pay attention in class, to understand better. Once he raised his hand in class, to answer the teacher's question, and solved the problem immediately. The teacher did not even have time to be very much surprised. He asked several more questions and Palacitos, a little frightened and stammering by now, answered correctly.

I saw that his companions had neither the time nor the opportunity to bother him with their curiosity or amazement at his sudden "sea change." At recess time he sought out Romero and Iño and me. Romero, the champ, quite tall and popular, was faithful to him. He played with him and talked to him. And Romero's shadow sheltered Palacitos and allowed him to develop in peace.

Now he was awaiting his father's arrival with a feeling of great accomplishment, foreseeing a triumph.

"Will your father believe you? Will he like the *daños?*" I asked him.

"He'll believe me, little brother! I'll make his heart stand still. I remember everything. I'll tell him about the books—about arithmetic, about geometry. About geometry, brother! He might even get scared. He won't know me. *Ja . . . jayllas, jajayllas . . . !*"

Together we ran off to the playground. I was lucky to have met him that night, when he was triumphant.

But Antero grew away from me. His new friend Gerardo became the recently-arrived hero. He beat everyone, even Romero, at hop-skip-and-jump and at pole vaulting. He destroyed his opponents at boxing. He played center forward like an eel or an arrow. Only at sprinting and in the running broad jump was he unable to surpass Romero. "Romero, you're great!" he told him on the playground before everyone. Romero was the defensive leader of the soccer team, having replaced Lleras, and Gerardo led the offense. The Rector was already planning a trip to Cuzco to challenge the public school team.

"On to Cuzco!" shouted the priest after a practice game in Condebamba. And he walked between Romero and Gerardo, arm in arm with them. He looked young with his white hair standing up, smiling as he marched across the field.

We applauded them.

"I'm learning from Gerardo," Antero told me in the schoolyard during afternoon recess. "Women! He knows them."

"Women?"

I had never heard him speak of them like that before. He'd call them girls, or kids, the way I did, and lately there had only been one name—Salvinia—and in second place, another—Alcira.

"Yes, women," he answered. "He knows; he's an expert. He's already had two of them in love with him. We've left Salvinia for nobody."

"What do you mean, for nobody?"

"I've got one girl, and another in prospect. But we've got Salvinia fenced in. She's become forbidden territory, forbidden by me and Gerardo. No one is allowed to trespass. Gerardo already had one over at the Mariño River. He made her cry, the bum. He sampled her. I—"

"You what?" I shouted.

"Nothing, brother," he told me. "We're punishing Salvinia. You saw how she was laughing with Pablo, Gerardo's brother, didn't you? You saw her. Now she gives both of us frightened looks. She looks at both of us the same way! Isn't that treachery?"

"You two are just showing off. You're already almost as bad as Lleras," I told him.

As I spoke he gave me a look that was part horror and part curiosity.

"You don't abuse them. You're not evil. But you're worse than Lleras, even dirtier, lying in wait for the girls, like dogs. Why are you frightening Salvinia?"

"Just tell me she didn't laugh. Deny she was flirting!"

"I don't know, Markask'a. You're bigger than I am. You ought to know. But this afternoon I'm giving you back the *zumbayllu*. I've thought it over. I can make some more just like it."

"What are you talking about?" asked Gerardo, jumping down from the porch into the courtyard.

One of his eyes had an iris as large as that of a purebred horse. And it was not the same color as the other one, which was a bright brown; this iris was light green, a green floating amid other diffuse colors, with perhaps the same bright, joyous brown hue predominating in the background.

"Ernesto doesn't understand; he's still a baby," said Antero. "He's angry because I told him we've got Salvinia fenced in and that you already had one girl from Abancay."

"Fenced in! Now I know you're like a panting dog that goes sniffing about in the streets. Hadn't you better leave Salvinia alone?" I told him.

"A panting dog? We'll protect Salvinia. No one will even get near her door," Gerardo answered. "It's not my way of doing things, but Antero decided to do it like that. I told him he had

better get right down to it, the way I do with women. They don't
like anything else."

"What don't they like?"

"Well, being worshipped," answered Antero. "They're crazy
about Gerardo because he's a positivist, because he wants their
bodies."

"That's a lie, you dog! A lie, you thief! You're filthy!" I yelled
at him.

"A lie? They follow me around. They write notes to me. They'll
go anywhere I want them to."

"Then you're nothing but a lost soul, Gerardo, like Wig! If
Wig were brave he'd kick you to pieces, and take your good looks
and your women away from you. He'd made you crawl through all
the streets on your knees after him, the way you deserve. He'd
make you his servant while he abuses the idiot. Didn't Antero say
you make them all cry? Get out of here, son of a soldier! You pig!"

He rushed at me. Antero managed to grab him by the jacket. I
was waiting for him, ready to smash into him. A crowd of clamoring students surrounded us. Blind with rage, I managed to give the
Comandante's son one good kick before they grabbed me from
behind.

"What's going on here?" I heard the Rector say as he came down
the porch steps.

Several boys, fearing the Rector, withdrew to the back of the
playground. The three of us stayed together.

"What's the trouble?" asked the priest, looking at us one by one.

"Nothing, Father," Gerardo answered firmly.

"Ernesto insulted Gerardo, he even kicked him," said Wig. "I
saw him."

Everyone looked at Wig. He laughed, with the strange expression of a remorseful fool, looking as if he were about to burst into
tears. No one paid any attention to him.

"He's lying," said Gerardo. "It was just a joke."

"You, first. Get out of here and go to class. You surely need it!"
the priest ordered Wig. "Ring the bell!"

Recess had ended.

The Rector was left with the three of us.

"Father," I begged, "let me go up to the dormitory for a moment, I have to get something for Antero right away."

"Go on," he agreed.

I bounded up the stairs two at a time, opened my trunk, and
took my only *zumbayllu* out of the bottom of it. The dormitory
was in semidarkness; the wooden rafters, which had never been

covered with a ceiling, were visible in the light from the half-opened window. An American nightingale, the *jukucha pesk'o*, tiny and restless, sang as it hopped about on a beam and then flew out the window.

"*Zumbayllu, zumbayllu*! *Adiós*! I feel sorry for you," I said to the top. "You're going to fall into dirty hands and pockets. The boy who made you is now a godchild of the devil."

I went downstairs. The Rector was still talking with Gerardo and Antero. They looked tall and fleshy to me, and rather jaundiced. I thought the spot in Gerardo's eye was going to spurt pus or some other unhealthy liquid.

I approached them. The presence of the Rector made me hesitate a moment. But I decided to show the *zumbayllu*.

"I'm giving it back to you, Antero," I told him. "It's better to do it now, with the Rector as a witness."

I startled him. He took the little top from me without thinking. But I saw a whirlpool in his eyes, as if the pure water of our first days together were returning. His face grew more handsome, suffused with the light of a childhood reborn. The trace of cynicism, of brutality, vanished from his lips, which reddened.

"No, brother," he said to me. "I gave him that *zumbayllu*, Father. He shouldn't give it back to me!"

Gerardo became confused and uneasy. He noticed Antero's change of expression. The Rector realized something had happened between us. He peered into our eyes. Gerardo remained uncertain, almost lost among the three of us. The spot in his eye floated, unconsciously, like the dilated pupil of a cat's eye in the darkness, without any will or intelligence of its own. I no longer despised him; my anger had cooled. I looked at him and he blinked.

"Why are you returning the top? Wasn't it a memento?" asked the priest.

The attention he was paying us was plainly a tribute to the Comandante's son, to the new hero, Gerardo.

"It was a souvenir of Abancay," I told him. "He's already taken it, but if he wants to give it back to me now . . ."

Antero handed back the *zumbayllu* as if it might burn him.

"A souvenir of Abancay? How's that?" asked the priest.

"It's because of the *zumbayllu* that I'm from Abancay, Father!" I replied. "They don't have them in any other town."

He looked at the three of us again.

"Settle the dispute among yourselves," he said. "I believe it's a child's affair. But promise you won't fight any more. Besides, it's a small matter. You are almost young men. Such young men!"

The Rector flattered them as he was accustomed to flattering those who held power in the valley. He was quite skillful at dealing with this class of people; he chose his words carefully and used appropriate gestures when he was with them. I was aware of the inflections people used when they spoke; I understood them very well. I had been brought up among people who hated one another and hated me; they could not always brandish clubs, or strike with their hands, or set dogs on their enemies. They also used words, injuring one another with these, imbuing their tone of voice, rather than their words, with their mild or virulent poisons.

Antero and his friend left first, after respectfully taking leave of the Rector. Antero followed Gerardo. They did not shake hands with me.

"Go on, you little madman!" the Rector told me. "And don't bother Gerardo; you'll see how we make a clean sweep of all the soccer teams and athletes in Cuzco. I hope that makes you happy!"

I put the *zumbayllu* in my jacket pocket. I caressed its cold paw and its eyes, with which it danced and hummed. It remained quiet and still in the rough cotton cloth of my pocket amid the bread and brown sugar crumbs. But when the town boys left I would spin it again in the main courtyard on the stone pavement, and then it would be the quickest, the liveliest and luckiest, the finest creature to move in the light of the sun.

The next day neither of the two youths spoke to me. They ignored me. Once again Antero's lips had grown brutal, more hardened than any of his other features. His birthmarks, especially the ones on his upper lip and neck, seemed to be joined to his lips by some secret inner current. On the hides of ruttish boars I had seen similar spots that looked exactly the way these birthmarks did now.

Gerardo did not come to call me to account for the way I had insulted him in the presence of witnesses on the playground. I learned that Antero had said that I was a slightly "touched" stranger. They devoted themselves to training for the athletic events. Antero was best at throwing. The boys came to admire Gerardo more and more. He was friendly and kind to the little boys. He trained them in jumping and running and in other exercises which, according to him, developed agility and resistance. Palacitos participated in the games; he was becoming more self-confident.

Pablo, Gerardo's brother, became friendly with Valle. He cultivated elegance and erudition. He also made a conquest of Martel, of a boy called Garmendia, and of a slender, pale youth with a foreign surname who did not mix with the plebeians either. They all were careful about the way they dressed and would not go to the dusty courtyard. During recess they went up onto the balcony. The Rector tolerated them. They even occupied the part of the balcony just outside the Rector's private parlor, over the school's arched entryway, and the Rector did not chase them away. Meeting in this exclusive spot, immaculate, with their shirt cuffs starched and their silk neckties carefully arranged in the *k'ompo* knots Valle had introduced into daily wear, this group of students gave the impression of being a group of stylishly dressed visitors to the school. They were all upperclassmen. The debates and orations they produced on that lofty stage seemed false and stilted to me, although it was Valle who gestured the most. The posture of the others seemed more natural, even the expressions of calm disdain with which they regarded us.

It often happened that when the bell rang Gerardo would come running into the main courtyard, sweaty and unkempt, his clothes covered with dust. He'd look at the learned, polished youths on the balcony slyly, and laugh uproariously.

"Such gentlemen! Such gentlemen!" he would say, and then burst into laughter again.

And neither his words nor his gestures were malicious. He was a strong, cheerful boy. He would laugh at those who were excluded. He would run circles around Wig, at a great speed, saying, "Let's see if I can't wipe that crybaby expression off your face," without meaning to hurt his feelings either.

Wig turned his head to watch him as he ran. The big spot in Gerardo's left eye brightened when he stopped in front of Wig; it conveyed an impression of cruel and domineering joy.

The boys on the balcony treated Gerardo rather condescendingly, unable to conceal their anxiety, and perhaps their envy, even though, with the exception of Valle and the Comandante's son,[2] they really seemed to be reasonable young men, shy and studious by nature. But their faces trembled noticeably when they heard Gerardo's amorous and sporting exploits discussed, and when he laughed boisterously at them.

Romero also let himself be influenced by Gerardo.

"There's no question about it," he said. "On the Coast they know a lot more than we do; they're ahead of us in everything."

He did not play his harmonica for several evenings. I noticed he was worried and followed him about. Palacitos was absorbed with his new discoveries.

---

2. That is, the Comandante's other son, Pablo.—Trans.

"I can't play. Just don't feel like it," Romero told me one night.

"There wouldn't be any team or anything without you. And all you know about is Abancay and Andahuaylas and the road between," I told him.

"So you don't think they're ahead of us on the Coast?"

"Yes, I think they're ahead of us. But who can beat you at the broad jump? Who's better on defense? Is Gerardo? Haven't I noticed how you make him look silly or leave him with his mouth open on the soccer field, and how the ball is always at your feet?"

Romero was naive, tall and strong, and religious.

That night he suddenly began to play *huaynos* again.

"You're almost ashamed of the *huayno*, aren't you?" I asked him.

"Could that be it?" he asked.

"I've been on the Coast, brother," I told him. "In the port of Lomas. The church is a cave the fishermen have taken away from the seals, and the tower is a whale skeleton. A beautiful port, little brother! But sad, and with a rough sea preaching to you in the night like a herd of bulls."

"That Gerardo talks to you and makes you do different things. It's not that you get tired of *huaynos*. But he doesn't know Quechua; I don't know whether or not he despises me when he hears me talking Quechua with the other boys. But he doesn't understand, and I think sometimes he just stands there looking at me as if I were a llama. To hell with him! Let's play a *huayno de chuto*,[3] real *de chuto*," he said enthusiastically. He put the harmonica to his mouth, almost swallowing the instrument, and began to play the rhythm on the bass, as if it were his own big chest, his own great heart that sang. I recognized the tune from the first notes; the words began with these lines:

Vaquillachallaykita tiyay watakuykuy	Tie up your little heifer, auntie,
torillochallaymi suelto kacharisk'a.	My little bull is running loose.

"Hey," Romero asked me presently, "is it really true that the women are dying for Gerardo? It must be the novelty, and because he's the champ. They chase after him."

"Let's not talk about that, Romero; keep on playing. Palacito's father is coming tomorrow . . ."

It was cruel to hear him say the girls were fighting over Ge-

3. Indian.—Author

rardo. It was cruel to have it confirmed like that, after having heard
him speaking with his friend Antero in confidence. Didn't the
girls know anything? Didn't they know the son of the Comandante
was just the same as Wig and no better? Just as disgusting—although without the impatience, without that ungovernable rage—
but with the same froglike drool, and cautious and treacherous,
and so contagious that Markask'a's face and birthmarks had been
tinged with that trace of Gerardo's brutality.

"Wait for me, Romerito," I told him.

"It must surely be his destiny, the destiny of his blood!" I said,
thinking of Antero, as I walked slowly toward the playground. At
the end of the dark courtyard I dug a hole with my fingers, using
a sharp piece of glass to help deepen it. And there I buried the
zumbayllu. I laid it to rest in the bottom of the hole, patted it, and
buried it. Trampling the dirt down firmly, I felt relieved.

"What could have happened?" asked Wig, who was hanging
around in the passageway. "She hasn't come for eight days."

"You mean the idiot?"

"Yes. The cook says that she's been shivering with fever for six
days. And the priests—they don't even know or care!"

"With a high fever?"

"She says she's trembling. Why don't you go to see her? The
cook will let you in."

"Tomorrow early, Wig; I'll go real early."

We returned to the stone-paved courtyard together. Romero was
still playing the melody that had accompanied me as I buried the
zumbayllu, the dancer that had introduced me to the valley and its
soil, particle by particle, from the icy mountain peaks to the sand
at the bottom of the Pachachaca and the Apurímac, God of Rivers.
Now I would find a new *winku* in the neighborhood shops. I had
been looking at them. In the idiot's presence, and with the cook's
help, I would scorch out the top's eyes with a red-hot nail. I'd
make an orangewood tip for it. Then I'd go down to the river and
spin it for the first time on the bridge. From the bottom of the
gorge the *winku* would sing, above the sound of the river. And
immediately after its first song I'd go down to the banks of the
Pachachaca and christen the humming top with water, right out in
the middle of the stream. I'd temper it the way blacksmiths temper fine steel blades.

"Listen," Wig said in a mysterious tone, just as we reached the
porch, "watch out for Gerardo. Didn't you see his eyes? You think
they look like a Christian's? It was awful the way you insulted
him. The *guardias* could take you a long way off and they could

cut your throat. In a little while the dogs and buzzards would eat you all up. These *guardias* know everything; they're trained. They're not like the policemen who went around with the *chicheras*. Be careful, stranger! Who would even ask about you? Didn't you say your father is a hundred leagues from here? What if they threw your body into the Pachachaca in the night? 'Pig, son of a soldier,' you called him. That's not something easily forgotten. And as for them, don't you see, they're the *papachas* here, in Abancay.''

He spoke incoherently, but the meaning came through to me. His throat swelled as he pronounced the words gravely and solemnly. I listened to him attentively.

"You think they'd throw my body into the Pachachaca?" I asked.

"Your dead body."

"Does the body die?"

"What did you say?"

"Water is dead, Wig. Don't you think so?"

"It's something else."

"If water's not dead it would be better for them to take my body to the Pachachaca. Maybe the river would care for me in some woods, or underwater, in its pools. Don't you think so?" I asked.

"If you were a woman, maybe. You're not making any sense!"

"But I'm still not so bad as you. Maybe it would carry me a long way off, into the *montaña*; maybe it would change me into a black duck or a sand-eating fish."

"Honestly, I believe you're crazy. Listen, Ernesto; if I were you, after the way you insulted the son of the Comandante and after he hasn't even looked at you for two weeks and your friend Markask'a won't either because he agrees with Gerardo and won't even speak to you, I'd run away, far away to where my father was. It's easy to go somewhere else. But here they're sure to do something to you! Do you think the Rector would inquire as to your whereabouts?" he continued. "And don't trust them. They'll wait. It won't be to-morrow, nor the next day . . . But I won't forget about you. It'll be any day now . . ."

"And would you run away too, after what you've told me?"

"Why? All I did was tell you, that's all. It's bound to happen. If someone else doesn't tell the Comandante, Gerardo will."

"You'll go and tell him, the way you told the Rector!" I shouted.

"Me, little brother! Me, little brother? I'm a dog, maybe, but how could I do that? Don't you believe it; take care of yourself. I'll look after you too."

"Why?"

"God has permitted me to warn you. He's punishing me. I'm with you now because of that, just like lost souls are chained together. Dear God! Don't go very far from Abancay; don't go into the cane fields; don't go down to the Pachachaca!"

I left him whimpering.

Romero had stopped playing and was talking with Chipro.

"What did Wig tell you?"

"He says the idiot has a fever."

"Really?"

"A high fever."

"Listen," said Chipro, his voice breaking, "I know that on the other side of the river, on the Ninabamba hacienda, people are dying. Something is happening! They had Father Augusto over there to say mass! All that did was to make the fever spread to the other villages, they say. I'm from a town above Ninabamba; people came to visit me yesterday. I'm about to leave for the other side of the cordillera, with my family. They think it's the plague! You mustn't go down into the valleys. Fevers spread without mercy in the heat."

"And why don't they know anything about it in Abancay?"

"Why? It must be because the regiment was here, because everyone was so busy amusing themselves. But by now they must know about it and be getting ready for it."

Iño and the boy from Pampachiri came up to us.

"He says the Pampachirino heard that the *guardias* have set up a control post at the bridge."

"A control post? Who can control the fever?" asked Chipro.

"Stories!" exclaimed Romero. "Ever since the regiment came they've been making up these stories all over town. About the plague coming, about the 'black battle,' about the Chunchos."

"Ninabamba is the poorest hacienda and it's the one that's the farthest from Abancay, almost in the highlands. We'll see!" answered Chipro. "If it's the fever it'll spread from one cane field to another, like a fire with the wind behind it. Me it won't catch. I'll go beyond the cordillera . . ."

They called us to go up to the dormitory. We climbed the steps quietly, without shoving, being careful not to make any noise.

The Rector entered the dormitory and had us say our prayers. As he walked toward the door to leave, the boy from Pampachiri called him.

"Father," he said, "they've sent word to me the fever has broken out on the other side of the river. Do you know anything about it?"

"What?" asked the Rector.

"The fever, Father. Typhus. It's broken out in Ninabamba; they say it's coming down to the other haciendas. The *colonos* are already eating the lice from the dead people. That's what they say . . ."

"I don't know anything about it. I don't know anything! It must be the *chicheras* making up stories to frighten people. Be quiet! Go back to your prayers."

He made us say our prayers again. And his voice changed. When he realized that he was imploring God too earnestly, he went back to his usual singsong tone of voice. But at the end, when he made the sign of the cross, he intoned the words solemnly.

"Sleep well, my boys."

He said good night, walked slowly to the door, and turned out the light.

I thought the boarders, all of them, would get out of bed, or sit up and keep on asking and inquiring about the plague. That they'd gather round Chipro's or the Pampachirino's bed. I had always seen how easily they became excited, almost competing with one another in exaggerating rumors, telling stories, and inventing or guessing things. But this time they covered their heads with their blankets and quieted down immediately, isolating themselves. I was left alone, as the others must have been. We must have all seen the plague at least once, in our own home towns. It was probably our memories of it that created the abyss between one bed and another.

"The fever is spreading!" Every fiber of my body tingled with the news. In two towns, Querobamba and Sañayca, I had seen people dying by the hundreds from the plague. In those days I had been terrified every time a fly crawled over my body, or whenever a spider fell, dangling from a roof or a bush. I would stare at them until my eyes burned. The townspeople thought of them as death itself. They would shoo away the hens that cackled in the patios or in the backyards, throwing sticks or rocks at them. They killed them. They also suspected them of being harbingers of death when they cackled like that. The hen's raucous, uneven voices broke happily through the silence that was maintained in every house. The wind must not blow too strongly, because people knew that death came in with the dust. They would not put the carcasses of slaughtered sheep out in the sun, because the *chiririnka* lays its eggs in their flesh; it is a dark blue fly that buzzes, even in the darkness, and announces death; hours before it happens, it senses those who are about to become corpses, and hovers around them. Anything that moved violently or suddenly was greatly feared. And since the bells tolled day and night, and those who sat up with the dead sang hymns in a falsetto that chilled the marrow of our bones, the days and weeks that the plague lasted were lifeless. The sun seemed to be eclipsed. Some of the *comuneros* who were still hopeful burned straw and brush on the hilltops. In the daytime, the pall of smoke made us drowsy; at night the light of the fires descended into the depths of our hearts. We were amazed to see that the huge eucalyptus trees were not felled also by the plague, and that in the mud the worms still survived, crawling about.

I cringed in my bed. If the plague came it would enter the filthy hacienda quarters and kill everyone. "It must not cross the bridge!" I screamed.

Some of the boys sat up.

"That's right! It must not cross the bridge!" said the Pampachirino.

"Yes, let the people on the other side of the river just die like dogs," answered Chipro.

"You said they're already eating the dead people's lice. How's that, little brother? How's that?"

As I was questioning the boy from Pampachiri, my blood grew cold; I felt frozen in that heated dormitory.

"Yes, The families come together and remove the lice from the corpse's feet, and from all his clothing; and with their teeth, brother, they crush them. They don't eat them."

"You said they ate them."

"They bite them first. They crush their heads. I don't know if they eat them or not. They call this *usa waykuy*. It's to fight the plague. They detest the lice but they do it to resist death."

"Do they know the louse carries the fever, brother?"

"They don't know it. Do they carry the fever? But the dead, who knows why, are crawling with lice, and they say that God puts wings on the lice when there's a plague. He puts wings on them, little brother! They say the wings are tiny, just big enough for them to get from one man to another, from an infant to his father, or from a father to his little child."

"It must be the devil!" I told him.

"No! It's God; only God sends death! The devil has a tail; death is bigger than he is. With his tail he tempts us, all of us who are hot-blooded."

"Have you ever seen the wings on a fever louse?"

"No one has, little brother. No one. More transparent than glass they are, they say. And when the louse flies up into the air the wings move, they say, and you can't see them. Let's pray, little brothers."

"Silently!" shouted Valle. "Silently!" he repeated, entreating us.

"All together, like in church, would be better," said Wig, kneeling.

"Be quiet! You're as bad as broody hens," said Romero, firmly. "This uproar is all because of the idiot. There isn't any plague anywhere. The *chicheras* are defending themselves or taking revenge with their mouths. I hope they give them another beating!"

After that no one said anything else. Many of them must have been reassured by Romero. Wig went back to bed. They all fell asleep. Some of them moaned in their sleep. All during the night I could hear the boys breathing. Groups of people went by in the street, talking. Three times I heard the word *plague*. I did not understand what was being said, but the word came in to me clearly, plainly spoken. Some of the boarders woke up around midnight; they sat up and lay back down again. They seemed to feel hot, but in my bed the chill continued.

I waited, motionless, for daybreak. Once, I shook myself, believing that I had "gone beyond" from holding my body so rigid. I did not trust the roosters. They crow all night; they make mistakes; if one of them crows because he is upset, or sick, many more follow his example, misled by the first call. I waited for the birds, the *jukucha pesk'os* that dwelt in the eaves. One lived inside the dormitory, in the rafters. He'd come out at dawn, hopping from beam to beam, fluttering his little wings that were almost like a hummingbird's, and fly out through the window that was left open to let in the air.

The nightingale finally got up. He flew down to a wooden beam and hopped about there for a while, turning completely around. He was the same color as a squirrel, and just as restless. I never saw him pause to contemplate the ground or the sky. He hopped and frisked about, opening and closing his wings, amusing himself for a while on a board where the sunlight from the window shone. His incessant activity brought warmth to my heart, which had almost stopped beating. If I looked for them, I could see his eyes. No river, or diamond, or even the noblest of stars sparkles the way the eyes of that Andean nightingale did that morning! He flew away, finally, escaping through the window. The daylight shone in, first on the things in the dormitory and then on me. I got out of bed and managed to dress quietly. Thinking of the time

Chauca had gone out to flagellate himself in the chapel doorway, I opened the dormitory door, raising it so as not to make any noise.

When I reached the courtyard I was captivated by the sky, which was beginning to brighten with the tender joyfulness shown by nature in the warm valleys at the break of day. I thought, then, that perhaps I should spin my *zumbayllu*, as I had that early morning when I first felt myself to be a child of the Pachachaca. "I'll rescue it!" I said. "It might have learned some other sounds, since it has been sleeping underground."

I ran to the inner courtyard. The door to the passage leading to the kitchen and to the idiot's room was not closed. All of my fears were revived. "Her!" I said.

I entered the narrow passageway, and came to the little yard where they kept the firewood. The stone-paved ditch, with the foul water from the toilets, ran through there. The door to the cubbyhole where the idiot slept was half open. I pushed on it. The cook peered out at me; it seemed that she, too, had just come in; her eyes filled with tears.

The idiot's body lay on some sheepskins. I moved closer. On the end of one of the poles that held up the tin and thatch roof was Doña Felipa's shawl, covering some other tattered clothing.

I saw the sick woman's face. I saw her hair, close up, and the filthy blouse that covered her chest up to the neck.

"*Mamita*," I said to the cook. "*Mamita*! Tell her farewell! Say good-bye to me too!"

I knelt on the ground, my mind made up.

The idiot's hair and blouse swarmed with lice; they crawled along slowly, dangling from every hair on her head, from those that hung down over her forehead and face; on the hems of her blouse and in the seams I could see them moving along in a line, one behind the other, toward a world without end.

"*Imam? Imam?*" asked the cook.

"Be calm; go to the doorway and pray from there. She's dying," I told her.

She knew it. She knelt and began to pray the Lord's Prayer in Quechua.

As if by the light of a great sun that illumined my native village, I saw plainly the cascade of clear water where the bereaved relatives of those who had died of the fever washed the clothing of the dead, and the eucalyptus tree in whose shadow they wept in the plaza while they rested the bier.

"This creature who has suffered—gather her unto you, great Lord," the cook prayed to God in her own words, in Quechua,

having concluded the Lord's Prayer. "She has suffered, she has
suffered! Walking or sitting, doing or not doing, she has suffered.
Now you will put a light in her mind; now you will make her an
angel and have her sing to your glory, great Lord . . . !"

"I'm going to go and tell the Rector," I told her. "Don't go into
the hut anymore, until I return."

When I got to the main courtyard, I stopped. I felt as though
thousands of lice were crawling over my body and heating it up.

"How can I give him the disease, how could I do this to him?"
I exclaimed, hesitating. But I had to save the others. "I'll shout
to him and run away," I said.

I climbed the stairs slowly so as not to make the boards creak. I
rapped on the Rector's bedroom window. He heard me.

"Father," I said. "The idiot Marcelina has died. From typhus,
Father! Have her taken out of the school!"

I went down the steps, almost running.

The cook was still on her knees, in the doorway of the hut.

I entered, and with sudden joy, saw Doña Felipa's shawl. Taking it down from the roof pole, I gave it to the cook.

"Keep it for me, *señora*, it's a keepsake for me," I begged her.

She got up and went to put the cloak away in the kitchen.

When she returned, I was sitting on the ground by the idiot's
sheepskins.

"If I die, you must wash my clothing," I told the cook.

She looked at me wonderingly, without answering.

I raised the idiot's arms and crossed them upon her chest; her
hands were very heavy. I told the cook this was strange.

"It's from all she's worked and all she's suffered," she answered
me.

A *chiririnka* began to buzz around my head. I was not afraid.
They can smell corpses from a great distance and come to hover
around them with their melancholy little music. I spoke to the fly
as it circled at roof level. "Sit on my head," I told it. "Then you
can spit in the dead woman's ear or nose."

The idiot grew quite pale. Her features sharpened.

I begged her pardon in the name of all the students. As I spoke
I felt the heat from the lice abating. Her face was growing beautiful, losing its deformity. She had already closed her eyes by herself.

The Rector came.

"Get out!" he shouted at me. "Get out of here, you miserable
little wretch!"

"Not now, Father," I begged him. "Not now, not me."

He took me by the collar and dragged me out. Two men with sheets in their hands stood behind him. They quickly wrapped up the dead woman, picked her up, and hurried off with her. I followed them.

One of the men held her by the head and the other held her by the feet. It was still early morning. It only took them a second to cross the stone-paved courtyard and pass into the shade of the archway. The porter held the little door in the gate open for them. They went out.

I cried as the Rector shoved me along, driving me with a stick toward the little concrete sink next to the toilets. From outside he ordered me to undress. The porter washed my body with a rag, covered me with another sheet, and carried me off to Brother Miguel's still empty cell.

From the balcony I saw the sun rising behind the cliffs on the other side of the valley.

They put me in the friar's bed. The priest soaked my hair in creosol and wrapped a white towel around my head.

"She went with Father Augusto to Ninabamba, it must have been about two weeks ago," I told him. "I saw them crossing the bridge over the Pachachaca. Doña Marcelina climbed the stone cross like a bear. Surely she was marked for death then, just as I am now."

"The wretched woman, the beast! She must have been with the hacienda Indians, with the sick people," said the Rector in an angry outburst, unable to control himself.

"Then the plague is already here, Father! The plague is already here! I'm going to die. Have them wash my clothing, not burn it. Have someone sing me a farewell song in the cemetery. They know how to do it here," I told him.

"You miserable child!" he shouted. "How long had you been there with her?"

"Since daybreak."

"Did you get into her bed? Confess!"

"Into her bed, Father?"

His eyes glared at me; there was a disgusting fire in them.

"Father!" I screamed. "You have hell in your eyes!"

I covered my face with the blanket.

"Did you lie with her? Tell me, did you get into bed with her?" he kept asking me. He was panting. I could hear the wheezing in his chest.

Hell exists. It was there, rasping away at my side like a blacksmith's bellows.

"Answer me, you little madman! Did you get into bed with her?"

"Padrecito!" I screamed at him again, sitting up. "Padrecito! Don't ask me. Don't get me dirty! The rivers might sweep you away; they're on my side. The Pachachaca might come!"

"What?" he said. He came even closer to me. I could smell the pomade on his hair. "Then you didn't get into bed with her? You didn't? Answer me!"

I realized he was frightened; I think he was so confused it was beginning to make him dizzy. He was furious.

He took my hands and stared at me for such a long time that I turned to face him. That repugnant tension, which had made him seem like a hot-blooded animal, had left his eyes. I spoke, still looking at him.

"I prayed by her side; I crossed her hands on her chest. I said farewell to her, for all of us. She died peacefully. Now she is dead, fortunately. Now, even though I come down with the fever, you must let me go to my father."

"Always the same! You lost creature. You don't have any lice, not a single one. We got to you in time. Perhaps I shouldn't have asked you things, those things. I'll be back!"

And suddenly he left. I could hear him locking the door with a key.

I had to conjure up the torrent of the Apurímac, the clumps of reeds that grow up and wave their plumes along its banks, the gulls that shriek for joy above the light of its waters. And Brother Miguel. His blackness; his hair that curled so tightly it revealed the shape of his head. He would not have questioned me as the Rector had; he would have had them serve me a cup of chocolate with muffins; he would have gazed at me with his eyes that were white and mild, like those of all beings who truly love the world.

I covered my head with the blankets and could not help weeping, weeping for joy, as though I had just escaped from some danger, from being contaminated by the devil. And afterwards, once I felt better, I sat up to inspect the little room, and the religious pictures on the walls. I recognized one of the Virgin Mary, and began to speak to the friar:

"Brother Miguel, I'm going to tell you about the time in Huamanga a lady where I was staying gave me a Madonna like the one that presides over your room. It had a little glass frame. I kept it in my jacket pocket all the time that I was in Huamanga. At night, I'd hang the little picture up on the wall, at the head of my bed. My father went on ahead to Cangallo. He had some mule drivers come after me the next week, and sent me a pretty blue donkey. But the mule drivers had other freight; they begged me to lend them the donkey; and they offered to let me ride on a bored-looking mule with big ears, because he was tame. I felt sorry for the mule and preferred to walk. I'm a great one for hiking, Brother. We set out at three in the morning from Ayacucho so we could climb the long slope, reach the summit by dawn, and cross the plain of the Morochucos in the daylight. You know what bandits those bearded horsemen are, Brother. We left in such a hurry and confusion that I forgot my image of the Virgin and left her on the wall. I remembered her near the summit, as the sun appeared. 'I'll catch up with you, for sure!' I told the mule drivers, and went back the two leagues to the city. I ran through the courtyard and into the little room where I had been staying. There was the Madonna. I took her down; she was awfully small, even with her glass frame. The lady who owned the house kissed me when she saw me coming out with the image and gave me an orange for the road. I caught up with the muleteers, Brother, right out in the middle of the plain, at noon. They were moving along rapidly, driving the herd of mules. They lifted me up onto the mule's back and made much of me when I showed them the Madonna. She might protect them from the highwaymen. Three years later a scoundrel in my home village broke the frame and threw the picture in my face. You must know who it was, Brother. I hope a snake gets into his bed and spits venom into his eyes. I hope he goes blind and stumbles off to hell, unable to find it for years and years. Maybe that would be worse for him than being burnt in the fire. I know it would!"

I heard the footsteps of many people on the balcony. By then they must have been all upset. The noise had begun while I was speaking to the friar.

I removed the towel from my head. It was white. I could not find a single louse. It smelled of disinfectant.

"Brother Miguel!" I continued. "Maybe I won't get the fever! Perhaps I'll be saved. The idiot Marcelina must be praying for me up in heaven. She'll burn off the lice's wings and save us. But now I can't go down to the Pachachaca. I'll have to go round by way of Cuzco."

I sprang out of bed. When I saw that I was naked, I covered myself with a blanket. I walked about, testing my strength. "I don't have the fever! I'm going to escape it. The Rector has saved me. Like the others, he had filth in his soul, but he cared for me. God preserve him."

I lay down again. I felt sheltered by the bed. "It's Brother Miguel's spirit," I thought. "Let them close the bridge. The only thing they can do now is to close the bridge!" I exclaimed.

I tried to get out to help run errands, to go down to the river with the *guardias*, although I wondered if those gaudy soldiers with boots and hats could stand the sun in the gorge, and the permanent guard duty. But the cell was locked tightly.

"The *colonos* will come down like a landslide from the other side of the river," I thought to myself. "Or else they'll just die peacefully in their thatched huts! They have no fear of death. They receive it with mournful hymns, even though no one else pays any attention to an Indian's death. In the Indian communities they wear mourning, but the *colonos* don't even know about that any more; they teem in the alien earth like worms; they weep like little children; like Christians they take orders from the overseer who represents God, who is the master, the son of God, as unattainable as He is. If one of those masters were to say 'Feed your tongue to my dog,' the *colono* would open his mouth and offer his tongue to the dog. They will die, trembling, like the idiot Marcelina, and go to heaven to sing eternally! They won't go down to the bridge," I said. "They won't dare! And if one of them does go down and sees the *guardias* armed with their rifles, and with those wide-brimmed hats and leather leggings and spurs, he will fear them worse than death."

I did not hear the bell. Nor did I hear any of the town students arrive. I remembered it was Saturday. They brought my breakfast. Father Cárpena entered the room.

"Let's have a look," he said, taking a long time to inspect my head.

"Not a one," he said. "But you shan't go out until tomorrow. They put more creosol on than you needed."

He made me wash my head in a bucket of water, with a foul-smelling soap.

"The day-pupils didn't come to school, Father," I told him.

"They're practicing football and other sports. The boarders have gone out too. They already know you're sick."

"Sick?"

"Yes, with the grippe. You must not be alarmed. I took the idiot's body to the hospital. It was a heart attack."

"An attack? What about the lice?"

"They always have them."

"Are they going to let the servants in there? All of them?"

"The cook isn't there any more, as a precaution. The idiot's

clothing has been burned. The kitchen has been swept with creosol. The whole thing with creosol, without leaving a corner. The
porter has also been disinfected, even though he doesn't even sleep
nearby."

"Why, if there isn't any plague?"

"Plague? Lice multiply on any dirty body, especially if it's sick."

"No, Father. It's the fever. Tell them to close the bridge. I've
seen people die of typhus in other towns. They looked just like
Doña Marcelina did. And just as everybody says about the plague,
Doña Marcelina's body was swarming with lice."

" 'Doña'? Why do you say 'Doña'? You're delirious, and no
wonder. But calm down, my boy, for the sake of Brother Miguel,
whom you love."

But there was nothing they could do about it. In the afternoon
the boarders hung around the door to my room. Someone must
have been watching them because they did not speak to me from
outside.

During the night the courtyard was quiet. Except for a few
moments when I heard Romero's harmonica. He played the *huayno* from Huanta, the one about Colonel Ramírez who massacred
the Indians in the cemetery. Father Cárpena brought me my dinner.

"Don't talk," he ordered.

I ate in silence, once more tormented by my premonitions.

Late that night someone knocked at my door.

"Do you have a fever?" a voice asked. It was Abraham, the
gatekeeper.

"Do you have a fever?" he asked me again.

"No!" I said.

"I do, child. I'm going back to my home town to die."

"Don't." I told him. "You'll spread the disease. Where are you
going?"

"To Quishuara! On the other side of the Pachachaca. People are
dying there already. The Rector has already burnt up all of my
lice! Now I won't carry the infection; he says it's carried by lice.
They were running around all over my body and my head, too," he
said in Quechua, in a faint voice. "There aren't any more left
now."

I wanted to ask him if he had slept with the idiot, but I thought
better of it and kept quiet.

"In Ninabamba it started," I told him.

"From there the departed one brought it up. As for me, well, I
used to go in there once in a while. How unfortunate, how un-

fortunate! That's how death comes, child. The departed one will keep watch over the other people from heaven, but she'll be calling me to her, because I slept in her bed when she was coming down with the fever. She'll be calling me! No matter where I am she'll find me, too. God's helping her now. There's no hope. I'd like to drown myself in a pool; to the great jungle I could go, but it wouldn't do any good. It's better for me to go back to my home town to die."

Indians and mestizos love to talk about death; we do too. But when you hear it discussed in Quechua, you embrace death almost as if it were a rag doll, or an icy shadow that oppresses your chest, brushing against your heart, filling it with sudden dread; even though it comes like the softest of lily leaves, or like snow, like snow from the mountain peaks, where life does not exist.

"Abraham! Here you can get well again! The idiot doesn't have to request your death. Once she gets to heaven she won't remember how she suffered," I pleaded.

"It's not her, child," he answered. "It's God! I have slept with a sick woman. She didn't want to do it. She didn't want to, child. Surely it must have been the devil who got into her bed, and not me. The hotter her body was, the more I wanted her. The road to the graveyard is the only one for me. It's not far now! After a few years they're sure to put my skull in a niche in the graveyard. If you go to my home town, when you're big, look for it, child. It will have a green spot on the forehead. Break that part with a stone and bury me, even if it's not very deep. Farewell, child! I came to make this request of you. You'll get to Quishuara sometime even if it takes twenty years. Thank you, *papay*! The demon that is in my body must die. *Adiós, papay*!"

I heard him leaving. "Good-bye," I said.

He went down the stairs. At that moment I could have heard his footfalls even if, by the devil's handiwork, he had been changed into a centipede or a snake. After a few moments, he opened the little door in the gate and then closed it immediately. He would walk down to the bridge rapidly, and come upon it while it was still night. At the foot of the cross he would take off his hat and bow. No one would be able to stop him. He'd get home to his village to die.

I couldn't go to sleep after that leave-taking. More groups of people walked the streets that night. Brother Miguel's room was quite dark; only one small, high window, a skylight, opened onto the street. I heard people hurrying by; I could hear the footfalls even of those who were barefooted. I lay still in bed, listening intently. Death, wearing a mantle, was coming closer; she was advancing from the other side of the river. "They'll have to demolish the bridge," I thought, "blow it up with dynamite, knock down its three arches. I hope they attack the fever from behind." Because she was coming with her face turned toward Abancay.

I awoke in the morning to the sound of my door being opened.

"Oh!" Father Cárpena exclaimed in alarm when he saw me.

I had slept stretched out on my back, in the position used to lay out the dead.

I got out of bed.

"What about Abraham, Father?" I asked him.

"Abraham?" he said, staring at me.

Father Cárpena enjoyed excellent health; his ears were red, and beneath his shaggy brows his eyes were always sparkling with joy.

"Why do you ask?"

"He's gone, Father," I said. "He had the fever and came to say good-bye to me; but he'll make it home to his own village. The fever won't overtake him on the way. It couldn't!"

The priest sat down in a chair, and stared at me.

"But you're not sick," he said, looking at me.

"Not me. Abraham came to say good-bye to me because I took care of the idiot when she was dying and crossed her arms. Surely he must have known about it."

"There are rumors all over town and on the haciendas. People get frightened easily, you know?" he said. "Wig has been expelled from school because he was howling like a dog on the playground, near the latrines. I think he has lost his mind. Simeón, the boy from Pampachiri, has run away. Tomorrow the boarders are leaving. You are to stay here."

"Wig was howling, Father?"

"Yes, son, howling."

"His mother must have heard howling when she was carrying him in her womb; he must have been brought up in some dreary place where dogs were suffering."

"Perhaps, son. Three of his relatives carried him off all bound up with leather thongs. He had the whole town in an uproar. I think he'll probably have a stroke."

The priest spoke to me anxiously. He was the one who had kicked Wig and knocked him down on the playground.

"Brother," I told him, "the Rector thought . . . I was a devil, that I was hot-blooded. This must be the punishment."

"But don't you leave."

"I'm leaving! Everyone's going to go away."

"Tomorrow," he said. "The school will be closed for a month."

They would not let me out of the bedroom. At first I kicked on the door, trying to break the lock. But Father Cárpena spoke to me from the balcony.

"What could you do outside, except witness the despair that people are undergoing? In there Brother Miguel's spirit will keep you company."

"I'll wait," I answered him, "as long as it takes."

Next morning some horses entered the courtyard. Many times people went down the stairs, whispering, trying not to make any noise.

"They must be afraid the fever is developing in my blood," I reflected. "That's why they don't let me out. They let my friends go off without saying good-bye to me."

The horses left the courtyard at a walk. I counted ten of them.

Around noon I heard someone coming up to my room. They stopped outside the door. Whoever it was rolled in two gold coins, worth a pound each, through a crack under the door, and pushed in a little folded piece of paper. It was Palacitos! I jumped out of bed.

"I'm leaving with my father, little brother! Good-bye!" he whispered hurriedly. And off he went.

I didn't even have time to answer him. He ran off before I could speak. I picked up the paper. It, too, was written hastily. I read: "My father sends you this for your journey. If you're not saved, for your funeral. Good-bye, little brother Ernesto."

I heard them going down the stairs. I picked up the two gold pieces and went back to bed.

Palacitos was just like the Indians and mestizos from the communities. He worried about his funeral. If it were not conducted by a richly attired priest, and if no masses were sung, then the devil would win the contest and drag his soul away with him. He had meant to remove all my fears with his farewell gift when he wrote "for your funeral"!

But if I felt the fever coming on I would do what Abraham had done—run away. Maybe I could not get to Coracora, but I could reach my home village, which was a closer journey by three days. I would take the red dirt road down Huayrala Hill. From that fine clay I'd model the figure of a dog to help me cross the river that separates this life from the next. Trembling, I'd enter my village without a single louse, with my head shaved. And I'd die in any house but the one where they had raised me, hating me because I was someone else's child. The whole town would sing as they followed the little bier that carried me to the cemetery. Birds would come to the roadside walls and bushes to sing for an innocent child. In my father's absence, the staff-bearing Indian *alcalde* would cast the first handful of dirt on my body. And they'd cover the little mound with flowers. "It's better to die that way!" I thought, recalling Wig's madness and the Rector's murky, polluted eyes, and thinking of Markask'a, so suddenly changed into a pig, his birthmarks swelling as if they were oozing grease. On my way out of the city I would go through Condebamba, and on Salvinia's doorstep I'd lay a lily that I would have picked in the plaza, a purple one, from Abancay. "Don't trust anyone," I'd write on a big envelope, and sign my name.

That's what Abraham had come for, surely, so that with his departure everything would become clear to me.

I stood there happily inspecting the gold pieces. Hardly anyone spent those gold coins any more. Palacitos's father flattered the Rector by paying the school fees in gold. He did it solemnly, like one nobleman paying tribute to another. The first time he had left his son one of those coins was when Palacitos, imitating his father, had wished to honor Romero and show him his gratitude. And now I held two of them in my hands. For my funeral or for my journey. Palacitos—"the Indian Palacios" as he was sometimes called by those who were arrogant or by his enemies—had rolled into my prison the gold coins that would enable me to reach either of two heavens—my father, or that which they say is waiting in the next life for those who have suffered.

Gold is something that human beings discover deep down in the rocks, or in the sands of the rivers. Everyone is exalted by its dull gleam, even if we only fancy we see some similar glow in the sand or in the streaks of minerals on the dark walls of a cave. I knew that its working is difficult, that it is refined by the grace of fire and some arcane compounds discovered by engineers and alchemists through long and secret research. But a gold piece in the hands of a boy transforms him into a king, into one of those hummingbirds that, by instincts peculiar to them, fly straight up towards the sun. I have seen them glowing iridescently, their wings whirring as they rise upwards.

In spite of the message that accompanied them, the coins helped to dissipate my gloomy fears. I tossed the coins into the air to make them whir; I looked at both sides of them, and at their indented edges. The plumed crest of the Inca warrior engraved on the back of the coins pleased me.

"I'll never spend them," I said. "I'll just show them in the villages and they'll take care of me. They'll think I'm the wandering son of some prince or a messenger of the Lord who travels around testing the honesty of his creatures."

The coins were heavy. I have never seen a worn gold piece. They're always new. Mine had a better shine and ring to them because of the silence around me.

"It's because of you, Brother Miguel," I thought. "I'm in your room. Surely that's why Palacitos came here, as if to a temple, to leave his gold. It won't be for my funeral!"

Tuesday, at noon, the Rector opened the door to the bedroom, and hurried over to my bed.

"You're going to go to your Uncle Manuel Jesús's haciendas," he told me. "I've already got permission from your father. There aren't any horses. You're to go on foot, the way you say you like to travel."

I sat down on the bed. He remained standing.

"To the Old Man's, Father? To the Old Man's?" I asked.

The Rector gave me a telegram to read, from my father. It told me to leave Abancay for the Huayhuay hacienda and to return when the school called me back.

"I suppose that two days on the road is nothing to you. The haciendas are up above the Apurímac, in the highlands."

"In the highlands, Father?"

"There are rocky cliffs between the river and the haciendas. But a road, which only the Indians can traverse, comes down like a corkscrew to the river. The old gentleman invited us there three years ago. You'll be able to get down—"

"The Old Man won't give me anything to eat, Father," I interrupted. "He won't feed me. He's stingier than Judas."

The Rector's cheeks reddened.

"Stingy!" he said, indignantly. "Did you say he's stingy?"

"I know him. He lets fruit spoil rather than give it to his servants. My father—"

"You're out of your mind! Don Manuel Jesús takes missions of Franciscan priests to his haciendas every year. He treats them like princes!"

"Missions of Franciscan priests . . . ? Then he must have a lot of *colonos*, Father?"

"Five hundred in Huayhuay, one hundred fifty in Parhuasi, in Sijllabamba . . ."

"I'll go, Father!" I told him. "Let me go right now!"

He looked at me in even greater astonishment.

"I don't understand you, boy," he told me. "I don't understand you now any more than I did the other times. You are to leave tomorrow at daybreak."

"Father. Does the Old Man speak Quechua with his *colonos* in Huayhuay?"

"Sometimes. But you won't be able to speak with the Indians. I'm warning you! Don Manuel Jesús is stern and magnanimous; he's a great Christian. On his haciendas the Indians don't get drunk or play those devilish flutes and drums; they pray morning and evening; then they go to bed in their quarters. The peace and silence of God prevail on his haciendas."

"And the Apurímac, Father?"

"What does that have to do with it?"

"Don't the Indians even go down to the river to sing at carnival time?"

"I told you the *patrón* is a religious man. You must observe the rules of the hacienda—work, silence, piety."

"I'm familiar with them, Father. I shall go. Did you say two days? I'll get there in a day and a half. I shall pray with the *colonos* and live with them. Have all the boarding students gone?"

"All of them."

"And Antero?"

"He's gone too."

"And the major's sons?"

"They've all gone; only the sons of the poor will stay here."

"What about the fever, Father?"

"It's still raging on the hacienda on the other side of the river. It's getting worse."

"And the bridge?"

"They've walled it off with adobe. They made a door in the wall. Medicine gets through."

"And the cook, Father?"

"I don't know."

"She died!" I said, for it seemed to me that his too sudden reply gave him away.

"Yes, but in the hospital, in isolation."

"With her head shaved, without her hair they buried her?"

"That's right, son. How did you know that?"

"I had a presentiment about it, Father. Abraham has gone home to Quishuara to die. The fever must have gotten there by now."

"You're not to leave the school!" he exclaimed, with unexpected anger. "I'm going to bring in an alarm clock for you. It will ring at four in the morning. There is a new gatekeeper. He sleeps in the kitchen."

"Won't you let me out to say farewell to Abancay?"

"I promised your father . . ."

His tone of voice had turned strange when I mentioned Abraham. He stared at me. He gave me a piercing look, becoming more and more lost in space, like anyone who is misled by signs suggested to him by his own confusion and misconceptions.

I showed him the two gold coins. Perhaps I did it in the heat of the malign unrest that he himself aroused in me when he was troubled.

"What's that?" he asked.

"Two gold pieces, Father."

"You didn't steal them, did you?"

"With these I'll go down the road like the son of a king, Father. I'll show them to the Old Man. I'll test whether or not God hears him . . ."

As I said these unexpected words, the image of Cuzco came into my mind, the voice of the María Angola welling out as if from the bottom of a lake; the image of Our Lord of the Earthquakes and of the deep mirrors that shine in the semidarkness of the cathedral.

The priest came closer. There was a dullness to his eyes. A kind of cloudy liquid rippled in them, revealing his confusion, the still undefined longings that were growing in his soul.

"Did you steal them, my boy?" he asked me.

He was wise and forceful, and yet his voice quavered; there were centuries of suspicion weighing upon him, and a fearful thirst to punish someone. I felt as if the flame of evil itself were licking at me.

"Read this, Padrecito," I told him. "It's a gift from a friend. He must have gotten to his village by now."

The Rector read Palacitos's note. He leaned against the head of the cot and stared at me. I think his first impulse was to punish me violently. I was expecting it. But his eyes cleared.

"I shall let you go out. We have suffered a great deal lately. The school is empty. Now you will see Abancay. I'll have them bring in your clothing. Your friend Palacitos's father went off ecstatic over his son, despite his fear of the plague."

"Did you test him? Did he have you give Palacios an exam?"

"It wasn't necessary. The boy showed him Añuco's gift, that collection of red *daños*, and a letter from Brother Miguel, congratulating and blessing him. And while I was there, he himself spoke to his father about history, natural science, and geometry. You should be pleased, my boy! Palacios dazzled his father; he looked quite respectable."

"Had Romero gone already?"

"Yes."

"And Chipro?"

"He's gone too . . . 'You'll be an engineer,' his father told him, and after that I left them in the office."

"Then he must have asked for the gold coins for me when they were alone. Did they leave right away?"

"No, a little while later. The boy went up to the dormitory for his books and his saddlebag. When he said good-bye to me he didn't cry. Nor did he say anything to me about you, even though I had locked you up, and that seemed strange to me."

"He had already been here."

"You must be careful with the gold pieces; you're going to be traveling alone."

"I'll never spend them, Father."

"Wait a little while; I'll send your clothing."

He went out of the room, leaving the door open. He was tall, and walked majestically, with his white hair standing up. When nothing serious was troubling him, his face and his whole figure radiated kindliness; at such a time he could, with a hug or by laying his hand upon a head, cheer and console some little boy who might be suffering from anger, despair, or some physical pain. Perhaps I was the only boarder who had seen the shadow of what there also was in him of gloom, of remorselessness.

Wearing my new suit I went out in the afternoon, going down into the courtyard.

Neither Palacitos, Antero, the idiot, Wig, Romero, Añuco, the cook, nor Abraham were there any longer. I realized I was alone in the big school building.

I sat down for a moment on the porch steps, facing the little fountain.

Then I walked slowly to the playground. I was more attentive to memories than to external things.

There were three of the little wooden privies; and another larger one that housed the small sink and another toilet. That's where they had attacked the feeble-minded woman. Finding myself in front of that door without having meant to go there, I opened it. The weeds that grew in the damp corner, by the wall, had even more flowers on them. A bouquet could be made from the *ayak'-zapatillas*. I picked all of them; then I pulled up the plant, shook the dirt from the roots, and threw it into the water running in the ditch. After that I left the courtyard.

The cemetery was a long way from town. I would have liked to have hung that bunch of flowers on its gate, since no one could tell which of the mounds of dirt on the common people's tombs belonged to Doña Marcelina. On my way to the room where she had died, I went down the little passageway and looked into the kitchen. There I saw two men. They did not hear me go by. The little yard still smelled of disinfectant. They had closed up the room with a little red padlock. I did not find any mourning bands crossed on the door, as is the custom in the small towns when someone dies. I fastened the bunch of flowers to the latch.

The sun would soon wilt those fragile yellow blossoms. But I believed that once that plant had been pulled up, its roots and the earth that had nourished it thrown into the water, and the flowers burned, the only living witness to the human brutality the madwoman had unleashed at God's command would have disappeared. She would no longer come back, futilely, to try to kill that weed with her wraithlike hands which could do nothing against the cause of the curses or sins of this life. I looked at the bunch of flowers on her door, content, almost as if I were a hero; I took the gold coins out of my pocket. My departure from Abancay was assured! Just as she did in heaven, I felt freed of all guilt, of all pangs of conscience.

I ran out into the courtyard. The men from the kitchen followed me. I wanted to see the town, to go to Patibamba, and to go down to the Pachachaca. Perhaps on the road I would meet the plague, climbing up the hill. She would come in the guise of an old woman, on foot or on horseback. I knew it now. I was prepared to put an end to her. I would bring her down from her horse with a stone, on which I had made the sign of the cross with spit; if she came on foot I would grab her by the long cloak she wore that streamed out behind her in the wind. Praying the Yayaku[4] I would squeeze her wormlike throat and knock her down without letting go of her. Still praying, I would drag her to the bridge; and then throw her from the cross into the mainstream of the Pachachaca. Doña Marcelina's purified spirit would help me.

I ran to the gate to the Patibamba road. Three *guardias* with rifles blocked the entrance.

"Nobody goes through," said one of them.

"Why, sir?" I asked. "I have permission to go to the bridge."

4. The Lord's Prayer.—Author

"Permission? From whom?"

He wasn't about to understand me. I did not trust him.

"Let me go through. It's a free road," I told him.

"Don't you see that the city is in a state of emergency? It's dangerous."

"Has the plague already gotten here?"

"It will come in by the thousands. Now, boy! Turn back. Go home."

I could have entered the sugar-cane fields in a hundred different places. What did I care about the road? But the *guardia* had said something mysterious. How could the plague come in by the thousands if there were only one of her? I turned back. I'd go to Huanupata and find out.

The *chicha* bars and the doors of all the houses were closed. I saw people going up the mountain, toward the Apurímac. They went on foot, on horseback, and on donkeys. They carried their little children; the dogs followed along behind. Even the little bars that sold fermented cane juice to the Indians and the mestizo travelers were closed. The wind winnowed the roof straw, and whirled the dust around in the streets. There was always a breeze like that in the valley in the afternoon. But this time, with the neighborhood empty, the wind wrapped itself around me and, as I was walking rapidly, I went through the streets as if I were floating. I looked into one doorway after another. I saw an opening in a reed fence and went into that house.

The yard was covered with animal dung. Flies were everywhere. The sun shone directly down on some old blankets that were spread out at the end of the porch, in front of the kitchen. There was the frame for a bed, made of thick, dry logs. I went up to it. I found an old woman lying on the ground, with her head resting on a round chunk of wood. She was wearing a *makitu*, an old-fashioned Indian garment of woolen homespun that covered her arms; they had wrapped a rag around her head. Her face looked mummified; the skin clung to her bones and her nose appeared sharp and yellowed. Coca-leaf juice oozed from her thin lips. When she saw me, she managed to wave her arm to frighten me off. "It's the plague," I thought. And I did not leave. I went closer. I could see, then, that this bed was identical to others upon which I had seen old people laid out to die in the Indian towns.

"Who are you?" I shouted at her in Quechua.

"I am going to die," she answered me.

"What about your family?"

"They've gone."

Her voice was barely audible.

"Why didn't they take you along?" I asked thoughtlessly.

"Because I am going to die."

She motioned with her arm again, to frighten me away, and I realized I was bothering her. But I could not make up my mind, so quickly, to obey her. They had abandoned her, doubtlessly with her own consent.

"*Adiós, señora!*" I said respectfully, and went out quietly, not running away.

From the street I spied a family going up the hill nearest town on the Apurímac road. I ran to catch up with them.

"Why are you leaving?" I asked, when I was only a few steps behind them.

The man stopped and looked at me in surprise. They had loaded a donkey with pots and blankets. The man had more things on his back and the woman carried a little girl; a boy of about six walked beside his father.

"They've come across from the other side of the river on a rope bridge, in hanging baskets. With ten hanging baskets! They're arriving now," he said.

"Who?" I asked.

"The *colonos*. From fifteen haciendas. Didn't you know, boy? Last night a *guardia* died. They say he cut down a hanging basket by hacking at it with his saber when the *colonos* were coming across. But there were only a few left on the other side. They say eight fell into the Pachachaca; the *guardia* did too. They meant to corral the *colonos* down along the river; they couldn't do it. The Indians from this side of the river went down, like ants, and converged on the *guardias*. Poor things! There were only three of them. They didn't shoot; the others didn't do anything to the *guardias* either. The *guardias civiles* have arrived now. They're getting ready. They say all the *guardias* are going to go now and hold the *colonos* back on the road with machine-gun fire. It's a lie, child! They'll never be able to do it. They'll be climbing up over all the hillsides. I was a corporal in the army . . ."

"Did you say the *colonos* converged on the *guardias civiles*? The *colonos*?"

"Yes, the *colonos*."

"That's a lie! They couldn't do it. They couldn't. Didn't they get scared when they saw the *guardias*?"

"*Ja caraya*, boy! It's not that simple. The *colonos* are like chickens, only worse. They just lie down and die. But the plague is a curse. Who sends the plague? It's a curse! They say the *colonos* are crying, 'Church, church; mass, Padrecito!' There's no escaping the plague, now; they want a high mass, they say, from the great Father of Abancay. Then they'll sit down and be still; shivering, they'll die and be still. Until then they'll push hard, even if the *guardias* should come in a cloud, or like the wind. They'll get here, all right. They must be coming into town now!"

"Do they believe that without mass they'll be damned?"

"Naturally, of course they do! That's the way it is. They'd be damned. They'd fill up the whole gorge with lost souls. Oh God, think of that! They'd crawl around like big lice, bigger than merino sheep; they'd eat up the little animals alive, finishing the people off first. *Padrecito!*"

"That's why you're leaving. You're leaving now!"

"What about the louse, boy? There's sure to be a mass. The *colonos* will come into Abancay tonight. Maybe the Indians will be saved when they hear mass. They're coming, leaving their little children behind—they are little angels! With their women they'll come. They'll be saved! But they'll leave their lice in the plaza, in the church, on the streets, in the doorways. From there the lice will rise up like a curse upon a curse. The town will be crawling with them. They'll devour us. You think people in Abancay will crush the lice with their teeth the way the *colonos* do? You think they're going to chew them up? They're sure to rise up out of all the corners, long lines of them! That's how the sick man's louse is."

"You're scared, corporal!" I said. "I think you're feeding your own fear by whining . . . Just the opposite of the *colonos*."

He answered me in Quechua.

"*Onk'ok' usank'a jukmantan miran* . . . (The sick man's louse reproduces itself in a different way. We can only go far away from here. What use is a brave heart against that?)"

When I tried to return to town, he wanted to stop me, to take me with him. The woman said to me in Quechua, "You're a handsome little boy. Why are you going back of your own free will to let the lice defecate on you?"

They were terrified.

"Tomorrow morning before daybreak I'll be climbing this hill too," I told them.

I said good-bye to them, and ran back down the hill to town.

Far from Abancay I came out of the cane fields into Patibamba. I was perspiring. I had walked, hunched over, under the sugar cane plantings that were ablaze in the sun, all day long. Afraid that I would be discovered, I had avoided the wide lanes that separated the blocks. It was through these spaces that the hacienda mules carried the cane to the big sugar-mill yard.

Crawling over the cane trash, I reached the Indian quarters. They were empty; there was no one at all. I looked down on it from the top of a stack of cane trash. The wasps buzzed around, their feet dangling. They kept me from seeing properly. The doors of the huts were closed; the roof thatch rustled in the wind. "I'm coming down!" I said. "I'm coming in!" I got to my feet and went down to the alley.

I knocked on the first door. I heard a scurrying inside and peeped through a crack. Three children fled into a corner.

I knocked again.

"*Mánan!*" answered the largest, without my having asked him anything.

They hid in the darkness, crowding together in a corner of the hut.

"*Mánan!*" the same child shouted again.

I went off, looking for another house. They answered me in the same way.

I went the whole way down the street quietly, without making any noise. I went up to a hut at the other end of the alley. I crouched down on the ground and looked in through the crack under the door. The sun shone into the house splendidly, through an opening in the roof. It was late afternoon; the light was turning golden.

Near the hearth a girl about twelve years old was probing the body of another smaller girl with a long needle; she was sticking it into her buttocks. The little girl moved her legs without crying; her body was naked. They were both quite close to the hearth. The older one raised the needle to the light. I looked intently and could see on the point of the needle a nest of chigoe[5] larva, a big nest, perhaps a cluster of them. She moved aside to throw the clump of nests into the fire. Then I saw that the little girl's anus, her little private parts, were covered with enormous, white, insect-bitten swellings; the white sacs hung down as they did from the rear quarters of the filthiest, most abandoned hogs in that treacly valley. I lay my head on the ground; I smelled the stench coming from the

5. South American sand flea; the female burrows into the skin and lays eggs, causing serious lesions.—Trans.

hut and waited there for my heart to stop, for the sun's light to be extinguished, for torrents of rain to fall and wash away the earth. The older sister began to sharpen a knife.

I got up and ran away. I felt more energetic than I had when I bade farewell to the dead Doña Marcelina, in her hut that was devoid of mourning decoration, adorned only with the bunch of flowers I had fastened to the latch. I reached the iron fence that went around the hacienda mansion. And from the gate I called out in a loud voice.

"*Yauúú* . . . ! *Yauúúa* . . . !"

The hacienda house was empty too. I shouted again, more loudly this time, clinging to the bars.

It seemed that the light of the setting sun flowed from my mouth and shone futilely on the bars and the whole static valley beyond. I feared I might become insane, or that my lungs might burst if I kept shouting. And I turned toward the river.

I ran down, taking a short cut for I was afraid it might get dark. Far down the hill I met a troop of *guardias* with a sergeant. They caught me.

"Look there!" said the sergeant. He took me to a bend in the road.

The *colonos* were really coming up the hill like a herd of sheep, like thousands of sheep. They had spilled out over the edges of the road and were climbing up through the brush, between the bushes, clambering over the stone or adobe walls that enclosed the sugarcane fields.

"Look there!" repeated the sergeant. "I have orders now to let them pass. They'll ruin the church and the city for many days. Father Linares, the saint, will hold a midnight mass for them and see them off to the other world."

I grew calm when I saw them approaching.

"They won't die," I told him.

"Who are you?" the sergeant asked me.

I told him my name.

"You're the friend of Gerardo, the Comandante's son," he answered. "I'm supposed to look after you."

"Did he ask you to?"

"Yes. He's a fine boy. We're falling back as the Indians advance. You get out of the way now and go up the hill quietly. Why did you come?"

"Are you a friend of Gerardo's?" I asked him.

"I already told you so. He's a fine boy!"

"Then let me go with you."

"The town crier must have already read the proclamation ordering all the people in Abancay to close the doors of their houses. But
you can still get into the school."

"I'm going with them, sergeant. I'm going to pray with them."

"Why? Why you?"

"Look at me," I told him. "Gerardo's not like me, neither is Antero, Gerardo's friend. I was brought up by the Indians, by other
men, better than these, better than the *colonos*."

"Better men, you say? Maybe for some things, but not for defy-
ing death. Look at them coming, neither the river nor the bullets
stopped them. They'll get to Abancay!"

"Yes, sergeant. You're opening the road for them by retreating.
Maybe I'd better go back and tell the Rector."

"Tell them I'll have them come in around midnight. I'll send a
messenger when we're half a mile out."

He grasped my hand. I was startled, almost bewildered.

I returned, singing, as the sunlight faded.

As I neared the gate of the hacienda house, after dark, I loudly
sang a song of defiance, a carnival song from Pampachiri, a cold
town, the last one on the southwest end of the Apurímac.

I went down the road from the hacienda to the city in triumph.
I crushed the *pisonay* flowers underfoot; even in the night the red
mantles of those flowers appeared, and stood out more clearly.

When I reached the school, the Rector called me "madman" and
"wanderer," half in anger and half in jest. It was late, the priests
had already had their supper. He threatened to lock me up again.
But he cooled off when he learned from me that the Indians were
coming, that the sergeant was trying to control their approach so
that they would arrive at midnight.

"Did you see them yourself?" he asked me, breathing heavily.

I realized that until that moment he had been sustained by the
hope that the *colonos* would retreat when the *guardias* fired at them.

"Did you see whether the *guardias* had machine-guns?"

"No. I don't think they did," I answered.

"Yes," he answered me curtly. "They must have had them hidden in the bushes."

"They haven't shot at them, Father," I told him. "They didn't
say they had killed anyone."

"The blood . . ."

He didn't finish the sentence. But I had guessed it.

"When so many of them are pushing forward, so many . . . it
doesn't frighten them!" I said.

"No?" he exclaimed sharply. "It's that to die now, like that, asking for mass, coming for mass . . . But on any other occasion a single whiplash across the face is enough . . . Yes! You shall help me. You don't seem to be afraid; you're almost demented. You shall help me with the mass if the sacristan does not appear. You shall ring the bells."

"Yes, Father!" I said, hugging him. "I rang the bells in my town when I saw the priest coming down the hill from Huayrala. I'll do it the same way."

"Get to your knees!" he told me.

We were on the balcony, in the light of the electric bulb that illuminated the doorway of his bedroom.

I knelt on the floor. The Rector said a few words in Latin.

"I've given you absolution," he told me. "We'll wait in the school until the sergeant's messenger arrives."

The sacristan showed up before the messenger. Taking me by the arm, the Rector led me to Brother Miguel's room. He put my clothing in a saddlebag and hung it over my shoulder.

"I'm responsible for your life," he told me. "I'm going to lock you in. After mass I'll open the door."

He wound a clock he had had them bring me from his bedroom; it was a tall clock, made of yellow metal.

"It will awaken you at four," he told me. "You're to get up, go to the kitchen, and call the new gatekeeper; he'll accompany you to the entryway; after you go out he'll close the little door in the gate. In three hours' time you will have reached the summit; you should get to Huanipaca before nightfall; they'll be waiting for you there. The next day by lunchtime you should be able to see your uncle's hacienda, just a short distance from the road."

"Will they ring the bells at twelve o'clock, Father?"

"Before twelve. The Abancay people know that the call to mass will not be for them."

"Will you preach a sermon to the Indians?"

"I shall comfort them. They will weep until they have unburdened themselves. I shall restore their faith in God and ask them to pray on their way back across the city."

"They'll go out in triumph, Father, the same way they are climbing the mountain now. I won't see them! I'll hear their prayers from here."

"You long for death, strange child," he told me. "Peace be with you; go to bed. The bells will awaken you."

He took my face in his hands and stared at me for a long while, as if I were a still pool on the Pachachaca. I felt his gaze, bright and piercing.

"May the world not be cruel to you, my son," he said, addressing me again. "May your spirit find peace on this broken ground whose shadows you perceive only too well."

His forehead crowned with white hair, his eyes, even his cheeks, and the hands he had placed under my chin conveyed peace; they calmed the desperation I had felt when it became evident that I would not be able to see the arrival of the *colonos*, their entrance into the church with their tousled hair standing on end and their eyes glowing like coals.

The priest waited for me to go to bed. He went out without locking the door. I would not disobey him.

At midnight the bells were rung three times. None of them could have had gold, silver, or human fat in them, because their voices were harsh and dissonant.

Beneath the ugly clangor of the bells of Abancay the *colonos* must have been coming into town. And yet I heard no sound of footsteps, no singing, no shouting, for a long time. Ordinary animals have hoofs that resound on the paving stones or on the ground; the *colono* walks with his foot soles bare, stealthily. They must have run to the church in a silent mob. I was to hear nothing all night long.

I waited. It was a short mass. Half an hour after the bells stopped ringing I heard a deep rumble of voices drawing nearer.

"They're praying!" I said.

The direct cross street from the plaza to the Patibamba road was less than a hundred yards from the school. The rumbling became louder. I knelt. The sound of a chorus came on the wind.

"They're leaving now. They have a long way to go, Brother Miguel!" I said aloud.

I began to say the Lord's Prayer. I said it over twice. The murmuring grew louder and I raised my voice, "*Yayaku, hanak' pachapi kak'* ..."

Suddenly, as the prayers were coming to an end, I heard other voices. I went to the door, opened it, and went out onto the balcony. From there I could hear the voices better.

"Out, plague! *Way jiebre! Waaay* ... !"

"*Ripuy, ripuy! Kañask'aykin! Waaay!*" [6]

6. "Go away, go away! I must burn you up!"—Author

Far from the plaza by now, they called out to the plague, threatening it.

The women began to sing. They improvised the words to a dismal tune used for funerals:

Mamay María wañauchisunki	My mother Mary shall kill thee,
Taytay Jesús kañachisunki	My father Jesus shall burn thee up,
Niñuchantarik' sek'ochisunki	Our little child shall hang thee,
Ay, way, jiebre!	Ai, wai, plague!
Ay, way, jiebre!	Ai, wai, plague!

They would keep on singing until they reached the edge of town. The chorus moved off into the distance, becoming detached from me.

They would reach Huanupata and sing or shout the final cry of the *jarahui* together, directing it to the worlds and unknown substances that precipitate the reproduction of the lice, the slow and so minute movement of death. Perhaps the cry would reach the mother of the fever and pierce her, causing her to explode, changing her into a harmless dust that would vanish behind the trees. Perhaps.

I went back into the bedroom.

Once they reached Patibamba, the throng of Indians would scatter to the other haciendas, each *colono* to his own master.

I would be leaving the next day. Ai, wai, plague! Those who were already ill and had to die would be buried in the hacienda graveyards, which had neither walls, nor façades, nor crosses, but those who lived might perhaps be able to conquer the plague after that night.

The curses against the plague re-echoed through my bedroom for hours and hours.

I was awake when the Rector's gilded clock played a crystalline European march, a reveille that was repeated three times.

I turned on the light and went over to the clock. It was a model of a palace façade. Its columns ended in capitals carved with a vine-leaf pattern. It kept on playing. I dressed rapidly. That music reminded me of the army band march; it opened, before my eyes, a happy avenue to the unknown, not to something to be feared. "I'll hang a bunch of lilies on Salvinia's gate," I said. "I know now that I shall never return."

The mestizo gatekeeper was awake. He put on a poncho and accompanied me to the entry. I left the school. The clock's reveille bathed it, flowing across the porches, flooding its dark corners, bringing it peace, forever.

I picked some lilies in the plaza. The *colonos* had not trampled them. They must not have overflowed into the park. Probably they had marched along in triumph, like an orderly funeral procession. I went toward the poplar grove. There were only three flowers in the bouquet, and I held it carefully, as if it were the softness of Salvinia's hands.

It was easy to fasten the bouquet to the gate, to the sound of the beautiful music that still accompanied me. The night was bright with dense clusters of stars. I went off. "It's for you, Salvinia, for your eyes," I said, in the shade of the mulberry trees. "Color of *zumbayllu*, color of *zumbayllu*! *Adiós*, Abancay."

I started up the hill. Then I remembered the Rector's advice and Antero's stories.

"The Old Man!" I said. "The Old Man!"

How he had prayed before the altar of Our Lord of Earthquakes, in Cuzco. And how he had stared at me, in his parlor, with his steely eyes. The *pongo* who had remained standing outside on the balcony could have been destroyed at the Old Man's command. I turned back.

The Pachachaca roared in the darkness, in the depths of the immense gorge. The bushes trembled in the wind.

The plague must, at that very moment, be almost frozen to death from the Indians' prayers, from their songs and the final wave of *jarahuis* which must have penetrated to the rocks, reaching down even to the tiniest roots of the trees.

"I'd better drop down into the canyon," I exclaimed.

"I'll cross it, go to Toraya, and from there to the cordillera. The plague won't catch me."

I ran across the city.

On the hanging bridge at Auquibamba, I crossed over the river in the afternoon. If the *colonos*, with their curses and their songs, had annihilated the fever, perhaps from the height of the bridge I would see it float by, swept along by the current, in the shadow of the trees. It would pass by caught on a branch of *chachacomo*, or of gorse, floating on the layers of *pisonay* flowers that these deep rivers always bring. The river would take it off to the Great Jungle, the country of the dead. Like Lleras!

Afterword

Dreams and Magic in José María Arguedas

The connecting thread that is woven through the episodes of this nostalgic and, at times, passionate book is that of a child tortured by a double origin, a child with roots in two hostile worlds. The son of white people who was brought up by the Indians and then returned to the white world, Ernesto, the narrator of *Deep Rivers*, is a misfit and a loner. He is also in a privileged position to evoke the tragic opposition of two mutually unfamiliar worlds that reject one another and are unable to coexist painlessly even within his own person.

At the beginning of the novel, in the shadow of those Cuzco stones where the Indian and Spanish cultures come harshly in contact with one another, as they do in Ernesto (and in José María Arguedas), the boy's destiny is sealed. He will not change again and, throughout the story, will be a simple presence, bewildered by the violence with which at every moment, and in a thousand subtle or devious ways, two races, two cultures, two classes clash in the solemn setting of the Andes.

Subjectively he identifies himself with the Indians who brought him up ("I was brought up by the Indians, by other men, better than these"), and who represent a lost paradise to him, as we shall see. But he is distant from them because of his position in society, which objectively identifies him with those whites in the town of Abancay whose unjust, foolish, or simply blind attitude toward the Indians angers and saddens him. Ernesto finds the world of men an impossible contradiction. It is not strange that the feelings which inspire him should be confusion and, at times, a horror so profound that he comes to imagine he springs from some non-human species and asks himself if the song of the lark is "the stuff of which I am made, that nebulous region from which I was torn to be cast in among men." One must live, however, and Ernesto, who cannot escape his situation, must find a way to endure it. To do this he has two weapons. The first is his inner refuge of dreams; the second is a desperate desire to communicate with nature, with what is left of the world once men have been excluded. Ernesto's personality is formed by these two attitudes, and they are curiously projected in the book's structure.

Why this inner withdrawal? What strength does Ernesto have within himself that enables him to live? There was once a time when he was still unconscious of the duality that was to wreck his destiny, when he lived in innocent complicity with men, doubtlessly content, sheltered by that "community that grew corn in the smallest, happiest valley I have ever known" where "the *mamakunas* of the community protected me and instilled in me that kindness in which I live and which I can never repay." And the two leaders of that Indian community, Pablo Maywa and Victor Pusa, are the protecting shadows which the boy secretly calls on in the Abancay boarding school to conjure away his sufferings. The current of nostalgia flowing through this book originates in the continual melancholy remembrance of that time when Ernesto was ignorant of the strength of the "sad and powerful current that buffets children who must face, all alone, a world fraught with monsters and fire." That confrontation with "the world fraught with monsters and fire" coincides with his arrival in Abancay and his entering the school where the city's well-to-do boys are educated. When he meets them Ernesto discovers the abysmal differences that separate him from the others—his loneliness, his exiled condition: "My rubber shoes, my long shirt cuffs, and my necktie embarrassed and upset me. I couldn't feel at home. Where to sit, and with whom?" He cannot turn back to his Indian community; and now he also knows that he is not an Indian. He cannot return, but, in spite of himself, he will try madly and will live like one possessed by the spectacle of his lost "innocence." As he is constantly nostalgic and trying to recall the past, the reality vividly reflected in *Deep Rivers* can never be the immediate one Ernesto faces in the course of the novel's main plot, situated in Abancay. Rather it is another past reality, decanted, diluted, and enriched by memory. This also determines some of the novel's formal characteristics: the lyrical purity of the writing, its poetic and reminiscent tone, and the constant idealization of objects and beings, which are presented to us just as Ernesto remembers them.

In the last chapter of *Deep Rivers*, Ernesto walks about the schoolyard "more attentive to memories than to external things." He is almost always like this; even when his attention falls on something that seems to absorb it, his mind is confronting the present experience with a past one, and he uses the present as a base from which to move backwards. In the first pages of the novel the boy sadly laments that his father would always "decide to leave one town for another just when the mountains, the roads, the playing fields, the places where the birds sleep, and the details of the town were beginning to become a part of me." We may assume that from then on he is fiercely determined to capture that fleeting reality and to keep alive in his spirit the image of those landscapes and towns where he can never remain. Later he will live on those images. Amazingly precise memories crop up in Ernesto's mind on every occasion, as if he were an old man ("the *charango* became a whirlwind that recorded the words and music of the songs in my memory"); he is a person wholly dedicated to the task of remembering because the past is his main reason for living. In school (where the Rector symptomatically calls him "madman" and "wandering fool" because he is not like the others) he dreams of running away to find his father. But he does not, and waits, "observing everything, storing it all up in my memory." One could say of a novel so clearly autobiographical that Arguedas has transplanted his own trials into the narrative in a symbolic fashion. The child whom the author calls up and extracts from the past, from an earlier experience in his life, is presented in an identical situation—also living in the past. Like those Chinese boxes, each of which contains a smaller box, the book *Deep Rivers* originates in the author's memory; from it comes the story in which the main character, in turn, is nourished by a frail reality, alive only in his own memory.

Through that process of constantly recalling the past, Ernesto discovers his longing for a reality which was no better than the present one, but was lived in innocence, even unconsciously, when he was still ignorant of evil (even though he was submerged in it and was its victim). On holidays the boy frequents the taverns in Abancay, listens to the music, and there remembers "the fields and stones, the squares and churches, and the streams where I had once been happy." Here his idea of happiness already seems to be more closely associated with a natural than with a social order; he speaks of fields, stones, and streams. Because this is the other wellspring of his spirit, his strongest link with present reality.

In a way Ernesto is conscious that he rejects the present and lives in the past, and he sees intuitively how this will affect his future. On Sundays his schoolmates court the girls in the main square of Abancay, but he prefers to wander about the countryside, thinking of that tall young girl "with the beautiful countenance who lived in the cruel village with the *capulí* orchards." Then he dreams of someday deserving the love of a woman who "could divine and take for her own my dreams, the memory of my journeys, of the rivers and mountains I had seen." He speaks of himself in the past tense, as if he were speaking of the dead, because he himself is a kind of dead man; he lives with phantoms and aspires to having his future companion live with him, amid those familiar departed shadows.

But he is only half-dead, because even though an invisible wall isolates him from the men he rubs elbows with, there is something that still ties him, like an umbilical cord, to the present—the landscape. That "kindness . . . I can never repay"—which the boy resists imparting to his cruel companions or to the school's religious hypocrites or fanatics, and has no real chance of repaying to the Indians, being a prisoner of a social class that practices, without admitting it, a severe racial segregation—will be lavished on the air, plants, and animals of the Andes. This is why the Andean landscape plays such an important role in this book and is the most outstanding character in the novel.

Is it not significant that the title, *Deep Rivers*, refers exclusively to nature? But in the novel the natural order does not appear in opposition to or conflict with human society. On the contrary, it is humanized to an extent that surpasses simple metaphor and invades the realm of magic. In an instinctive, obscure way Ernesto tends to substitute one order for another, to transfer peculiarly human values to that area of the world he does not reject. We have already seen he sometimes imagines a filial relation between himself and the song of a bird. On another occasion he rails angrily against the men who slaughter the birds and parrots with slings, and in the first chapter of the novel he mourns bitterly for a little *cedrón* tree the children of Cuzco had "made a martyr of." Later he protests furiously against those who would kill a cricket, "a messenger, a visitor from the enchanted surface of the earth," and in Abancay one night he devotes himself to removing the crickets from the sidewalk "where they were in such danger." In the chapter entitled

"Zumbayllu" there is a long, extremely beautiful and tender elegy to the *tankayllu*, that insect with a "velvety body" that disappears in the light and whose honey makes children who taste it "feel for the rest of their lives the brush of its comforting warmth on their hearts, protecting them from hatred and melancholy." Whenever he describes flowers, insects, stones, and streams, Arguedas's language takes on its best temper, its most successful rhythm. His vocabulary loses all harshness, he joins the most delicate and fragile of words, speaks animatedly, becomes sweetly musical, and elates the reader with his impassioned imagery. "The Abancay lemon, large, thick-skinned, edible within and easy to peel, contains a juice which, when mixed with brown sugar, makes the most delicious and potent food in the world. It is burning and sweet. It instills happiness. It is as if one were drinking sunlight." This boundless enthusiasm for nature is based on and counterbalanced by a mystical ecstasy. The spectacle of the sun's appearance between scattered showers leaves the boy "uncertain" and unable to reason. That rapture contains a real alienation, concealing the seed of an animistic vision of the world. Natural reality heightens Ernesto's sensitivity to the point of complete self-absorption and leads him to a pagan idealization of plants, animals, and things. He attributes divine as well as human properties to them, making them sacred objects. Many of Ernesto's superstitions derive from his early childhood; they are the spiritual legacy of his Indian upbringing and the boy clings to them, subconsciously showing loyalty to that culture. His own situation, moreover, explains and favors this tendency to reject reason as a tie to reality, and to prefer obscure intuition and magic. In his personal situation Ernesto duplicates a process that the Indians have experienced collectively; that is why he is a symbolic character. Reality can hardly be "logical" for the exploited Indian peasant, scorned and humiliated all his life and defenseless against disease and poverty; nor can the world be rational for the outcast child, rootless among men, forever exiled. On the contrary it is essentially absurd. This is the source of his fatalistic irrationality, his animism, and that secret fetishism which leads him to venerate the strangest objects with religious unction. One thing, in particular, plays a totemic role throughout the novel—the *zumbayllu*, that whistling top which is for him "a new kind of being, an apparition in a hostile world, a tie that bound me to the courtyard I hated, to that vale of sorrow, to the school."

His feeling of helplessness feeds Ernesto's superstitions. For him the world is a stage where dark forces do battle with defense-

less, frightened mankind, who sees the presence of death everywhere. It is announced by the *chiririnka*, a blue fly that buzzes, even
in the darkness, and that "hours before it happens, . . . senses those
who are about to become corpses, and hovers around them." In
addition there is the plague, that at any moment might come
"climbing up the hill. . . . in the guise of an old woman, on foot or
on horseback." So threatened mankind can only take refuge in
vague magic-religious exorcisms that make his situation even more
humiliating. The Indians "detest the lice." Nevertheless they
crush the insects' heads with their teeth, "but they do it to resist
death." When the idiot dies, Ernesto picks the flowers in the school
playground where the boys came to copulate with the wretched
woman because he believes that "once that plant had been pulled
up, its roots and the earth that had nourished it thrown into the
water, and the flowers burned, the only living witness to the human
brutality the madwoman had unleashed at God's command would
have disappeared."

Not only is he diametrically opposed to the actions and feelings
of the other boys; Ernesto reacts the same way toward that which
the others believe and adore—his faith is not theirs, their God is
not his. The lonely boy sets up a personal religion, a secret cult, a
god of his own, in the middle of the Christian world in which he
is immersed. Hence his hostility to ministers of the "enemy" religion; the Rector of the boarding school, the Saint of Abancay, is presented to the reader as the incarnation of human duplicity and the
accomplice of injustice. *Deep Rivers* erupts in a wave of fury whenever this person appears. The masochistic sermon the Rector
preaches to the Indians of Patibamba and his unctuous, deceitful
speech to placate the rioting women are nearly caricatures. Neither
the landowner who exploits the Indians nor the soldiers who re-
press them are so harshly portrayed as the priest who teaches them
resignation and combats their sporadic rebellions with dogma. This
is understandable; the novel, as already stated, is based on an inner
reality in which religion shows its subtle and efficient powers. The
exploitative landowner appears only in passing, even though the
problem of feudalism in the Andes is mentioned frequently, and
even represented allegorically by the city of Abancay, "a prisoner of
the hacienda, on whose alien land it was built."

From his inner refuge Ernesto participates emotionally in the terrible struggle between the Indians and their masters. Two of the
main episodes of the novel bear witness to this age-old war no one
mentions—the insurrection of the marketwomen and the ravages
of the plague. These are the two moments of greatest intensity in

the novel, two centers that radiate a powerful current of energy to
the rest of the book, dynamizing the other incidents which are almost always drawn as static and independent pictures. And it seems
as if the scalding lava flowing from these two sources might even
overwhelm the narrator, transforming him from a retiring, intro-
verted boy into another person. When the Abancay marketwomen
rebel and the respectable townspeople become frightened and shut
themselves up in their houses, Ernesto dashes out into the street,
excitedly rejoicing amid the varicolored skirts of the Indian women,
singing in Quechua just as they do. And later, with his propensity
to make something sacred of what he has done and to project his
experience of the world in myth, Ernesto makes Felipa, the ringleader of the bar-women, a symbol of redemption: "You're like the
river, *señora*. . . . They'll never catch you. *Jajayllas!* And you'll return. I will see your face, powerful as the noonday sun. We'll set
fires. We'll burn everything down!"

It's curious how an introspective book that uses the contempla-
tion of nature and a child's aching loneliness as its raw material can
suddenly take on an unbearable violence. Arguedas does not seem
to be very much worried by the technical aspects of the novel and
sometimes commits errors of construction, as in the chapter "Stone
and Lime," where the story's point of view is moved, for no reason,
from the first to the third person, but in spite of this his intuition
usually guides him well in the use of his material. The small clots
of raw violence, for instance, strategically inserted in the tranquil
and moderate body of the narrative, are a real triumph of form.
From the first time I read *Deep Rivers* six years ago, I have had a
vivid memory of the terrible impression made by those incidents
that light up the story like a conflagration—for instance, the image
of the little girl, in the plague-stricken town, with "her little private
parts . . . covered with enormous, white, insect-bitten swellings."
These tiny active craters scattered over the smooth surface of the
novel create a current of emotions, tensions, and events that enrich
its beauty with an unrestrainable flow of life.

A tormented conscience? A boy whose impossible contradictions
isolate him from other people and cloister him in a past, remembered reality? A predominance of nature over society? There will be
no lack of people who say that this is an alienated account of the
Andes, that Arguedas falsifies the problem when, rather than de-
nouncing the mystifications of Andean reality, he transposes them
in fiction. This is a mistaken reproach; it is legitimate to require
any author who speaks of the Andes to give an account of the in-
justices on which life there is based, but not to demand that he do

it in a certain way. All the horror of the highlands is to be found in *Deep Rivers*; it is the prior condition, the basic premise without which Ernesto's suffering would be incomprehensible. The boy's personal tragedy bears witness unequivocally to that horror; it is its product. The deep roots of the evil may be seen showing through his bewilderment, his loneliness, his fear, and his naïve, magical approach to plants and insects. The story does bear witness to social and economic reality by refracting it, registering the repercussions of historical events and great social problems at a *personal* level; this is the only way literary testimony can be *living* and not crystallize into dead symbols.

At the end of 1969 José María Arguedas committed suicide by shooting himself. In his last letter he wrote: "I withdraw now because I feel, and I am sure of it, that I no longer have the necessary energy and inspiration to continue to work and consequently to justify my existence." We shall never know if this was true, if he really no longer had the strength and will to continue to write books like the ones he has left us. What we do know, however, is that by pulling the trigger at the very moment he felt his vocation endangered he has set us the greatest example of honesty a writer could give.

Mario Vargas Llosa

Glossary

adiós (S) : good-bye.
akatank'a (Q) : dung beetle.
Alameda (S) : name given to a poplar-lined avenue.
alaymosca (Q) : a granitic rock.
alcalde (S) : an Indian community leader.
alk'o (Q) : dog.
amank'ay (Q) : a yellow lily.
amaru (Q) : snake.
Amaru Cancha (Q) : "Snake Enclosure," the palace of the Inca
    Huayna Capac.
apank'ora (Q) : a tarantula spider.
apasanka (Q) : a tarantula spider.
apu (Q) : a regional god; also an honorific title meaning "lord."
Apurímac Mayu (Q) : Apurímac River.
atatauya (Q) : an exclamation of disgust.
awankay (Q) : the soaring flight of large birds.
ayak'zapatilla (Q+S) : literally, "corpse-slipper"; a yellow flower.
ayllu (Q) : Indian community.

Q: Quechua S: Spanish E: English

When letters are in combination they are shared by the languages. The first
letter indicates the language from which the other language(s) borrowed
the word. Letters joined by + indicate a word which is a combination of
two languages; Quechua often borrows a root word from Spanish and
adds its own endings.

calandria (S): calendar lark (*tuya* in Quechua).

capulí (S): a rosaceous tree with cherrylike fruit; also a kind of grass.

Castilian cloth (E): coarse, fuzzy, factory-made woolen cloth.

cedrón (S): lemon verbena, whose leaves are used for tea.

-cha (Q): a diminutive suffix which may be added to a person's name to show respect, affection, or to make the person "more one's own"; using this form in personal address is a way of drawing closer to the person for whom it is used. This syllable also has religious connotations and is used as a suffix for the names of gods, spirits, and other supernatural beings, in which case it may be translated "Great." For instance, *mamacha*, meaning the Virgin Mary.

chachacomo (Q): a bush found in the Andes between 2,700 and 3,800 meters of altitude.

Chanka (Q): an ethnic group living in the Cuzco area. Chanka Quechua was the type of Quechua spoken by José María Arguedas.

charango (Q): an instrument like a mandolin.

chicha (SQ): a mild alcoholic drink made from corn.

chichera (S): a woman who works in a *chicha* bar.

chichería (S): a bar-restaurant selling *chicha*.

chigoe (E): South American sand flea; the pregnant female burrows into the skin and lays eggs, causing serious lesions.

chihuaco (Q): a bird similar to a thrush.

chipro (Q): nickname for one whose face is pitted with smallpox scars.

chirimía (S): a wooden reed instrument of European origin similar to a recorder or flageolet.

chiririnka (Q): a dark blue fly which, in the book, is a harbinger of death.

cholo, chola (Q): an Indian who has adopted the speech, clothing, and manners of the whites; a term applied by whites to Indians and servants.

chullu (Q): a cap that covers the head and part of the face.

colono (S): an Indian belonging to an hacienda.

comadres (S): godmothers with respect to one another; women connected by a religious tie by which they promise to help each other's children and also, in effect, each other; intimate friends.

comandante (S): commanding officer, major.

comparsa (S): a group of people in masquerade who parade, singing and dancing, to the music of drums and other instruments at carnival time.

comunero (S) : a member of an Indian *ayllu*, or community.

concertado (S) : a worker who is paid by the year.

cordillera (SE) : the high mountain ranges of the Andes.

daños (S) : damages; the name given to animals which stray onto someone else's land and are held by the landowner. In Peru many white landowners illegally forced the Indians onto the high, bleak wastelands and then confiscated their animals for damages when the animals returned in search of good pasture. In this book, it refers to winnings in a game of marbles.

danza (S) : a type of dance.

danzak' (S+Q) : a ritual dancer.

de chuto (S) : Indian; in the Indian style.

don, doña (S) : a respectful title of address used before the Christian name.

erk'e (Q) : a crying child under five years of age.

fuga (S) : the last, liveliest part of certain types of dances.

guardia civil, guardia (S) : a member of the national rural police.

hacendado (S) : owner of an hacienda.

hacienda (SE) : a large, traditionally operated landholding.

huaman (Q) : eagle.

huaranhuay (Q) : a tree native to the Andes.

huayno (Q) : a folk song and dance of Inca origin.

huayquear (Q+S) : for many people to beat one person.

huayronk'o (Q) : bumblebee.

huayruro (Q) : a kind of red and black colored seed native to Peru; the nickname given to the *guardias civiles* because of the red and black colors of their uniform.

illa (Q) : a vibrating kind of light; a monster with a birth defect caused by moonbeams. See first paragraph of chapter 6 for the author's comprehensive definition.

illapa (Q) : a ray of light.

illariy (Q) : the light of dawn.

imachá? (Q) : What can it be?

imam? (Q) : what?

indigenista (S) : belonging to a pro-Indian literary movement.

-ito (S) : a diminutive suffix; used by Quechua speakers speaking Spanish where they would use *-cha* in Quechua. See *-cha*.

ja caraya (QS) : a strong interjection.

jajayllas (Q) : expression of scornful derision.

jarahui (Q) : a short, mournful commemorative folk song usually sung by a small chorus of women.

jaylli (Q) : a song of triumph sung at the end of battles or on completion of important tasks, especially agricultural; this music is also used for dancing.

jukucha pesk'o (Q) : American nightingale.

kachi (Q) : salt.

k'anra (Q) : disgustingly dirty.

k'echa (Q) : literally, "diarrhea"; Arguedas translates it as *meon*, a person who is continually making water.

k'eñwa (Q) : a low tree with red bark.

killa (Q) : the moon.

killincho (Q) : a kestrel or sparrow hawk.

kimichu (Q) : an Indian musician who journeys from one town to another as a pilgrim, carrying a case of glass and wood containing a portrait of the Virgin Mary and begging for alms.

k'ompo (Q) : a bulky knot.

lambra (Q) : a tree with twisted, thorny branches.

layk'a (Q) : sorcerer.

llipta (Q) : lime or *quinua* ashes; chewing *llipta* mixed with semi-dry or toasted coca leaves produces a chemical reaction which liberates the cocaine from the coca, anesthetizing the stomach and mouth. It permits people to withstand great fatigue without feeling hunger or thirst.

lúcumo (S) : a fruit tree native to Peru and Chile.

makitu (Q) : an Indian garment of woolen homespun.

maltón (Q) : a puppy, a cub.

mamachakuna (Q) : diminutive form of *mamakuna*.

mamacita (S) : diminutive form of *mamá*, "mother."

mámak (Q) : a thick jungle reed named after the mother, the source, the creator.

mamakuna (Q) : nowadays the oldest and most competent women of the Indian communities; originally a term for the Inca's concubines or the oldest Virgins of the Sun.

mamita (S) : diminutive form of *mamá*, "mother."

mánan (Q) : no.

marinera (S) : a coastal folk dance formerly called the *zamba chilena*.

mestizo (SE) : a person of mixed Indian and white ancestry.

montaña (S) : the lower eastern slopes of the Andes on the edge of the Amazon jungle.

nakak (Q) : a mythological character who goes around slitting throats at night and eating human flesh.

ñujchu (Q) : a delicate red flower.

pacae (Q) : a tree with silky pods, whose pulp is eaten.

Padrecito (S): an affectionate way of addressing a priest; little Father.

pampa (QSE): a level plain or wide field.

papacha (S+Q): great father, a term of respect.

papacito (S): little father; similar to *papay, tatay, padrecito*.

papay (S+Q): my father; respectful term of address used by Indian serfs to address their master.

pati (Q): a tree native to the Andes.

patrón (S): master, in the feudal sense of a lord in relation to his serfs; boss.

patroncito (S): diminutive form of *patrón*.

pejerrey (S): a small, silvery fish with a blue stripe.

perdoncito (S): a little pardon, an affectionate way of saying "excuse me."

picantería (S): a place where hot, peppery food is sold; for instance, a *chicha* bar.

picantes (S): hot, peppery food.

pinkuyllu (Q): a giant, five-holed flute the southern Indians of Peru play at community celebrations. See chapter 6.

piruchan (Q): a dance.

pisonay (Q): a tree found in the Andes between 2,200 and 2,600 meters of altitude. It grows rapidly and has red flowers and leguminous pods two and one-half inches long.

pongo (QS): an hacienda Indian who is obliged to work as an unpaid servant in the landowner's house.

puna (QSE): a high, cold, arid plateau, as in the Andes.

quena (Q): a reed flute with a slot in one end which the musician blows across.

quijllu (Q): a crevasse.

quinua (Q): a species of goosefoot with a small, edible seed, domesticated by the Andean Indians.

quirquincho (Q): a ten-stringed instrument like a mandolin made from an armadillo shell, similar to a *charango*.

Rukana Quechua (Q): one of the dialects of Quechua; Rukana is the name of an ethnic group.

runa (Q): people.

Saint's day (E): a church festival in honor of a saint.

salud (S): health; your health.

sampedrano sheepskin (S): a highly esteemed type of sheepskin from the city of San Pedro.

sanku (Q): cornmeal cooked in water, a very old kind of porridge in Peru.

saywa (Q): a heap of stones which travelers pile up in the mountain passes.

señor (S): a title used to address an important man; used in small towns to address a notable or by Indians to describe a member of the provincial upper class in the sense of "lord" or "master."

señora (S): a lady, gentlewoman, or married woman.

señorita (S): a young lady; miss.

tambo (Q): an inn where country people, mule drivers, and mestizo travelers stay. In pre-Hispanic times it was the name for way stations on the Inca highways.

tankayllu (Q): a heavy-bodied buzzing insect that flies through the fields sipping nectar from the flowers.

tara (Q): a thorny, leguminous tree whose fruit is used for dyeing cloth or curing hides.

tatallay tayta (Q): "O father, my father," an expression commonly used in difficult or distressing situations.

tayta (Q): father; also used as an affectionate and respectful form of address.

tullpa (Q): a stone hearth.

tuya (Q): calendar lark (*calandria* in Spanish).

ukuku (Q): a ritual dancer dressed as a bear.

upallay (Q): be quiet.

usa waykuy (Q): one who cooks lice.

wak'rapuku (Q): a trumpet made of bull's horn, fitted with a silver or brass mouthpiece.

wamancha (Q): sparrow hawk, kestrel.

werak'ocha (Q): one of the principal gods of Inca mythology, who was bearded and white; also used nowadays by Indians to mean "sir," "gentleman," or "boss."

winku, winko (Q): deformity in objects that should be round.

wiswis (Q): grimy, greasy.

yanawiku (Q): a wild duck.

Yayaku (Q): the Lord's Prayer.

zumbayllero (Q + S): a top spinner.

zumbayllu (Q): a top.